MYSTERIES OF HEAVEN

Prophecy Revealed

John Natale

Contents

Endorsements   vii

Introduction   xi

PART I
Prophetic Words — 2013   1

PART II
Prophetic Words — 2014   5

PART III
Prophetic Words — 2015   17

PART IV
Prophetic Words — 2016   53

PART V
Prophetic Words — 2017   89

PART VI
Prophetic Words — 2018   151

PART VII
Prophetic Words — 2019   197

PART VIII
Prophetic Words — 2020   243

PART IX
Prophetic Words — 2021   283

PART X
Prophetic Words — 2022   311

PART XI
Prophetic Words — 2023   339

Final Words   353

Thank You!   357
About the Author   359

Published by Dominion Unlimited Publications.
P.O. Box 1412, Manteca, California 95336
www.dominionunlimited.org

I would like to thank the following people that have inspired me, challenged me, and pushed me to continue the journey and fight the good fight of faith!

My wife Nancy, I am so thankful for your heart, your sensitivity that Holy Spirit gifted you with, and your constant reminder that we must remain focused on Jesus at all times! You have been a source of strength for me, and always by my side! It has been an honor to be your husband, and walk together throughout all these years, and the many more to come!

Our six Children, CJ, Ryan, Chase, Noah, Luke, and Jacob, you all have been a reminder to me to keep pressing in, and never give up! Your lives remind me everyday of perseverance, diligence, and destiny! We have travelled together, ministered together, and pushed each other! Thank you for the influence and impact you all have made in my life!

To Ron and Renee Joelson, your unconditional love, friendship, and spiritual insight have been such a blessing to me in more ways than I can speak! Thank you for your role in my life, and how Holy Spirit uses you both!

My desire is that this book of prophetic words given to me by Holy Spirit to release to the church, to nations, and governments, is a source of hope, strength, and guidance that the reader can use at any time, anywhere!

It could not have been done without Him, it was all Him! I am just a voice in the wilderness! For this, I am so honored to be used by Jesus to help advance the Kingdom of Heaven!

Endorsements

I wholeheartedly endorse John Natale, a dedicated servant of Christ, a remarkable father and husband, and an impactful author whose message has the potential to transform lives. John's book carries profound truths that can ignite a powerful change within your heart. His dedication to reviving hearts and cities has impacted me and I know his message will impact you. His prophetic insights shine through his life and ministry. I am honored to know this man of God and witness firsthand how God flows through his life. I encourage you to read his book and allow its message to resonate within you, fostering positive change and growth in your life. Get ready to change the world!

Dr Brian Simmons
Passion & Fire Ministries
The Passion Translation

Endorsements

Prophet John Natale and I go back almost 20 years. He was the wedding officiant / minister that presided over the wedding ceremony of my wife and I. I had the privilege of traveling with John as he ministered in the Northeast region of the United States. We wrote a book together entitled, *Listen. Learn. Obey.*

For as long as I have known John, he has always been a tender-hearted and loving man who deeply loves Jesus and others. He always seeks to encourage and lift up others. Prophet John Natale has done this with me personally, at conferences, at prophetic schools, at various churches and at the local church (Rescue Church) that I pastor.

Many times, over the years he has spoken the right word, at the right time, for the right reasons! His newest book is meant to encourage and challenge you to seek and follow Jesus.

Pastor Adam LiVecchi,
Founder of We See Jesus Ministries
and Lead Pastor of Rescue Church

I have read, watched and listened to Prophet John Natale's prophetic words for more than three years. When details are presented, I found them to be accurate and impactful. From comments from his many followers including me, it is clear that John edifies the body as mandated in Scripture (1 Corinthians 14:4). Every prophecy is carefully considered so that only words that have been released are presented. John has become a good friend and I have also observed that he carries the right heart for the prophetic office that he walks in! As a loving father and husband, John understands the importance of our relationships, and this permeates his entire ministry.

He cares deeply about the church and, with his wife Nancy, goes where he is assigned. He speaks words with wisdom and discernment and in God's timing. I encourage you, the reader, to delve carefully into this book. You will learn about the church, our nation, the world and most of all, through John's revelations, about God himself. I have even had the joy of watching John get a prophetic word while we were watching a movie together with our spouses. John had a surprised look on his face as he quickly exited the theater to record the word he just received. It was a special moment to see how the Lord reveals himself to John.

How wonderful now to see his prophecies in one place in this book. I heartily endorse it!

Ron Joelson
Former EVP and Chief Investment Officer
Northwestern Mutual

Introduction

One of the phrases that has come to be a normal occurrence in my everyday speech is "Cmon, God." As my relationship increased, and my sensitivity to Holy Spirit began strengthening, something very unusual started! Every time I hear Holy Spirit speak to me, I respond automatically with those words!

It's like He has chosen them already, and desires for me to engage! It's our connector when there is something significant that is being released to me! It's the "WoW" moment when Jesus overwhelms me, and takes me by surprise!

Over the past 20 years, there have been many words spoken over my life about ministry, calling, authority, and the books that would be written. It has been an incredible journey walking this path with Jesus, my wife, and family. I could not have done it without them! They all have been used significantly to support, encourage, and even correct me. It's not easy living with an individual called to an office of a prophet, the path has not been easy, and at times, it seemed extremely lonely, and set apart. I can identify with the life of Elijah.

Introduction

He experienced some very challenging times during the course of his calling, but God!

As the journey continued, I was assigned by Holy Spirit to carry the office of an Evangelist, Pastor, and now the office of a Prophet. As stated earlier, it didn't come without a very high price! The testing, the trials, the molding! I have travelled to many places, many churches, preaching wherever Holy Spirit led me. Each season that went by, I was learning more and more, and understanding my calling on a greater level. With each new day, I came to recognize what was imparted inside of me to release was not just increasing, but increasing in authority and platform.

Throughout the years, I received many prophecies that the ministry would be used for Government, and Law Enforcement Agencies. I began to see fulfillment in 2015-2016. The Holy Spirit started using me significantly in Governmental prophetic words and I also started United States Law Enforcement org. It has been an honor to be used this way, and in this capacity! It has always been my hope that with each word released, it would bring hope, encouragement, and inspiration to people worldwide!

So as this book came into fruition, I had no idea that through the many years that we have been used to prophesy, that Holy Spirit had a plan to put them into a book form for people to have ready to read at any time! Ten years of prophetic words that I hope will be a source of strength, even guidance, as you start each day, or end each night, to help you understand the *Mysteries of Heaven.*

Part One
Prophetic Words — 2013

John Natale

10/29/2013— Lazarus is Alive

There has been a shift in the atmosphere as Holy Spirit has shown me that the hearts of the people have been revived and are ready for a fresh awakening. The sound of the heartbeat can be heard. Lazarus was raised for one reason....to break the barrier of religion and doubt and to show that there is power over death, both physically and spiritually. A religious spirit that has carried subtle deception is broken. This season, Holy Spirit says, *"Your grave clothes have been removed and the dead things in your life are now alive again."*

Many will say, *"How can this be? What has caused this great sudden change?"* You have entered into a new realm of glory and peace. As with Lazarus, you too will see a brand new day and cause a great stirring with many.

Holy Spirit says, *"Remove the stone. Lazarus, come forth and see your King!"* Your days have not ceased, but just begun!

11/21/2013— Everything Is Going To Be Ok

Today His voice came forth and said these words. *"Tell them today is a good day and everything is going to be ok."*

BE ANXIOUS FOR NOTHING, BUT IN EVERYTHING BY PRAYER AND SUPPLICATION, WITH THANKSGIVING, LET YOUR REQUESTS BE MADE KNOWN TO GOD; AND THE PEACE OF GOD, WHICH SURPASSES ALL UNDERSTANDING, WILL GUARD YOUR HEARTS AND MINDS THROUGH CHRIST JESUS. Philippians 4:6,7

11/24/2013

Expect sudden blessings to come your way, surprises about to knock on your door. Holy Spirit says, *"Do not be discouraged or dismayed, I have all things in My hand."*

12/1/2013

Watch as new doors open this month. As with Joseph, he too did not know when the door was to open. The opportunity will come suddenly and your victory shall be present.

12/4/2013

It's time for the ones who have been neglected, mistreated, and spiritually abused to shine. You have not been forgotten but misled, misguided, and wrongfully judged. It is your time to rise up and take your place. Many say the Spirit is leading them, but this is not so. They have been deceived and hear only their voice and not Mine. They have hindered many lives and caused delay and distraction, but this day is your day of restoration and hope. I have not forgotten, but have seen all. My hand has cleared your path and made every crooked place straight and the road clear for your forward progress.

12/5/2013

Holy Spirit says, *"My presence is more than enough. I love you unconditionally and I do not make mistakes. It does not matter what others think, because I made you!"*

12/9/2013

2014 will be marked as the year that the church gets a greater revelation of unity and purpose. Holy Spirit will be directing many leaders to humble themselves and become Kingdom, not with just the church, but with their personal relationships. It is a YEAR OF SUBMISSION TO OWNERSHIP.

John Natale

"That which you call yours is not so," says the Lord. *"You must advance My Kingdom without fear or compromise. Release My words that come forth as a sword. Did I not tell you that you would be persecuted for following Me? Be a light in a dark place and see the nation changed. Beloved you must act with a Holy desperation that releases a greater glory on the earth. Now is the time to speak, now is the time to act! My Comforter, Holy Spirit will guide and direct you. So do not be afraid, but be bold as a lion and watch the Glory manifest among the people. I see a nation shaken and empowered that will reveal My name in a greater way! Now go and proclaim that I Am alive!"*

12/11/2013

A sound from Heaven will come in the year called 2014 that has not been heard. There will be a rumbling and the skies will manifest with glory that is unfamiliar to the eyes of men.

12/30/2013— Restoration

Many will cry out and pray regarding restoration for their families. They have suffered with discouragement and weariness. Holy Spirit has spoken these words, *"Suddenlies will come forth in this new season that will bring vindication, restoration and resolution. Peace, joy and laughter will accompany these things. My voice has commanded these things to align properly. My voice has brought justice! You have not been forgotten. I see all things and I am Lord over all!"*

Part Two
Prophetic Words — 2014

1/6/2014-Do Not Give Up

Holy Spirit spoke these words to me tonight. You have been through much difficulty and hardship but I am here to comfort you and get you through your time of pain. I will restore your peace and joy, and of this you can be sure. Know that I love you and this will soon come to an end. You will rise up and stand firm on solid ground.

1/8/2014

Sudden surprises and breakthroughs will take place as the week comes to an end. Allow Holy Spirit to refresh you and revive your faith. It will finish well.

1/15/2014-The Year of Pursuit

The definition of *Pursuit*- The action of following or pursuing someone or something. As Israel received her freedom and left the bondage of Egypt, you too will march forward to your promised land. During the course of the year called 2014, you will see the hand and provision of God separate the waters that are blocking your triumphant journey. You must remain strong and be relentless in your course. Many will choose to stay complacent and comfortable.

I say to you this day, look forward to the bigger picture and bigger plan for your life. I move you forward, not just to bless you, but to make My name known to the nations. As you are set free, rise up and be a voice in a lost world that needs My freedom. My will is that all My Children find their freedom and that freedom is everlasting life! I came that not one should perish. This year My church will be a bride that looks outside the walls of religion and sees inside the hearts of lost men.

1/20/2014

Learn to listen to My still, small voice. There are many things that I want to share with you about the plans for your life. Press in to discern My voice from the voice of the deceiver. This week is pivotal for your forward progress. You will overcome and surge forward as you seek Me with all your heart.

1/21/2014

In a dream last night I was shown a wall of water that was coming to the shore. Holy Spirit spoke to me these words, *"This next great surge of Glory that is suddenly going to appear will not be like anything anyone has seen or heard, and that man must get out of the way. This next move of the Spirit must not be violated or hindered. It comes to awaken, restore, refresh and save that which is lost. It will come when you least expect and it comes to revive a nation!"*

1/27/2014

The year called 2014 — a fresh revival and awakening is desired by Holy Spirit, where true hunger lingers and remains obedient to the cause. In John 21, Jesus calls out to Peter to throw the nets on the other side of the boat. Several significant things are on the forecast for this year:

1. Discouragement and weariness will leave the saints individually and corporately.
2. Steps will be taken when you thought you did not have the strength to take them.
3. Provision out of obedience.
4. Holy Spirit will awaken the passion for the harvest.

As the story ends in John 21, Jesus reminds Peter three times with these very special words: *"Simon son of Jonah, do you love Me? Feed My sheep."*

At the end of the day when the dust settles, Jesus reminds him of the price He paid and what He truly came for.

1/31/2014-Destination Unknown

Israel had no idea the fixed point or exact location of where they were actually going when they left Egypt, but there was one thing for sure, they knew they had purpose and their journey was not going to end without seeing that come to fruition.

This day you might not know exactly where you're going right now in your life, but eventually you're going to get there, and when you get there you'll look back and see how it was all worth it.

2/9/2014

The thief comes only to steal, kill, and destroy but I have come to give you life ad give it to the full. Relationships in your life this season will take on a new meaning and purpose. There will be a revival in these relationships that will produce great fruit. Watch and see as many are encouraged and refreshed. I have placed these sons and daughters in your life for purpose. My purpose! You all will prosper because I know your hearts and your hearts are pure. This will be very beneficial to the plans for this year. You are being aligned to see this come to pass and behold it shall come quickly!

2/27/14

It's a good year that will bring about sudden opportunities. Doors are beginning to close. Do not be discouraged, for this is My will. These changes will come and reveal itself in the season called Spring. Start to prepare and remove fear of change. Look ahead to Promise!

3/3/14

The awakening will come, the revival will begin when the church stops grumbling with each other, stops debating each other, and just cries out to God to shake our nation. The lost need what we have. They don't need to see a people divided among themselves. They need to see a people unified!

If My people who are called by My name will humble themselves, and pray and seek My face, and turn from their wicked ways, then I will hear from heaven, and will forgive their sin and heal their land. 2Chronicles 7:14

3/9/14

Holy Spirit says that, *"The joy of the Lord shall be reinstated in My church."* Rejoice Children, there is much to be happy for. Enter into His gates with thanksgiving, And into His courts with praise. Be thankful to Him, and bless His name. For the Lord is good; His mercy is everlasting, And His truth endures to all generations.

3/11/14

Was awakened by Holy Spirit speaking these words, *"My Church must represent Me well. They must put their focus on those who do not follow*

Me. *Light cannot penetrate darkness if it is hidden in secluded places. Tell them these things!"*

"No one, when he has lit a lamp, puts it in a secret place or under a basket, but on a Lamp stand, that those who come in may see the light." (Luke 11:33)

3/17/14

It does not matter how many keys people have to give you. Their keys do not open the doors to your destiny. The only key that you need is the key that King Jesus Himself hands to you. For that key opens many doors!

3/19/14

Holy Spirit says that there are things that need to be released in order for fresh, sudden blessing to come forth. Take time to evaluate specific things that are happening in your life right now, and be sensitive to the Holy Spirit as He makes known to you these things that you will let go.

3/20/14

Get used to the fact that this is going to be one of the greatest years of your life. The priests have gathered the stones. The memorial is set in place. Remember where you came from. The land of milk and honey is just ahead of you.

3/21/14

The enemy is trying to delay things. Holy Spirit says, *"Do not be discouraged. These things shall take place in its proper time. All things are in order. You shall see things move, and move swiftly on your behalf. Be prepared, all is in alignment with My plan that is for you."*

3/22/14

One very special key is about to open one very special door in your life.

HE WHO HAS THE KEY OF DAVID, HE WHO OPENS AND NO ONE SHUTS, AND SHUTS AND NO ONE OPENS. Revelation 3:7

3/25/14

There's a time when a Father desires his Children to sit at his feet and just wait for his command. Holy Spirit has directed us to release this word to many right now. Just wait on God and be patient, for His Rhema word shall come mightily.

3/27/14

Press through the turbulence as it will only last a short while. Change is critical in this hour, and you must not be distracted by the noise. Keep your faith and stand tall.

3/29/14

Staying complacent and not taking a step to move forward will not only cause your future to be hindered but the generation behind you that is seeking your guidance. Don't be afraid to take the step that will ultimately prove to be worth your risk.

3/31/14

Sometimes the waters seem so rough that crossing is impossible. Holy Spirit changed the process from going through as Israel did, to now rising above and walking on the water. Today Holy Spirit wants you to understand that He is going to cause you to rise above your situation and not drown in it. Victory is looking in the eyes of Jesus first, and then you take the step out of the boat called Comfort.

———

4/1/14

His blessing and favor over you and those after you doesn't change. You will fully get the revelation that He is a King that keeps His promises and prepares a table for His Children. Therefore know that the Lord your God, He is God, the faithful God who keeps covenant and mercy for a thousand generations with those who love Him and keep His commandments (Deuteronomy 7:9 NKJV).

4/2/14

Don't look back at the door or doors that have just closed in your life. The enemy wants to slow down the pursuit of the new door that is open for you to enter. Take big steps and walk confident. Holy Spirit will not disappoint you.

4/4/14

Tell the people they must not be gripped with fear of any kind. Fear is from the enemy and it does not come from Me. Do not confuse wisdom with fear. My people are called to be a people that are different from this world, that are not of this world. I tell you today that you must not act like the world, you must not have the same fears, but are the representatives of the Kingdom of the Most High God. You have been called to lead and not follow. You must carry a new mindset that operates in great faith and confidence, knowing that I have given you authority and power. Nothing has changed, as in the days of Peter and Paul, these men knew the authority that was given to them. That same authority has been given to you. Again I say, nothing has changed.

8/9/14

This morning my three-year old was used to inspire me to write to you. As I was drinking my morning coffee in the living room he awoke, came down the stairs and said, "You left me upstairs in my room." In response I said, "Jacob, Jesus never leaves us nor forsakes us, and Daddy was right here the whole time waiting for you to open your eyes."

This scenario has prophetically inspired me to speak over you and release comfort to you that Jesus never leaves you alone, is always with you, watching over you, guiding you, loving you, and even when there's times when you don't feel that His presence is near, He is right there sitting in the room watching over you!

Today, receive these words over your life. *I am with you always and I never walk away! You do not need to worry. You never have to call out to Me to show up as if I was somewhere else. That special day when you invited Me in your heart and life, there was a sound in Heaven that announced your victory and to let you know that you will never be alone!*

9/1/14

Holy Spirit is releasing a double portion of grace as you complete this storm. The winds will suddenly come to a calm and the water shall be still. In this present season of your life, growth and maturity has come and will reveal a bigger picture of your destiny. These things needed to take place as you have been in preparation for new assignments and new connections. Opportunities will come, and the glory of Jesus will be demonstrated through you to many lives near and far. *"Hold onto My word,"* says Holy Spirit, *"and renew your strength."* These words do not come back void, but hold true forever.

9/27/14

As we approach the last three months or quarter of 2014, this is what we have been released to speak forth to the church. As Abraham walked a hill relentlessly pursuing his promise and not giving up, even in the midst of answers and breakthrough that were not physically seen, there at the top of the hill was a *kairos* moment of time waiting to be born. These months ahead as October through December come forth will also produce that *kairos* moment for you, and great blessing will come to fruition as you continue to march to the top of the hill that is called Promise. Things will come into place as puzzle pieces are placed together to display the true image of what is being prepared for you—to prepare and facilitate a new beginning and opportunity for 2015.

Kairos (καιρός) is an ancient Greek word meaning the right or opportune moment (the supreme moment).

9/29/14

Jeremiah 13:1-11 The Lord is preparing now to remove the things that have been clinging to you and have kept you in bondage. As the sash was placed in the hole of the rock and later brought to ruins, this very thing that has held you back and has kept you gripped with fear, anxiety, frustration, and confusion, the Lord says, *"It's no longer. The sash profits a man nothing. You shall cling to me and I will be your source of strength, hope, and victory."* Now is your time of freedom and your time to move forward, possess the land and the blessing that God is giving you. Rejoice. Victory is here!

10/1/14

Get ready for sudden encounters with Holy Spirit that will encourage you to press forward and enter into your promise. Scenarios are about to be revealed and take place in your life that were not necessarily what you had planned. Holy Spirit is giving more than you expected in this new season. Sudden divine opportunities will enable you to engage and prosper in the many areas of your life. It's a time to reap what you have sowed!

Part Three
Prophetic Words — 2015

5/4/15

Holy Spirit revealed to me in the midnight hours that Washington D.C. was going to experience a shift, and breakthrough would come suddenly. There is a strong presence of God over the land. A deep stirring is in my heart to pray for our leaders, Government, and the people that live in the district. In the Spirit I heard, *"Pray for them, for many are seeking Me for answers, but need to seek Me for direction. There is a beauty there in the natural, and this beauty will manifest in the spirit as well."*

5/7/15

One of the hardest things in life is change. Many of you are in the midst of change right now, and it seems not only hard, but terrifying. Holy Spirit wanted me to tell you that you are not alone in this transition. It will all come together soon and you will remember the goodness of God and how He never fails!

5/18/15

There's been an unusual amount of warfare, torment, and depression that the enemy has been throwing your way, but there is good news! All is quiet again! Holy Spirit has released angels to fight and clear the atmosphere. There are times that you just don't have the strength to fight and feel like giving in, but He will never let you cave in. You are not going to fail. You are victorious and Jesus loves you just the way you are. He never sees a failing Child, but one that He so loves and adores.

5/20/15

Situations and scenarios will be presented today in an uncommonly good way. Things that you weren't expecting shall come forth and be a breath of fresh air to you and your family. Meditate on the word and give thanks to God. For some doors have opened, ones that you were not expecting.

"CALL UNTO ME AND I'LL SHOW YOU GREAT AND UNSEARCHABLE THINGS THAT YOU DO NOT KNOW." JEREMIAH 33:3

5/24/15

As we celebrate Pentecost, Holy Spirit desires one thing. Let him do whatever He wants to do and get out-of-the way. Great demonstration of power, deliverance and healing shall accompany those that allow the freedom of the Spirit to rule and reign in their congregations today. There you'll see significant breakthrough, signs, and wonders. Cities and nations shall be shaken.

5/25/15

Great peace is being released right now. God's favor is upon you. Strength, joy, and rest shall accompany you. You have overcome an intense season, but you have overcome adversity. Prepare for the door to open that has been prophesied over you. All things are aligned and prepared to be given unto you.

5/27/15

The fiery darts of the enemy are no match for the glory and power of God that is within and around you. The enemy has been trying to keep you held back, but Holy Spirit is your guide and source of strength. This is your season to shine, and shine you will. You will make it and you will overcome! It doesn't matter what you see right now. You have kept diligent, and have not given up! You are a conqueror! What does matter is He is in control and it will be good! For He is good and loves you so much! His love and peace is surrounding you right now!

John Natale

5/28/15

Open doors, Open doors, Open doors. Breakthrough, Breakthrough, Breakthrough. Today is the day of opportunity and promotion. Do not be discouraged about what you see in the natural. The light has removed the darkness and victory is at hand. *"You have been pursuing with your own strength, now pursue in the spirit and do not wrestle in the flesh any longer says the Lord. In this you will find certain victory that I have planned for you."*

6/1/15

Never underestimate your ability to achieve and overcome all things. God has a great plan for you. When others say you are not equipped, God says you can do all things! Today you are being reminded that you shall see many things come to pass in your life that man said would not! *"WHEN THEY SAW THE COURAGE OF PETER AND JOHN AND REALIZED THAT THEY WERE UNSCHOOLED, ORDINARY MEN, THEY WERE ASTONISHED AND THEY TOOK NOTE THAT THESE MEN HAD BEEN WITH JESUS." ACTS 4:13*

6/3/15

One of the tools that the enemy uses against the body of Christ is deception. In the spirit, I heard the Lord say He was removing all deception that is causing hindrance, delay, and distraction in the believers' lives. Today, this word is for you. Know that this demonic spirit has been broken and freedom has come to your door. Take this opportunity to move forward, have better clarity and understanding as you progress in your destiny today! You are victorious and you are an Overcomer!

6/6/15

Unusual and unexpected circumstances that came your way and brought despair and frustration have lifted. When you thought this was the straw that would break the camel's back, Holy Spirit has spoken these words, *"The gates of hell shall not prevail against you. I am strengthening you and empowering you. Your faith has made you whole".*

6/9/15

Play Christmas Music! Then the sound of Heaven came down and these are the words that came forth.

"My people have endured much pain and anguish. They have suffered but they have not succumbed to the enemy and the plans for defeat. There are many things happening right now for them. Things they do not see. Many of you are in a closing season and you have done well. Greater than you think! I am pleased with you, My Child. Well pleased! I am opening doors for you right now and you will see great blessing come to you. These doors are for you to walk through now. So walk and do not look back!"

6/11/15

The door is closed. You have done well. The enemy will try to bring discouragement in the form of making a mistake. I am bringing clarity, confidence, and confirmation. Do not try to turn back and open it. This door has been removed completely only to push you to the one that is open now. Do not be afraid. This will not be as hard as you think it will be, but peaceful and refreshing. For you have made it through a long and strenuous season that did not come without sacrifice and persecution. These summer months will bring the resources and strength you need to get through, and prepare you for a wonderful and prosperous new journey!

6/15/15

Oh how I long to bless you and reward you for your diligence and perseverance. Even when you think you are not overcoming or prevailing, I am pleased by your faithfulness and strength. Many have believed this lie that you are not moving forward, but I say to you now that things move in the Spirit first before they move in the natural. Yes, things are moving for you! Just as I have planned for them to move. It has not been easy, but it has been fruitful in ways that you can see and not see. All that matters is what I see, and what I deem as righteousness. You are Mine, and what I have seen is beauty and a Child still fighting for what they know is truth. Now you have come to a place of victory, blessing, and vindication. It's yours My Child, it's yours! You have made it! Just like I knew you would!

6/16/15

Changing things as you read this. Holy Spirit is positioning things and aligning you for great blessing. You are beautiful just the way you are. Don't ever doubt yourself. Prepare for the sudden wind of God to take you to your promise land.

6/25/15

Yes, you have come to an end, to a Season of Sacrifice. Many things have come forth from this assignment, and you have finished well. Do not look back or be discouraged. For your reward has come. Heaviness has lifted and freedom has come! Declare and believe that doors are open for you and expect great things to arise! For a new assignment is now ready to be introduced to you. Take this time to catch your breath and rejoice My Child. You have done well. Even though you were expecting more response from your well doing, it is I that sees all things and makes all things come to an end and to begin again! You are where I have placed you and that placement is perfect! For this path and current time in your life is positioned perfectly for you to develop and operate in greatness.

Prepare and get ready for the unfolding of many wonderful things! Yes, it is that time Child! Get ready!

6/27/15

As we approach the month of July, things that needed to fall into place are now being positioned properly for your advancement and breakthrough. Take this time to prepare and listen carefully to what Holy Spirit is saying. What was once unsure and unclear is now in focus and ready to be revealed. The enemy tried to convince you that only destruction and despair would follow you all the days of your life, but God has made the way once again. The summer shall be filled with opportunity and promotion. Things will transpire in ways that you were not expecting, but will only come in a greater way, filled with a double portion of blessing and wonder!

7/2/15

Do not be concerned with what things look like in the natural. You have not done anything wrong, and you are on a path that I have chosen. What is happening in the Spirit realm right now will reveal in the moments ahead what is important. This hour Holy Spirit is aligning all the pieces necessary to fulfill a wondrous summer. You will not be discouraged any longer, and in the days ahead that come forth, you will see a great plan unfold that is filled with abundance, joy, and peace. Prepare as you are refreshed and filled with a new level of joy that only I can bring. It is a good time for you now. I have seen your hunger and desire for more of Me. You have pursued Me to reveal My will, and now is the time to release an overflow of My love.

7/4/15

Things are happening in the Spirit that have the reflections of sudden bursts of light. This day is a reminder that your faith has been diligent and filled with perseverance. The sound of heaven shall break forth in your life and the sight of My hand shall remove all obstacles and create new paths for a fresh start and new beginning. Rejoice for a great time has come in your life that has been hanging in the balance. There is a fresh outpouring being released to you now, so open up your heart and allow it to fill you.

7/6/15

For the many that are listening, I am your source of strength in time of need. I will not allow your heart to be torn any longer. I have been listening to your cries and to the words that you speak in the hours of your trial. But know this My Child, that in a wilderness comes great revelation and understanding. Many reject this place, but you have overcome much adversity and pain. In this hour I am preparing your next step into a beautiful land called Promise. It shall flow with milk and honey and be a place of healing, joy, and refreshment. Divine connections, opportunities and assignments are all here to establish you and cause you to soar into destiny! Prepare and watch as these things unfold quickly My Child!

7/11/15

Recently the Holy Spirit has revealed some answers and direction to your forward progress. The enemy has been hard at work to bring discouragement in the form of deception. I heard these words in the Spirit.

"You are only kidding yourself. Holy Spirit wants you to know that this is a lie and what has been revealed and given will not be stopped. You are right where you are supposed to be on this path, and step by step you will see all things unfold and placement shall be given to you. Rejoice, for I am

aligning all things according to its time, and you will be filled with laughter as these things are revealed to you."

7/14/15

Why do you worry My Child? Have you not heard My voice rise above the darkness and declare that your freedom has come? In this hour I am working out all things on your behalf and completing the stage that will be revealed to you soon enough. You must not worry, but be encouraged because it has come! I am not one that makes a promise and breaks that promise! You see my Child, I love you so much! I love you more than you know! in the days to come, things will unfold and take shape. They will come together swiftly and cause you to be filled with a heightened joy that has not been there presently. This joy will refresh you and confirm My word in this season. A Father that loves to surprise His Children!

7/17/15

What is this attack that comes to the doorsteps of My Children? For it is not so! Do you not know that these are Mine and the gates of hell will not prevail against them? Enough, says the Lord of Hosts! Their hearts and their eyes are fixed on Me! There is nothing that can separate them from the love of the Father. As you have pressed in My Child and fought with diligence and have continued to move forward with faith, I am pouring the foundation of something brand new for you. This will move quickly, and the walls shall be put in place to establish a new dwelling place that will be filled with the fragrance of Heaven. The slate has been cleaned, My Child. All things become new, and as you continue this journey you will see many things added to this new adventure that is called destiny! Arise and be glad, for your reward has come!

7/21/15

The time has come My Child, yes it has surely come when certain things in your life come to an end, and brand new things come to the surface and are revealed. The enemy has made a last minute effort to discourage you with fear and doubt. Very specific scenarios have made themselves known again and came to remind you that you are in fact not victorious, but defeated.

But I have given you strength and power to overcome all things. My presence is with you in this hour, and as these days unfold and the hours go by, you will see how this all unfolds in a glorious way for you. You are not alone My Child, I am always with you to comfort and guide you. The summer is not one that brings defeat only, but is accompanied by blessing, breakthrough, and favor. You will shine and you will prosper. Very significant prayers that have been on your heart are now ready to be answered in ways that you did not imagine. Rejoice My Child! It is here!

7/22/15

And this too shall pass. When these things around you bring concern and pain, I AM. It's nothing but a spirit of deception and delusion. It is not so, says God! You are running My Child and run you shall. To a place called promise! Nothing shall stop you for your breath and your strength comes from Me. The finish line is just ahead and you shall cross with your arms raised high. The celebration is coming My Child. Victory is right in front of you!

7/26/15

Just as was spoken earlier, the enemy has tried to come again and bring destruction to your house, but I have intervened on your behalf to bring peace and joy. There has been a shift in the atmosphere this day to bring you to another level of freedom. Do not be concerned how you will get there, just know that it is I that hold all things and have a wonderful plan of fruition for your life. Breakthrough and forward progress has been achieved in the spiritual realm, and suddenly you will see great breakthrough that you are seeking in the natural.

8/1/15

Many are traveling and pursuing their destiny. Much progress has been made and diligence and faith has been present. At this time, there are those that hear the sound of chariots coming to disrupt their course, and in the natural see a roadblock hindering their way. The enemy is trying to convince you that nothing will happen now and the forces behind you will soon overtake you and defeat you. But I say this, says the Lord, as with Moses, when they came to the sea, I will once again prove My power and love and cause the hindrance to separate and move aside. The path will be made clear and forward progress will once again be made. You will cross over, never to look back again!

8/5/15

Everything is going to be alright. Do not be deceived or distracted. The enemy tried to bring you into a place that looked and seemed like My will for your life, but I have revealed the darkness and have broken the chain that was made for a trap in this season. Your weariness will be replaced with strength, wisdom, and revelation. You are now in a season of great movement and progress. As you proceed through the August month, things will suddenly become easy and light. Preparation shall also accompany you as this month ends and September comes to bring a new door of breakthrough and opportunity. I have a plan that will not only surprise you, but the many that seek My will and desire for what I desire for this nation. For My plans are good and bring hope and joy. Rest My Child, and do not strive but take a breath and allow Me to comfort you with My peace. You are all right, and nothing will ever change that.

8/6/15

Beloved, there is a place that I desire for you to dwell. In this place peace, joy, comfort, and rest all dwell together. I am positioning you for great advancement and breakthrough. Did I not say that August would get lighter as it progressed through the days heading to September? For that month ahead you shall see things turn and become as beautiful as the leaves turn and display their beauty. Rejoice beloved, for that month comes and it will be one that is not forgotten.

8/7/15

I am with you always. Now and forevermore. You are not alone. There is no need to be afraid, My Child.

Oh how I love to see you worship. You bring Me joy and I laugh when you sing. There will be a day when we worship together. When we laugh together. That day comes quickly My Child.

8/10/15

These are the words that have been spoken tonight by Holy Spirit.

"Now you have come into a place of worship and intimacy. There has come a time now that in the secret place a paradigm shift has taken place. Breakthrough is now available to you and your family. Doors that were closed and paths that were blocked are now open and clear for you to move forward. The days that have been heavy are now days that will be light. Watch and see how this month ends far greater than it began. My will and purpose for you is to thrive, and not just exist. You shall finish this month well My Child."

8/12/15

This word is from Holy Spirit as a source of strength for those that have been struggling with unsaved loved ones. He is faithful and just to the righteous. His word never returns void and His promises are yes and amen. *"BUT THE LOVE OF THE LORD REMAINS FOREVER WITH THOSE WHO FEAR HIM. HIS SALVATION EXTENDS TO THE CHILDREN'S CHILDREN OF THOSE WHO ARE FAITHFUL TO HIS COVENANT, OF THOSE WHO OBEY HIS COMMANDMENTS!" PSALM 103:17-18*

8/16/15

Holy Spirit has spoken these words this evening. *"It's time now to leave dead things and stop trying to resuscitate them. Walk forward and chase after your future. You will not be disappointed."*

8/17/15

Life has endless possibilities for creativity and opportunity. Don't let setbacks and distractions stop your progress. Run the race with diligence and perseverance. Your reward is coming sooner than you think.

8/20/15

Can you see it My Child? Can you hear it? The sound of change and opportunity is here. The shifting has taken place and the adjustments to your life are now in process. Take this time to reflect on how you have overcome diversity and difficulties. The road now is straight and smooth. You will move quickly, and the necessary details to your inheritance and breakthrough will arise and manifest. Behold, your progress is moving like the wind and flows without interruption.

8/24/15

Align yourself with Me and do not worry, for the seasons change and adjustments are made, but I am forever constant and trustworthy. I am restoring you to a new level of thinking and doing. Fear and doubt are being broken off and being replaced with joy and peace. Now is a great time to rejoice, for opportunity and advancement are knocking at your door.

8/31/15

Do not be afraid My Children, for I am with you today and always. I will take care of you in times of need and times of plenty. Be sensitive to Holy Spirit and do exactly what is instructed to do. As you are obedient, times of refreshing and peace shall come.

9/2/15

The greater the expectation you have on My love, the closer you will come to the reality of your own individuality. My love is in you and will always fill your heart to overflowing rivers of peace and joy. I speak to you now, and I'm here to remind you that My desire is for you to flourish and shine. You have a wonderful destiny filled with opportunity and victory My Child, never forget that.

9/8/15

For I am not a God that brings distraction or despair. I am a God that is just, gracious, and filled with love. Why do so many of My Children worry about tomorrow when I have made it known to you that there is no worry or fear that you should have overshadow you? For in Me there is peace and joy. Did I not tell Peter that he should not have fear, but rejoice?

In this, I say this to My church now, Do not fear for what you see or hear. In Me, there is no fear and there is no worry. I rule and reign and I am moving in this nation in a powerful way. My people are praying and My people are singing. The hearts of many are crying out to Me for change and to revive this nation, and those cries have been heard. Nothing will stop this, and I say nothing will come against the plans that are in place and the things that are moving mightily in the Spirit realm. Do not be deceived and allow the enemy to taint what you see or what you hear. Holy Spirit is clearing the path of delusion and creating an atmosphere of clear, sound vision and revelatory hearing.

This nation is moving forward because My people are praying! They are singing! and their hearts desire is for My love to be poured out among people. This is being revealed more than ever. There is a stirring in the land which is now present that will facilitate a great awakening that is not far ahead, My Children, but moments ahead. This will be established quickly and be rooted in the soil that will not be quenched, but continue with more power and succession. Rejoice My Children, Great days are ahead!

9/9/15

These are the words that the Holy Spirit has spoken. *"For I am not a God that brings distraction or despair. I am a God that is just, gracious and filled with love. Why do so many of My Children worry about tomorrow when I have made it known to you that there is no worry or fear that you should have overshadow you. For in Me there is peace and joy. Did I not tell Peter that he should not have fear but rejoice?*

In this, I say this to My church now. Do not fear for what you see or hear. In Me, there is no fear and there is no worry. I rule and reign and I am moving in this nation in a powerful way. My people are praying and My people are singing. The hearts of many are crying out to Me for change and to revive this nation and those cries have been heard. Nothing will stop this and I say nothing will come against the plans that are in place and the things that are moving mightily in the Spirit realm.

Do not be deceived and allow the enemy to taint what you see or what you hear.

Holy Spirit is clearing the path of delusion and creating an atmosphere of clear, sound vision and revelatory hearing. This nation is moving forward because My people are praying! They are singing! and their hearts desire is for My love to be poured out among people. This is being revealed more than ever. There is a stirring in the land which is now present that will facilitate a great awakening that is not far ahead My Children, but moments ahead. This will be established quickly and be rooted in the soil that will not be quenched but continue with more power and succession.

Rejoice My Children, Great days are upon you and great days are ahead!

9/10/15

Prepare My Children, for the winds have shifted and the atmosphere is at peace. Angels are being released and the path is clear. I am making the way clear and positioning you for a great outpouring of My presence. Signs and wonders shall accompany you, and many people shall see My glory come forth in sudden ways. But I speak to you now, and tell you do not be distracted by the words of those that speak destruction and turmoil. For this is not so. For a great movement of healing and salvation is now upon this land. You shall see many people come to know me in the season called Autumn. As the leaves change and are filled with brilliant, colors, so will this season change for you. Get ready for a majestic season of brilliant change that reveals the most glorious colors of My beauty on your life.

9/11/15

I do not partner with the enemy to awaken the hearts of people. I am sovereign and I am just. I am full of love and full of grace. My name, My glory, and My power is used in this nation and the nations of the world through the hearts of young and old. Be a voice, show the love, and allow the peace that only I can give surpass all understanding.

9/12/15

The words will be silenced and the light shall shine. Darkness is removed and fear and doubt has been crushed. At this time, fear, worry, and anxiety has gripped My people with uncertainty. But I tell you this now, and in this, you can be sure. I Am, I Am; and I will silence the words that have brought a disturbance to My people. That once again, the enemy has used the spoken words of misleading false truths that come to bring disunity and confusion to My bride. This is not so! For you will not see destruction, but an establishment of My glory and My people operating in love and power. Not tomorrow, but today, and the days to come!

9/16/15

There has been much resistance. Many of my Children have been suffering in this hour. A great surge of discouragement and depression was released and brought confusion to the hearts of many. The enemy has been diligent and has attacked the mind, but I have brought peace and comfort. I have released a mighty wind of My presence. I have strengthened My bride. I have released confidence and comfort. I have restored the broken heart. I have strengthened the mind. I have released and equipped you with the spirit of a warrior that rises up and raises his sword in victory, and prophesies to the giant that he shall fall. Victory has been given and forward progress shall continue.

9/17/15

A Prophet is in need of our prayers and support. We believe in him and the ministry that he has been given to steward.

During prayer, I heard these words from Holy Spirit regarding Prophet Kim Clement.

"My son, I am with you always. I have never left your side. From the days of your youth you have always been a voice that was willing to speak and your passion came from My heart. Yes, you have overcome much adversity and trial and you shall see an even greater breakthrough that is revealed during this time of transition. You haven't been silenced as many would say, but only taken into a place of rest and companionship that will generate a new beginning of unprecedented favor and facilitation of My promises. Many of My Children have felt the burden of this trial and have been moved with compassion and love for you and your family. In this, I am revealing the love that you carry for My bride. Many that questioned you will now support you and call you friend. Their hearts have turned and during this season, you will be found victorious and restored. During the month of September, My glory shall move in supernatural, unexpected ways and be revealed in you at unexpected times. For the heart of the Father loves to surprise His Children. Over the next four days, there will be an increase that comes that will be a sign to you and those around you that I am in control, My Child."

9/21/15

Now you see and you hear. I am just and I rule with a sovereign hand. The voices are sent out to be My ambassadors, and to declare the beauty of My nature and My kingdom. There is peace on the land and there is opportunity. My desire is to fill this nation with such an outpouring of My love that has not been felt to the magnitude of which it shall come. There is a special place that has now come, My Children. The windows are open and the people are ready. Many have been praying and waiting for this hour to come. I have heard the prayers of those that have contended for this nation and it shall be so. That in the coming moments ahead, you shall see what you have been crying out for. Revival in America! These things in which you are hungry for shall come upon you suddenly.

9/24/15

Greater, far greater than you ever have seen before! The wind has come and pushed all distraction and resistance away from you. Yes, there will always be things you deal with My Child, and they will come and they will go. But I tell you this day that you do not have to be overwhelmed by the plans of the enemy, for he has already been defeated and you have already won! Have I not told you that I am with you and the plans for you are good and nothing will cause that to cease? So many have waited for these days to come and their wait is over. The season called Autumn is upon you now! This season will produce much joy within you. It will be a unusual season that surprises many. Will it be forgotten? No, for there will be specific signs to My church and in this nation that will set things in motion for a great ending to a great year. There will be great shifting and great progress. New open doors and new beginnings. Do not be discouraged for you have been faithful in what I have given you to do for Me. Remember, My Child, that you are never alone. My presence is more than enough for you. In this season, I am establishing with you new relationships that will advance My Kingdom on the earth. It is a time to rejoice and rejoice you shall! Laughter upon laughter shall fill the houses and a greater realm of joy shall overflow and bring great peace and satisfaction to the lives of many. Enjoy My presence and run with Me now! The gates are open for you!

9/29/15

A dream that I had regarding the presence of God and the outpouring that is about to come. I was in a boat waiting to leave the port. As we started heading out from the dock, I could see a large blue wave that was bigger than any other wave known to man behind me and was drawing closer. The color was such a beautiful blue that was indescribable. I heard Holy Spirit say these words.

"Get out of the boat and lay face down on the dock. The water which represents My presence and power is coming over you. Do not be afraid of this. You will see and experience a greater outpouring of My glory, My power and My presence in this season. I have asked My bride to lay down before Me as a prophetic posture to yield their will and surrender all that has been a distraction and hindrance to Me. To prepare for the weight of My glory. You will feel this wave hit you with a mighty force, but it will only saturate you and fill you to overflowing. This will prepare you for the days ahead that are coming quickly. There is a quickening and there is a stirring. The plans that I have purposed for in this hour are now ready to be released and shall come swiftly to you, My bride."

9/30/15

Remind them of My word. Tell them to call upon Me and I will tell them remarkable secrets that they do not know, for they are coming for them and their families. The day has come, My Children, that such an outpouring is upon you. As the clouds gather and are above you, so is this glory that is about to fall. Many have waited for this time and many have suffered much and yet they have persevered in well-doing. But a great peace is all around you. A great unity is here now. You will see these things unfold as the weeks go by, and the months fade. October shall be a significant season that produces new relationships and fruit. A great outpouring of love as there will be a new addition to your families. People that you never expected to be connected with, will now be established in your life. The ones that the enemy detached from you shall be restored and great healing shall be present with new joy and love. Things will take on new shape and new meaning in this month called October, My Child. For it shall come, and it shall be well.

10/7/15

You have been resilient and faithful during this time of perseverance. Presently, the fire has increased with intensity, but you have kept strong and full of courage. In this hour, you are coming out of the flames, and what the enemy planned for destruction, I have made perfection. As with the three men that came out as well, you too will be a living testimony in this season and those around you will see that the fire did not burn you, but only purify you as gold.

10/11/15

For the enemy has come suddenly to produce a quick attack that was not expected during your time of peace, but I have destroyed all his works and plans and what was intended for destruction has been replaced with multiplication. Great is your reward, for you have been found faithful and I love what I see in you My Child. I KNOW THE LORD IS ALWAYS WITH ME. I WILL NOT BE SHAKEN, FOR HE IS RIGHT BESIDE ME. PSALM 16:8 NLT

10/13/15

Keep your head up My Child. Things are about to change and change shall come in a glorious way! You have done well. You are victorious and you have overcome. I love you more than you know. I am always here for you. Not a day goes by that I do not think about you. I watch you and My gaze is always upon you. The time of your life that you presently walk in shall be called the season of Gratitude. October shall be the month that great Thanksgiving is established.

You say, 'Is not November the month that we sit and give thanks?'

Yes it is so, but this month is one that shall remain and captivate you with My presence, and that is My word for you in this hour. Get ready Child, October, October! As you pour into Me in a deeper realm I shall pour into you. There will be much to be thankful for in this month, and in this you can be sure. *The birds of the air are taken care of, and they rejoice with their song in the morning! You shall rejoice as well as the new day comes that will change all things!*

10/14/15

Humble yourselves and allow My word to deeply penetrate your inner man. For today I am speaking to you and guiding you. Don't let distractions come in the way of My leading. For this is a important time to listen and discern. Watch what unfolds as the week progresses. Time to move forward!

10/18/15

Don't be so concerned on how your victory and breakthrough will come. It is already finished and waiting for you. In its time, it will be revealed. Set your sight on today and enjoy My presence as you live your everyday life. Remember that as much as you seek change and change will come, that I am with you now, and that is good news. Make the most of your season now. There is much blessing in this present time and it shall be overflow and abundance.

10/19/15

Do not put any trust in man, but put all trust in Me. Many of My Children are placing too much emphasis on the comfort of approval and acceptance. It's time that you break free from these bondages that place a wall between you and I. Prepare for a new season that gives way to freedom and revived self confidence and self worth as you step into a new dimension of My love.

10/21/15

Prepare for change that causes swift movement and stability. Things are aligning for you now that will position you for the next big surge forward. What has been expectant shall arrive in its time. Do not be frustrated or concerned about the timing of your next move. It has already taken place in the spirit, soon to manifest in the natural.

10/23/15

Each of you are trying so hard to figure out your identity and the place where you fit in. I am here to tell you stop trying so hard! Receive strength, confidence and comfort from My love. Do not strive any longer to establish a place called success. You are already successful and victorious in Me. As you pursue and surrender your will to Me, I will establish you exactly where you are to be, and most of all what you are to be! This world does not bring comfort nor does any material thing, but will only bring disappointment. For it lasts only for a moment. My love and My plans for you last for an eternity. I will bring you peace and joy and in this you can be sure.

10/26/15

I watch you everyday of your life My Child. The things that keep you busy. It brings me such joy to see you overcoming the things that test your faith and inner man. You have come such a long way during this season of your life. Many times your strength was failing, but you called out to Me to be refreshed and strengthened. Your joy, your laughter, your tears, I have seen it all. I have not let a day go by without a plan and purpose for your well-being that is always at work and guiding you to peace and victory. My Child, you will see how this month of October ends in a glorious way. You have allowed concerns to enter your mind and worry to disrupt your progress, but you will see how My plans are far greater than anything that is made with the hands of man. Rise up and call unto Me! For your trust and faith that has been established by Me will be rewarded in many ways! Does not My word say, FAITH IS A SUBSTANCE OF THINGS HOPED FOR, THE EVIDENCE OF THINGS UNSEEN?

Do not be afraid, for I am with you and will never leave you.

10/28/15

My Child, you are so close! There are times that you get discouraged and frustrated that I am not speaking to you, but if you only knew what was really happening in the Spirit, you would be filled with such joy and peace. My Child, during those times when My voice is not heard, I am gazing into your eyes. Looking at a Child that I so dearly love. There are many times that a Father just wants to look at the beauty of a Child that brings such joy and laughter. A Father knows when a Child needs to hear His voice. Do not concerned any longer, and do not worry. You are heading into a glorious victory! You are moving forward! There will be times when this doesn't seem so, but do not be convinced of this because of what you see in the natural. All things will come into place as needed. Remember the words that were spoken earlier about October, and prepare for excellence in November. For in this month that is ahead, it shall be one that brings celebration! Great celebration!

10/30/15

You have been praying about specific situations in your life that needed change, and specific dates and times. There has been a conflict that in the natural you were greatly concerned with. These have been granted simply because they are all part of My will. What was concerning you shall not be a concern any longer. I know your heart. You never have to remind Me of that! It is your heart that fills Me with joy. It is your heart that is one with Me. I have your best interest in mind and it is well My Child. November is coming and it shall arrive in its beauty and it shall progress in peace and splendor.

11/1/15

I am always here to take care of you. One month has passed and another has come. It shall be well with you, and it shall be one that brings you that much closer to a grand finale to a year that released prosperity in the spirit realm as well as the natural realm. In this month called November you will learn and observe that your sacrifice and perseverance do not go unnoticed. It is through your faith that mountains have been removed, obstacles destroyed, and these things shall not be visible again.

You have made great strides to your destiny and promise land. Keep fighting and keep believing. You will finish strong and you will be amazed how strong and courageous you actually are. Much stronger than you thought. Greater faith than you thought. You have risen above your situation and you have conquered certain giants that held you back from abundance. Now is your time to rejoice. For I am rejoicing with you. Well done Child! Well done!

11/3/15

Call unto Me Child, call unto Me. For the wind has come and the cries of the Children are present. But, I say to you in this moment that you will not walk in defeat, but victory. For the enemy comes to steal, kill, and destroy but I have come to give you life and life more abundantly. My Children are not of this world and do not partake of its sufferings. I have given you all power to overcome all things. I am releasing to you a greater revelation of My love and authority. This revelation will cause you to see things in My ways and not yours. Sudden miracles, sudden manifestations of My glory! What once was will not be any longer. A renewed mindset that sees things the way I see things. You shall be stronger and your faith and expectation shall be changed. I am shutting doors in your life that gave room to the enemy to have access. These will shutM never to be opened again! It is time now that your countenance and your posture rises up and shines like the sun! A Warrior has been revived today, a Warrior that is not shaken, but prepared for victory. Child, I am stronger and I am greater than all circumstances and scenarios in your life! I Am and I Am all things and In this you can trust!

11/5/15

The enemy is trying diligently to steal your peace today, but I am with you to bring you strength and My presence will cause you to overcome.

"AND THE PEACE OF GOD, WHICH TRANSCENDS ALL UNDERSTANDING, WILL GUARD YOUR HEARTS AND YOUR MINDS IN CHRIST JESUS."

11/7/15

Do not take on anything that I have not spoken of or have not led you to. The enemy is trying to establish a foundation with specific circumstances and opportunities. Draw back, walk away, and shake the dust from your feet. You will learn much from this encounter.

11/9/15

My Child, the wind has blown and the direction has changed. Do not be concerned about plans that were on your schedule that you thought were coming to pass in the near future. These things will come to fruition in their time. I am setting a new course presently that requires immediate attention. Be sensitive to My voice as I lead you down this path. This change is not one that disrupts you, but only erupts with wonderful news and scenarios.

11/11/15

There is a difference between those that know Me and those that walk with Me. When you choose to surrender your will and choose Mine, all things are seen in a different perspective. What I see, you see and what I desire, you desire. I have placed inside of you power and a presence that can change the atmosphere at any time. Its all in your perspective! What do you want? What do you desire? Heroes are remembered, but Legends never die. Who wants to be Legendary? They will remember you by My power and My presence that flowed in your heart. Many people you have come in contact with throughout the years will remember simply because they saw Me, and that is good news!

11/12/15

Not only have you fought well, but you are victorious. What you thought was defeat is in fact a true victory. It is not what takes place in the natural realm that is most important, but what happens in the spirit. You have fought diligently and have overcome. You have done well Child, very well! Now it is time to rest! Enjoy this time as things become light and easy.

11/16/15

Come unto Me all that are weary and heavy laden and I will give you rest. There has been significant improvements that have been seen by My eyes simply because I am the one directing your path. All things are subject to change. Some very specific areas in your life are now finishing their course and closure is about to be completed. Get ready for a new beginning. The floor has been prepared for you to stand on!

11/18/15

The door is open for a new move in your life. Get ready and prepare as a new establishment is presented to you. There were two, now there is one.

This will bring much joy and peace, and will fulfill a very specific scenario in your life and the lives of your family.

11/20/15

There is an increased measure of activity in the atmosphere. A significant shift has taken place. Prepare for a surge of increase that has been waiting in the balance. The windows are open, the vats are open. You have said, "I have been waiting patiently, My Lord", and I have said, "Child, It is right on time."

11/23/15

I am opening the eyes in a greater way to understand My desires and My plans. It is not a time to become comfortable in what I have called you to do. I have not chosen you to operate in fear, but with authority. Do not be deceived. Many of My Children are not discerning My voice. My Child, you must remember that all that is given comes from My hands. It is spoken into existence through My voice. Do not take My love and My grace for granted. For I am a righteous Judge as well as a loving Father. In this moment, I am establishing My bride with a greater level of wisdom and discernment so you can truly understand your calling, destiny and accountability. My Child, it is time now, for in this time, it is a critical hour. Shake off the dust from your feet and walk with integrity, with power and with authority. Keep your eyes on Me and do not allow yourselves to be deceived.

11/24/15

For I have not told you to follow man but to follow Me. Many have put their trust in others and have allowed their calling and destiny to be dictated by the thoughts and desires of man. Enough of this! Why have you forgotten about what I have spoken to you regarding your own future and destiny?

There are plans that I have for you that have been delayed because of this. Do not give up and forget about what I have placed inside of you.

Do you not know that the future holds great promise and blessing for you? For there are rivers waiting for you to swim in. Refreshing waters that have been waiting for you. For I shall break the chains that hold you back and cause this soul tie that is not from Me to be broken.

11/29/15

Have I not told you that I am with you always! Times come and they go, but I am with you through all circumstances. Many have questions to uncertainty and there are those that wander through the valley of despair, but I am here to bring comfort to all situations in your life. There are things My Child that will not be answered in this life, and in time when we meet, all things will come to perspective and truth. You will understand in a greater way what took place and why. Today, I want you to lay down your mindset and seek Me with all your heart and allow Me to fill your mind with greater understanding and revelation. I am the God of peace that surpasses all understanding. I shall fill you with peace and I shall establish a foundation of joy.

12/1/15

Do you not know that I am ruler over all the Universe? Over all the nations? I Am! I have given authority to you by offering the Comforter. This authority is yours and has been given, not just for peace, but for power as well. My Child, you were victorious before the foundations of the earth were even established. I knew you and everything about you. I am Alpha and Omega, the beginning and the end. I say to you now, you were not born to be broken-hearted, not born to be defeated or discouraged. You were created with one thing in mind. To be My Ambassadors, to be My voice, to be Mine!

In this very moment, jump into My river and allow Me to fill you with a love and peace that is not comprehendible to man. It is My desire in this season to bring you to a greater level and a greater height. In this month that you call December, My birth and My life is celebrated and in this celebration, I celebrate your life as well. You are the apple of My eye! I love you and I have wonderful plans to bring to fruition. Do not wait, for the celebration has begun and what I see in you and what I have for you, is much to celebrate for.

12/4/15

Do not be discouraged by the words of men. The doors that I have opened and the blessing that I have for you will not be hindered or stolen. Your season of outpouring is upon you and I am the one who is in complete control of that. Do not allow the enemy to distract you, for it is only a lie and it will not have any power over you.

12/5/15

Light to every dark place. Peace to every troubled face. My Child, My presence and My grace is upon you to help you overcome every obstacle. You will see victory in your life that comes suddenly. Prepare and expect with faith as this shall come like rivers that flow to open waters.

12/8/15

Be on guard and alert as a controlling spirit has been prepared to be released to bring distraction and delay your progress. Be as Watchmen on the wall. Be sensitive to Holy Spirit, and do not allow yourselves to be deceived. As you press in to My presence and read My word, this too shall pass.

12/9/15

Faithful and true! You are soaring like an Eagle! Do not look back and do not be concerned by what could have been, or in your mind, what should have been. I am taking you to new places that are in agreement with My will. These things shall come to pass in their time. Watch and see how new things come into place like a puzzle. As each piece is put together by My hand, you shall understand and see the bigger picture before you even get there!

2/19/16-Trump Dream-Winter of 2015 in D.C. — Released on Social Media

In a dream that I had just recently, I saw Donald Trump walking. It looks like an evening setting, I'm all the sudden standing in a conference center hallway/auditorium like facility. I see two people walking towards me. They're much bigger than the average person. Looks to be as if they're like 8-feet tall. I see Donald Trump on the left and I see another individual on the right. What I was not allowed to see was the face of the individual on the right, but I knew it was the angel of the Lord because I could feel the presence of God around me.

As they approached me, I looked at Donald Trump and asked him, *"Are you prepared to be president of the United States?"* He gave me a kind of a grin, no answer, so I asked him again, *"Are you prepared to be president of United States?"* And he looked at me and smiled, and then continued walking. I knew when I woke up that the dream represented authority because of his height, but also represented protection because it was very intimidating.

12/9/15

Today I was overwhelmed by the presence of God and reminded by Holy Spirit of the outpouring that took place at Brownsville Assembly of God.

47

Tell them that My presence is surely enough. Tell them that My presence is greater than all things. Tell them that My presence shifts atmospheres and causes the mountains to tremble. This day I tell you, to remember what took place at Brownsville. Remember the glory that created an atmosphere of complete surrender. That revival will never be forgotten, because it was My presence that was welcomed. It will be cherished for a lifetime. Now, I tell you that a move of My Spirit is coming again to My church in a greater way. Seven times greater shall this come and manifest in My house. For those that sacrificed their lives for the advancement of My Kingdom, their cries have not gone unheard. Some have come and some have gone, but what was started is not finished. Many have said that this was over, but that is not so! For it was just a beginning and that time fast approaches again.

12/11/15

Romans 8:28 says, "And we know that all things work together for good to them that love God, to them who are the called according to his purpose."

Jacob was given a promise of great blessing, but he dealt with fear, doubt, and worry. When the enemy oppressed him with all these things, God used it to push Jacob towards the Father. This scenario gave him the opportunity to wrestle with God. The Father actually used the enemy to create the circumstances to allow him to move forward and break free from strongholds that held him back. Today, someone out there is dealing with the very same thing in their life and God is saying that you too will overcome these hindrances as you press in and fight for the very thing you are contending for. Breakthrough, Provision, and Opportunity!

12/14/15

And a time will come, yes, it shall surely come when My presence overwhelms the masses. Can it be that this day fast approaches? Yes, be it so! Today, My Child, you do not have to wait for that day! Go deeper with Me and enjoy My love. I am right beside you. I am near to you. I am filling you with peace and I am increasing your joy. You will be filled with an increase of My love and what was hindering you from receiving all that I have for you is broken off now. Peace shall fill your mind and understanding shall come in a greater way. You shall have an inner peace during this time that calms the waters. Worry shall be no longer and confidence shall be in your heart and mind, knowing that I am in control. I am increasing your laughter and delight, and I shall bring this to fruition simply because you are Mine!

12/18/15

Timing My Child is everything. Even when you know that blessing is on its way, the timing is most important. You must operate with increased sensitivity to My direction and My command. This day, I tell you that great blessing is coming to you. More than you were expecting. Lift your vision higher My Child. My gifts are good, and they are far greater than you can imagine.

12/21/15

I am a God of the Suddenlies. I am a God that has no boundaries. When you press in to My voice and My will, you will see that I have no limitations to the blessing that has been in existence for you before the foundations of time. You have always been on My mind. Now, I tell you My Children, that a greater presence is available to you, and I will demonstrate that with you! As you approach this new year that you call 2016, a manifestation of My glory will accompany you and My bride that will be much different than experienced before. This is not a desire My Child, but a command. My will is for My church to take hold and pursue My presence. Many will, but some won't, and they will continue to place more focus on themselves and their comfort. But for those that listen to My voice and seek Me with all their heart, they shall be filled with rivers of rushing water that flows to *no end. Take this opportunity to now change your heart attitude and sharpen your focus. Your new year ahead is one that has much delight and great opportunity!*

12/22/15

I am removing the injustice that you have been going through and the negative words that have kept you from moving forward. They are broken and silenced. Today will be filled with redemption and encouragement!"

12/24/15

Do not be alarmed or concerned by the sudden situations that have come presently. I am working all things for the good, and you will see vindication and justice knock at your door. Remain strong and focused. What is restored will be seven times greater than what was previously expected.

12/25/15

As you listen to My voice and seek My face, a greater level of understanding comes to you. This day, you celebrate My life, but I am here to tell you that I celebrate yours as well. I was born for you, and I died for you. You are the very reason I was brought to mankind, and you are the very reason that we will meet again! Today, many speak the words M ERRY CHRISTMAS to each other. This day, I speak them over you as well Child. These very words speak about life, and today is a great day to celebrate yours. You are loved more than you know, Child!

12/28/15

Every little bit matters. Everything you do, Child, has potential and significance. The enemy has tried to bring discouragement, but I have given you strength and freedom. Rest in Me and place your focus on My word. You are moving forward and victorious. You must remember that there is a fight against your future and destiny. Do not be quick to respond in the flesh. Do not fight the very thing that has been defeated. I am in control of your present and I am in control of your future. Surrender all to Me and watch Me grace you with peace, joy, and blessing.

12/30/15

Expect relationships that have been broken to be healed. Where hardship once ruled, peace now reigns. The fighting is over, and I tell you that you will be quite surprised how I bring about restoration. What was not expected shall be your sign to victory and joy in this new season.

Part Four

Prophetic Words — 2016

John Natale

1/5/16

This year will be one that is called "The Restored Wall" I am fixing the broken pieces. My church has been desolate to many. That which was called the "Ancient Ruins" has been in the present as well. There have been many that were called to bring about change and speak My truths, to help rebuild and build, but they were not about My business. Their desires were not My desires. My house has not been taken care of.

I do not speak of the physical walls of the building that will only crumble and fall, but about My people that have been broken. They have had their walls crushed and the enemy has caused them to walk away from their destiny. To believe there was no hope any longer. They have been waiting for a new beginning. Too much time has been wasted and a new day arises for them and their Children. Generations have waited for this day.

This day, this season, I am repairing that which was torn down. A great move of My Spirit upon My people that will cause such a stirring, and create an atmosphere of true unity. A new community of believers are rising that will work together to see the common good of mankind. There is coming such an outpouring of unity that has not been seen before. A brand new outpouring of the Spirit called "Kindred" is blowing on My Children. Many have thought that this was not possible any longer, for they have searched, but have not found.

But, I tell you now that this is not so. It is now, and it is available to My people. Many will come out from their caves and their places of hiding. They will appear, and their faces will shine like the sun simply because they have been given a fresh encounter of My love. AND THEY SHALL REBUILD THE OLD RUINS, THEY SHALL RAISE UP THE FORMER DESOLATIONS, AND THEY SHALL REPAIR THE RUINED CITIES, THE DESOLATIONS OF MANY GENERATIONS. Isaiah 61:4

As Nehemiah spoke these words, "Remember the instruction you gave Moses, saying, 'IF YOU ARE UNFAITHFUL, I WILL SCATTER YOU AMONG THE NATIONS, BUT IF YOUR RETURN TO ME AND OBEY MY COMMANDS, THEN EVEN

IF YOUR EXILED PEOPLE ARE AT THE FARTHEST HORIZON, I WILL GATHER THEM TO THE PLACE I HAVE CHOSEN AS A DWELLING FOR My NAME.'"

Many have been unfaithful to the commands that have been given, but their hearts have turned to Me. They have chosen to lay down their ideas and their desires. They have chosen to seek Me with all their heart. As with Nehemiah, he was given a heart of compassion and determination for change. Not for himself, but for the many. This great move of My Spirit upon My church in this new year that you call 2016 will come quickly and be established quickly. As with Nehemiah and the rebuilding of the wall that took 52 days, this too will be established in a short period of time. Great favor will accompany My church.

There will be opposition to this sudden advancement and it will come from within. Do not be discouraged or alarmed. For My presence will overcome all adversity and the hearts of those who come against you will be changed as the new walls are established. As with Nehemiah and the completion of the restoration, a new level of integrity and wisdom will be placed in My house. My word speaks these words, "THE FEAR OF THE LORD IS THE BEGINNING OF WISDOM" .

You will see in the days ahead a great change to My church and a restored Bride that is not concerned with the natural things of this world, but is alert and attentive in the Spirit. This is symbolic to the "Awakening" that will take place with My church. The Prophets are coming to prepare the people and sound the alarm. They will be used to gather the people and the work will begin. This will be a year of jubilee and much success. My Children will have the broken pieces of their life restored and they will dwell together in peace, unity and blessing. These days come quickly My Child, and what you are about to see and experience will be great glory and splendor. For I Am God!

1/8/16

Don't settle for what others have in mind for you. Push toward the plans that I have for you. Even in the little things, they are significant to Me. Rise up and watch how sudden diligence and determination comes upon you to contend for your breakthrough. It's time for your change.

1/9/16

For I know the plans I have for you. Plans to prosper you and not harm you. To give you a future and a hope. *My Child, do not give up on these plans. I have not given up on you. No harm shall come to you and you will see My great plans come to pass. Yes, there is a contention, and yes, there is a fight, but you have won already. In this you can trust.*

1/13/16

You see My Child, there are things that I do that come as a surprise. Do not fight so much in the natural what you do not understand. All things have purpose, even the little things that seem so insignificant to you matter to Me, and in that you can trust. There are many things that are now coming your way that you have not planned or considered. Allow them to bless you, for they come at a time in your life that is needed. Again I say to you, in this you can trust, and in this comes joy and peace.

1/14/16

Press in and stay strong. Be diligent and put a demand on your future. Like a warrior that has been trained in battle, you do not accept defeat but expect victory. You are that warrior, and you are victorious!

1/15/16

Open doors and breakthrough! It is here and is available to you. Watch, My Child, as opportunity comes to you that you have been faithful in waiting for. The contact will come, so be prepared and sensitive to My Spirit to act accordingly.

1/17/16

Take the authority that has been placed inside of you by Me, and command all oppression and torment to go in Jesus's name, and it shall leave.

1/18/16

I am changing all things and preparing you for a new thing. Even when you do not see things happening, I am moving on your behalf. You have been faithful, and My word speaks that the righteous will live by faith. So, get ready My Child, significant days are now upon you and you shall rejoice because faith has allowed blessing to flow.

1/19/16

My Child, oh how far you have come. What a joy it is to watch you travel your path. You are making more progress than you realize. You are closer than you think. Everyday you persevere and you endure the things that this world throws your way. You are an overcomer! January shall be filled with gifts and shall not be what you expected. For what is coming is far greater than is imaginable. Rejoice and prepare, Child, for it is coming. There shall be an excitement that suddenly fills you. This shall be My Spirit moving inside your very being, showing you and preparing you for great days ahead!

1/21/16

My Child, do not ever give up on yourself. I am the God of the second chance. Many question this, but My truth is that I never give up on you, and there is always a time for change to come to your situation. When your eyes and your mind dictate that present circumstances in your life show no hope or seem impossible, I am working on your behalf and preparing you for the possible!

Rise up, Child and posture yourself upright! Raise your hands in victory and praise Me! For great is your reward and great it shall be and you shall see this month called January end very well.

1/22/16

Peace and comfort, My Child. Oh how the enemy diligently tries to steal your joy, but enough is enough! You have persevered and fought faithfully. The time is now that your joy is restored and your laughter returned. The end to these assignments against you! The end has come and the victory has been won! My Spirit is releasing joy to you right now that flows like rivers! You are moving forward with immeasurable joy that is accompanied by unprecedented favor upon you, Child!

1/25/16

As with Noah, My child, he was taken and set upon a mountain to emerge victorious. But before that could happen, the waters had to recede. There was a storm that came, but through that came trust and peace. He was allowed to open the door after the water was completely unseen. I tell you now, that the storm that has affected your very being, that has tainted your peace and trust is over! It has been slowly sinking, no longer to be visible. It is your time now to rise up and walk out. The storm is over and the Son is shining. Remember Child, that when i speak to you and tell you to rise and walk, do not look back, for there is nothing to look back at!

1/28/16

And this too shall pass. Waiting on Me to move upon your behalf isn't as hard as you think, Child. There are things always taking place in the Spirit realm that you are not aware of. You just have to believe, and you have to place an expectation on the very things you are believing for. For in this hour, get ready for events to suddenly take shape and come to fruition. For the 11th hour is coming to an end, and a new day comes forth quickly. For I say to you now, that you have persevered in your hour of testing, and now that testing comes to an end. You have fought well, Child, and have overcome! Some of you have already been shown this through signs and sudden experiences with people that I have brought down your path. Some will experience this as the days unfold, but before this month that you call January ends, you will have received My word for your life in this season; and in this, you can rest and in this, you can find peace!

I HAVE TOLD YOU THESE THINGS, SO THAT IN ME YOU MAY HAVE PEACE. IN THIS WORLD YOU WILL HAVE TROUBLE. BUT TAKE HEART! I HAVE OVERCOME THE WORLD. John 16:33

1/29/16

Get ready to experience an exciting finish to the month called January. You have endured and you have persevered. It will be pivotal to the February month as you are aligned for great opportunity and abundance. There shall be a great calm and great peace. Light shall be your guide and it shall be more than you expect. Overflow and breakthrough is coming to you now.

John Natale

2/2/16

Today is your day of reconciliation! Today, you have overcome! Today, you have persevered all things that have come your way! Today, you shall see My power and My presence come in a greater way in your life! Today, I tell you that provision comes your way! Today, I tell you that you shall move forward and nothing shall stop you! Today, I tell you that you have begun a new season that brings supernatural provision to your family! Today Child, you are no longer waiting in the past, but filled in the future! What I see ahead of you is coming faster than you think! Get ready, get ready, get ready! It is coming and it shall be presented to you and it shall be good! For I am good!

2/3/16

This I say to you now. Have I not told you that you were not of this world? My words speaks very clearly that in this world you will have trouble, but rejoice, for I have overcome the world. My Child, it is time for My church to grab hold of a deeper revelation of your very existence and the power and authority that has been placed inside of you. You are not called to be like the world, but you were called to lead and to be the model of supernatural victorious living. I will awaken My church as many have prayed earnestly. They have prayed for revival and they have prayed for a harvest of souls, but what is coming first is a shaking with My Children and a fresh in-filling, so that their hearts and mindsets truly are shifted into a place of revelatory thinking and living. They will come to truly understand the power of My Holy Spirit.

When this takes place, the lives of many will take on a new perspective and confidence. They will rise up and take their place as warriors and they will march with a renewed heart and mind that takes them to another level of passion and expectancy. No more settling, My Child, you are a royal priesthood, a holy nation, a peculiar people, a chosen generation that you may declare the praises of him who called you out of darkness into his wonderful light. Now Child, rise up and with eyes to see and ears to hear, take your place and start your march!

2/6/16

Your setbacks can and will be used for your advancement. They are actually keys hidden behind the veil of discouragement. Certain keys will now be used to open specific doors. Watch as they open and show a clear path to breakthrough.

2/7/16

My light is to be a light that penetrates the darkness. Many have had their light so dim that it does not lead your path or blind the sight of the enemy. This day I tell you that I am reviving your light and setting that light ablaze. Watch and see how this all unfolds as My presence and power overwhelms and facilitates this change in your life.

2/11/16

A new source of provision is coming your way. It shall flow like running water. This shall come upon you suddenly and be revealed to you from a source that is not expected. You have persevered and you have been faithful. There have been many days that you have worried and considered giving up the fight, but I am here to rescue you from your doubt and unbelief. Just as My children wandered in the desert and cried out for water, they were satisfied with miraculous water that came from a rock. You too, My Child, you shall see living water come from a source that you would not have ever imagined or considered.

2/13/16

I will never lead you to opportunities that are not in the best interest of you and your family. In this season, there will be things that are a bit uncomfortable and not appealing to you. In your flesh, you will try to convince yourself that I am not working on your behalf. I tell you now, that suddenly, in a moment's time, you will get confirmation about your situation and beautiful peace will fall on you like the Summer rain.

2/14/16

Sudden distractions and attempts to steal your joy. The enemy has once again tried to rob you of your blessing, but I have caused your faith to remain strong and have increased your ability to persevere and overcome the test that you have just faced. You are an overcomer and you have proven again, that your trust is not in yourself and your own ability, but in the One that is above every situation and circumstance! Rejoice Child, well done!

2/15/16

It's not people that stop your forward progress. It's your mindset and belief system. Now, let Me take control. I will renew and I will revive your mind, and you will run to the finish line and achieve some very significant things that have been planned for you!

2/17/16 — In D.C.

And the Trump shall sound. And it shall be heard.

2/18/16

I know you are desperate for change and I know that you will do anything for that change to take place. I want you to know this; that I have prepared great change for you. Do not allow frustration to overwhelm you. It is coming and it will be here sooner than you think. That is why suddenly you are pursuing so hard right now. The enemy has spoken lies to mislead you and discourage you, but I am here to guide you and bless you. Trust Me. I will not fail you.

2/21/16

Sudden divine connections and establishments are being released to you now. Expect breakthrough to come in the moments ahead. You have been faithful and have been patient. Enjoy this time, My Child, for it will bring great increase.

2/22/16

It's here, Child! Many have been praying and waiting for the facilitation of breakthrough. Today shall be filed with increase and opportunities. Stay focused and be alert. Allow My Spirit to speak to you and guide you.

2/25/16

Do not get ahead of Me! Allow Me to guide you. Do not be discouraged! I am leading the way. Weariness is gone! Fatigue is gone! Your strength is being restored, and your determination sharpened! The flower has come forth and the colors shine like the sun! What you do not see, I can see! Always remember that, Child!

2/26/16

Do not trust everything you hear, Child. You must remember that a Father not only encourages His children, but corrects them as well. You will learn to discern what is Me and what is not. In the days ahead, your ability to understand and discern will be sharpened. Take what the prophets have spoken and activate what has been given.

2/27/16-In D.C.

Get ready for great change that is coming to this nation. For it shall come, and it will quickly gain momentum. A sound that has been silent shall no longer be hidden. It shall come forth and travel like a wave across America. You must trust that I am fine-tuning this sound. For it shall be sharper than before. Prepare now, for it shall come.

2/28/16

Listen to the Prophets, for they have sacrificed much for the advancement of the Kingdom. The enemy has tried to silence their voice, but they are now stronger than ever before.

2/29/16

What seemed to be another setback has taken on new meaning. You have gained a victory in a very specific area of your life. Now it is time to celebrate, for a new level of authority has been given.

3/1/16

It is time to March forward! An unexpected turn of events has come and will lead you to divine connections, favor, and success. Watch and see how this all unfolds for you and your family.

3/2/16

The enemy was hiding and waiting for an opportunity to steal your blessing. He was allowed to enter through discouragement, but I have exposed his plan and removed all threats.

3/4/16

The enemy thought he had you down for good, but a sudden, quick response and reaction has allowed you to escape the grip and move forward. You have won the battle even though you have been struggling and dealing with discouragement. You are stronger than you think, because I am helping you!

3/9/16

Things are going to pop today. Get ready for sudden opportunity and encouragement that brings promotion.

3/10/16

Advancing My Kingdom does not mean building your empire. You must remember that you are just a voice and everything is under My authority.

3/11/16

And it shall be in this year that you call 2016, that supernatural grace shall come and cover you like a blanket. For I shall sustain you in this year. What you have depended on presently shall not be your source, but a new stream of provision shall come and take you throughout this season. Rejoice, for I am the God of the suddenly! 1 Kings 17:7-16

3/13/16

You are free! Free indeed to overcome all obstacles that have come your way! This day, I am preparing a place for you that is filled with the splendor of Heaven. A place that has been waiting for you. Timing is everything, My Child, but in a moment's time, you will see how things unfold for you. For you have been so very patient, and even in your weariness, I have seen such faith and strength that you have not seen. Rejoice, My Child, the door of opportunity is upon you!

3/14/16

The widow gave the very last portion of oil and flour to the prophet and a supernatural stream of blessing and provision came to her and her son. This day, I say to you that you have given Me your all, and I have opened up the windows of blessing. Get ready for sudden increase that will facilitate direction and change.

3/16/16

As with Lazarus, I delayed My arrival simply because faith was being developed. Many of you have been discouraged and disappointed because your expectations have not been met. It is time now that your faith is activated to a new level and expectation becomes a reality. My timing is perfect and I am working on your behalf. You will see great breakthrough regarding your situation. In this you can trust.

3/17/16

God has big plans for you, don't give up now. The fun is about to begin.

3/19/16

I came so you can make an impact, but My church has created a safe haven.

3/19/16

The time has come now where your mindset has gained understanding. I have increased and sharpened your thought process, and you will now operate with revelation that facilitates expectation.

3/21/16

My Child, it might look and feel as if you are at your end, but I am here to tell you that I am with you at a new beginning.

3/23/16

Your determination and resilience can and will be used for your promotion. This will also activate the destiny of a certain individual that has been staying close to you, seeking answers for their own life.

3/26/16

Tell My people that as much as they will speak and write about Me this weekend, that the other 362 days of the year are just as important. My Church must be awakened, My Church will be awakened. My Church will be restored to the greater glory.

3/27/16

*Yes, I have risen and defeated the grave. I have opened up your graves as well. **Never return to that place of bondage.** You are free and you must never forget that.*

3/28/16

Just when you thought that you were going to sink and drown in discouragement, I have rescued you and pulled you up and out of the darkness and despair. I have restored your hope and filled you with a fresh anointing that will now accompany you in this new season.

3/30/16

My face is shining upon you today. That is a reminder for you, My Child. There are times when you do not feel My presence or sense My touch, but I am here to tell you that I never leave your side. I wanted to tell you today that I love you and have great things in store for you. You are not alone, and you are not abandoned! Even in this moment, I am restoring strength to you and reviving your wounded heart. You see, when I walked the earth with My disciples and friends, they too had their doubts, frustrations, and fears, but I silenced all their concerns because of My love for them. That same love is here right now for you and I will do the same as I did for them. So open up your arms and let My presence and My love fill you right now and give you everything you need today!

3/31/16

Never give up, My Child, never give up. Have faith and believe in Me. I am always here and will never leave you. I will turn your sadness into joy.

4/1/16

Yes, you will overcome all discouragement and depression, and yes, you will see glorious breakthrough in your life. It is a new day and a time to rejoice! The seasons have changed, My Child and that is also present in your situation. What you have been dealing with has changed in the spirit realm and will now suddenly manifest in the natural realm. Watch, for it comes quickly.

4/3/16

My church should not be divided and will not be divided, Enough! I will not allow the younger generation to be swayed by eloquent words that cause them to separate themselves from the older generation. A true revival and awakening is when young and old alike can worship Me together. I will cause a stirring that will penetrate the heart and bring about unity in My church. This day comes quickly and a new movement is about to begin.

4/5/16

Every situation and every obstacle can be defeated and removed from your life. You have been trying with your own strength to overcome this burden, but I Am here to tell you this truth, you must know this and believe this. My word speaks these words, BUT IN ALL THESE THINGS WE OVERWHELMINGLY CONQUER THROUGH HIM WHO LOVED US.

You will conquer this mountain because **My love is far greater than your trial.** I will strengthen you and empower you with the revelation of My love. I Am restoring your faith and reviving your heart. This day is a new beginning and one that will never be forgotten.

4/6/16

Things are about to suddenly change in your favor. The sound of laughter has been heard. There is rejoicing all around you for a great victory has been won.

4/7/16

Yes, all things are possible! Have I told you today that you are beautiful and precious in My sight? Everyday, these are the words that come from My mouth and speak to your heart. Many of My children have become cold and unable to hear these words, but I am here to remind you that what I see in you is beauty beyond description. And one more thing, Child, I will guide you and I will get you through every trial that you face. In this you can be sure!

4/9/16

Have I not told you that all things are possible? Your greatest hindrance is actually yourself. You must believe in yourself and remove all condemnation. All it takes is to press in a little more, and you will see breakthrough. It's that easy, My Child. Do not allow your thoughts to dictate your future. My plans are to prosper you and in this, you can be sure.

4/11/16

It's time to celebrate and not a time to be defeated. Your momentum will not be disrupted as you continue to fight and contend for your future and destiny. You have been questioning why there is still much resistance, but I am here to tell you that the pressure is decreasing and the assault of the enemy is coming to an end.

4/13/16

The Mysteries of Heaven revealed on earth and in your life. *Prepare, as of today, eternal rewards that have been positioned for release are ordered to move forward and meet you. Faithfulness has been given by My power and you have been found faithful. Now is a time to rejoice, for you are victorious and have overcome much adversity. Well done, Child!*

4/18/16

Beware of false teachers that deceive and misguide you. Self-promotion does not bring Me glory and only exhorts oneself. My gospel is not be entertaining. It is in place to be a source of strength, hope, trust, and guidance. My gospel is to direct all to Me, and in this you must use wisdom and discernment as many have come and will come in My name, like wolves in sheep clothing.

4/25/16

The time has come when all things that have been a distraction have been removed and swept away. Yes, new things have come and have taken their place. Do not be alarmed or concerned about what has now been activated in your life. Assignments have purpose and reason, far greater than you know. Allow the momentum to move, and watch how it generates speed and opportunity. Your season is good, and will only bring blessing to you and your family.

4/27/16

As Peter was asked to step out of the boat, this same message is spoken to you today. He was asked to do something that would require risk, and most importantly evaluate his faith and trust level in ME. Today, I have asked many of you to take such a risk and step out onto things that do not seem to reason well with your intellectual mindset, but you must trust in Me that what I have planned for you is good. Remember My words and hold them in your heart. And we know that all things work together for good to those who love God, to those who are called according to His purpose.

4/29/16

Joseph experienced many setbacks on a journey that he was not expecting. The key for today is that he never gave up and still kept his faith and trust. Many of you are on this same journey and the word for today is; You too will arise and come forth in victory and favor. It might not look good right now and in the natural make no sense, but great opportunity and blessing awaits you and soon will be part of your life.

5/3/16

Do not despise small beginnings and do not allow the enemy to convince you that your present situation is meaningless and insignificant. I am working on your behalf and My plans are in action. My word declares that all things work out for the good and in this you can have peace and hope. Be prepared as this week shall bring forth much fruit in your life and also unlock hidden answers that were waiting to be released.

5/7/16

Presently, many of you are questioning your present situation with uncertainty and doubt, but I am here to tell you that great things are coming and shall unfold before your very eyes. My word declares this hope, let us not grow weary while doing good, for in due season we shall reap if we do not lose heart. You will see why you have been placed in such a season as this and you will see the blessing as well. It is all for My glory, Child.

5/8/16

Whatever you are going through and the challenges that you face, a double portion of grace is upon you. You shall experience a sudden shift in your life and current situation that will facilitate change and increase. Faithfulness has played a powerful role in your life. The Lord smiles at you, and in His face reveals such love and excitement for the plans that are about to be revealed.

5/13/16

Never underestimate the opportunities given. It might not look and feel as if your current situation is filled with favor, but circumstances are about to change mightily and bring great opportunity.

5/16/16

Yes, the seasons do change and yes, all things come to an end. This day, I tell you this, you are setup for such surprises and suddenlies! Does not a Father love to surprise his children? You shall surely see My goodness in the land of the living! Make a shout unto Me and shout the victory! For you are victorious, My Child.

5/18/16

Sudden opportunities that come your way are not always what you were expecting or seeking. Learn to discern and act wisely as these will come in the days ahead!

5/20/16

Gaining understanding is not as hard as you think, My Child. You are wiser than you think you are and great revelation is about to come upon you. Many of you have fought the good fight and have persevered in your trial and struggle, even when you thought that you had no more fight in you. This day, these are the words that are spoken over you; **The warrior has been awakened, the warrior has risen and shall raise his sword high!**

You gain understanding at times just by being diligent Child! Yes, you have been diligent, and you must remember these words; I AM A REWARDER OF THOSE THAT DILIGENTLY SEEK ME.

10/3/16

It is time for you take a stand and pursue all that I have for you. Do you doubt in My ability to bring great opportunity and blessing to you? It is not so! Doubting is not from Me, but faith that can move mountains is inside of you. For you shall in this season reap a great harvest. For it has already begun, and you are not even aware of it! So rejoice, for in this day, you are in a time called Rosh Hashanah, a new year and a new beginning. For in this new year, a page has been turned in your life. A brand new season that has endless possibilities and opportunities. For you shall see many things come forth quickly and bring forth blessings that you cannot contain. Is this not good news? You can hear from Me! Never question your ability to hear from Me. I shall open up your eyes and ears to a new level of understanding. For the new season has come!!! It is good!! It is good!! Now receive!!!

10/7/16 — In D.C.

Turbulence and rumbling in the atmosphere shall cease when least expected. Watch and see how all things come to an end and very specific things are exposed in the month called October.

10/8/16— In D.C.

If you saw our post on 9/27/16 regarding the wind and skies, you must understand that this hurricane has spiritual connections to this upcoming election. There is turbulence in the atmosphere regarding the election and the candidates present. You will see over the next several days what unfolds and what is exposed. October 13th presents a very clear picture of what lies ahead. Watch and see! Watch and see! The clouds hold keys to answers not yet seen!

10/10/16— In D.C.

The atmosphere is clear but the anger of the enemy has risen significantly. Sudden scenarios of conflict shall rise, but quickly defused and peace shall reign over every situation. The skies are clear now and will reveal many things. October, October, your month has come filled with victories and you shall see the falling of what is not from Me.

10/10/16— In D.C.

There is a time coming, that comes quickly, when the Government seeks the Prophets for direction and wisdom.

10/12/16-In D.C.

One will weaken and the other shall strengthen. One will rise and the other shall fall. One will be a voice and the other be silent. For behold, one shall be recognized before the appointed time and you shall see the glory be released and the announcement of the one who shall be a pillar that will not be shaken.

10/14/16

Trusting that all things work for the good for those that love God, situations in your life will take a sudden turn in your favor and produce great blessing and opportunity. What looks small has enormous opportunity, and what looks discouraging, shall in a moments time, be very rewarding.

10/18/16

A word of hope that is spoken over you today. You have been known before your eyes had sight, and before there was sound in your ears. Whatever holds you back, whatever has caused you to fear, be strong and raise your head, for in this new day, your strength has been revived and restored. A new found hope, a new joy, a new freedom has come your way! Never doubt that peace will not show up to your heart, but rejoice and expect! All things are coming together now, what is unseen shall be seen in a moment's time.

10/21/16

The winds have ceased and the water has returned to its position. Now, there is opportunity that has come that must be learned and established within your heart. Prepare and open your arms, for in this time, a presentation of significant blessing shall be given to you.

10/22/16— In D.C.

In this season, My church has become fragmented by the current power struggle that is desiring to be a king in the nation that is called America. Today, this warning is coming to My church. You must humble yourself and turn from your wicked ways. What is desired from Me to lead must be one that will allow Me to use them, and most importantly, one that will reflect Me most. You will see as the days pass, who is for Me and who is against Me. Do not allow your flesh to get in the way of your ability to see and hear the truth. For in this time, you must discern wisely or the adversary will have his way, and that is not My will.

10/23/16

Yes, there is grace. But if My people who are called by My name do not humble themselves, repent and turn from their wicked ways, the grace will not be in blessing, but will be given in your time of suffering.

10/25/16

Take a look all around and you will see the beauty in the sky. The picture that's been painted today, as the sky shows its face. Look up, for the sun shines so bright, as does your life and your future. Always remember that there's another day for the sun to rise, and for light to be a source of hope for all people. You are that light, and you shine even when it seems the clouds have caused darkness to hinder you. Rejoice, for you will never lose your light!

10/26/16— In D.C.

It will be a November to remember. Simply because the scripture came to pass. "Now faith is the substance of things hoped for, the evidence of things not seen."

What was unseen and not believable shall be seen, and belief shall overwhelm and destroy all darkness and doubt.

10/28/16

You are reminded today how great you are. You are reminded today of what is inside of you and the heart of love that has been given. It is important that you understand that your ability to overcome all things is dependent on how your heart responds to the circumstances of life. Today, your reminder has come to inform you that what has been placed inside of you is a heart of gold, and in this, you can be certain. You can do anything and there is nothing that can hold you back! Remember that your natural strength will fail you, but I will never leave you and will always be there to help and guide you.

10/31/16

Unexpected situations have come and will manifest suddenly, and new relationships will come to help facilitate My will in your life. Watch and see how this unfolds, and how what was not expected becomes present in your life and family.

11/2/16— In D.C.

Yes, say it now! Yes, there is much to be pleased about! Much to be comforted by! What is not seen, shall be seen! The skies rejoice with justice, America! The people cry out for a sign, and a sign you will be given! You will look to the left and to the right, but it will not be there. You shall be taken by surprise, as what is coming shall be light, and that light shall prevail before you.

11/3/16

A sudden pause in your life has caused questions to come in your mind that have produced a wave of anxiety, but you will not be disappointed with the circumstances that arrive in the moments ahead. It is merely just a smoke screen trying to block your sight, but watch how it all clears and the skies show its color in your life.

11/4/16

Do you not know that light always conquers darkness? Do you not know that the hidden things are always revealed in its time? These things shall transpire in great measure over the next several days. The eyes will open, the hearts will turn, and the smoke that has blinded the eyes shall be cleared. Then at its appointed time, the sun shall release its rays and illuminate the atmosphere.

11/5/16

And so it begins, the month of surprises! What was once lost has been found! When you have lost your strength and ability to see promise and blessing, grace comes in like a flood! Unexpected favor has turned up at your doorstep and has been waiting for you all along. What was unseen, now has been revealed! But wait My Child, it does not end there! Others have been directed to assist you and the path you are on brings a double portion of grace! Now watch!! Watch!!!

Who brings justice? Who holds all things in the palm of the hand? As the clouds separate and reveal the sun, so will I separate one and reveal the other!

11/5/16

I have My eye on a man named Mel! He shall shake My church again! He has been given an insight to My Kingdom that brings passion and justice. Watch and see what unfolds as the months come to close. The voice shall rise again!

11/8/16

Church, you are a voice of reason! You are a sound! Today, let your sound be heard! Join in strength, join in unity! Join as one and be a catalyst that causes a rumbling in the land! You are not alone! It is your time!

11/9/16-In D.C.

The people have spoken and yes, the people have come together! The people have embraced unity! The people have come as one and have made their sound heard! Yes, it was spoken throughout the years of this day, and yes, My words came forth to remind you that an awakening would come!

Many believed, many did not believe, but the cries of the people were heard and the shift was made seen, even when those that did not listen, did not believe. Now they have seen and now they believe! Now embrace this time! For much celebration has been heard and much change is here!

11/9/16— In D.C.

Why do you question the very thing that you cry out for? Do you not remember that it was your heart that cried out for change? Do you not remember these words, "MY WAYS ARE NOT YOUR WAYS, AND MY THOUGHTS ARE NOT YOURS!"

You must trust Me in this hour! Do not respond in the flesh as if you are putting all your trust in Man! You must now pray and desire wisdom and understanding in this hour! Pray for this man that is called Trump, for he needs your prayers! This nation that is called America needs all of the people to come and humble their heart. Become one! See as One! Hear as one! Love unconditionally! Forgive unconditionally, and you will see the greatest of days!. In this, you can trust!

11/10/16— In D.C.

This day, you see a new man that will take his place in the house called White. This day, I ask you this very thing, "Why are you troubled? Why do you pray and not believe? Who are you listening to? Where do you put your trust?" If you humble yourself and believe, you will see the restoration of all things. In this, you can trust!

11/11/16— In D.C.

Who dares come up against what is in place! You wrestle and make war in the natural and you have no understanding what this fight is all about! You will see who is stronger and what is greater! Darkness will not prevail over light! Not only has great favor been placed and put in position, but divine protection is established. When the enemy is resisted, it flees in many ways! Do not fear for him that has been put in place! For he has many around him that guard day and night.

11/13/16— In D.C.

And it was declared before the foundations of the earth and before those that would inhabit this land called America, that there would be a day when a trump would be heard and the sound would carry throughout the nations. Now, I tell you these words, watch and see what is protecting this man. Watch and see how the enemy is shut down before his plans come to fruition. Watch and see, for you, that has unbelief will believe.

11/14/16

I laugh at the enemy when he tries to distract my children. Again, he has sent smoke in the atmosphere to blind your sight and choke out your encouragement. It shall not be so! My laughter has cleared the air, and My joy has penetrated your very being with renewed hope and peace! Now rise up and continue on, My Child. Your way has been made once again open and available to you!

11/16/16

Yes, you will see breakthrough today!!! You have been faithful in lack, and now you will be triumphant in much. Do not worry about the natural things, in the spirit, shifts have taken place for you and are now ready to be released.

11/18/16

As was bread and fish multiplied before the eyes of many, so will you see this very thing. How can it be? Many will say, from what way has this come? As it was done before, it shall be done again! Watch, for not just your home, but in the homes of many! You will see a great and mighty move of abundance and you shall know and see the power that is demonstrated with unconditional love.

11/20/16— In D.C.

Who dares defile my house? Who dares defile the sacred things? For you, who has corrupted my church, you will see the destruction of things to come! For you will see the worm eat the blessing that came your way.

For in its time, you shall see the delinquency of things to come. For the favor has been lost and for which was given has been taken away!

11/22/16— In D.C.

Your nation, called America, is being established and prepared for an awakening that will bring a surge of increase and prosperity. An army is being arranged, both natural and spiritual. You will see in the days ahead, the alignment of all things. Watch and see what the month called December brings! For a strange occurrence will come, for one that is not expected will suddenly come and join at the hip with the other, and unequalled strength shall accompany these that seek wisdom and fear nothing!

11/23/16— *In Honor for a Friend*

For what has happened today to a dear brother and Prophet in the Lord, I declare this day that the voice of the Lord shall roar like a lion and that sound shall cause such a violent storm of awakening in America! The Prophets shall come together as one and raise their voices in unity to bring one sound that shakes the atmosphere and destroys the plans of the enemy!

This was not a defeat, but a new beginning for those that carry the mysteries of Heaven."

11/27/16

Yes, the wind has spoken once again! The air is filled with joy and laughter! I have opened the windows of Heaven and allowed the floodgates to come! Do you not know or remember the scripture? I will pour out such a blessing that there will be not room enough to store it? These are signs of what has shifted in the atmosphere. The portals are open! The wind is free and favor is upon the land! The earth has cried for many seasons for this new glory to be poured out.

In My house, you shall see a great stirring and something brand new arise from the foundations. Again, I tell you this, there is a separation coming. What once was, shall be no longer and what has waited, shall come forward! They will say, "How can this be? What has happened?" I will divide from My eyes what is true and what is false and you shall see righteousness prevail. For in this time, righteousness and justice breaks out like a sword that does not dull. It shall pierce the wickedness and silence the deception of the enemy. What you are hearing and seeing is the beginning of new days that have been ordered by My hand. Rejoice, for in your sensitivity and discernment, you shall see wondrous days ahead that have no end!

11/28/16— In D.C.

And yes, they shall come against what has been put in place. With a fleeting hope that change will come and their king honored, but it shall not be so! For I am confusing them once again! They shall see a shaking like never before! It shall be one that causes all power to be restricted and silenced. Those that were a voice shall no longer be a voice. For there is a mighty wind among them that shall cause the raging waters to be calmed. It has been dealt with already in the Spirit, now you shall see it in the natural.

11/30/16

Grace is upon you. There is no need to worry about how you will get through your present situation. I have already made the way for your victory. Even though the waters might look overwhelming, as long as you look forward and into My eyes, nothing shall distract your progress or delay your journey. Now keep watch! For a celebration is about to arise!!!

12/1/16

For the days of old have passed away and the new day of restoration has come! Once was lost is now found! Be on guard, for the enemy has been on assignment to steal your passion and momentum, but this will not be so!. For you will continue strong and finish well. The month called December is all about new beginnings and you will begin a brand new thing that will bring great joy and harvest to many around you!

12/1/16— In D.C.

And yes, you shall see in the years to come, a Trump that shall sound for the next eight years! And they will say, how do we remove this Trump? And they will say, we must come together and dismantle this power, but it shall not be so! For not only will the sound carry for eight years, but will carry eight more. A new day has come and you will see great transition come forth as the House called white is filled with righteousness and power.

12/5/16

Today, the Lord has reminded me of Isaiah 61. For this word is spoken over your life today! "Prison doors are open! Freedom has been given and justice has been served on your behalf. This month, called December will bring great change and an opportunity that will not be quenched by anything or anyone! It will be the month that sets the new year called 2017 in motion!

12/7/16

The unexpected is here! The grace to help you overcome is here! The peace is here to calm your weary heart! The strength you need to persevere is here! This week, sudden gifts will come your way. God says you are worthy of a double portion of favor, simply because you are loved with open arms and unspeakable passion for your life! Bursts of blessing are about to come quickly! Your eyes will be filled with astonishment, your heart pounding with joy. You have never been forgotten! This is a kairos moment of time for you! Take this time, open your heart and receive this word and allow it to penetrate your heart and revive your spirit.

12/8/16

You shall be comforted and you shall find rest. You have fought diligently and you have been so strong! Oh, how it brings Me such joy to show such great love! Open your arms up, My Child, for your comfort has come!

12/8/16

Light always conquers darkness. Never allow the distractions of this world to discourage you or steal your joy! Keep looking up and you will see the glory that is always found in front of you.

12/14/16

There are many times that you wrestle with the very thing I have called you to. Everyday there are pressures that come your way to distract you and bring frustration and doubt, but there is good news!!! You have overcome and the enemy has lost again the battle in which he fights. Today is very significant in your life, you will see and experience a great increase of My presence and blessing that comes to those who are faithful. You have been faithful Child, even when you have doubted your own faith.

12/15/16

I am right beside you! Today and everyday! I am releasing a great realm of joy that will be like medicine to your heart! You have been trying to figure this thing out, but you just can't seem to do it. Guess what, My Child. It is I that is not allowing you to figure it out. I am strengthening you to trust me! Not allowing you to see the big picture. There is great news! The picture is big and the blessing carries a double portion of grace. So do not strive any longer, and do not worry or doubt. You are positioned right where I want you to be and you are doing what I want you to do, and I am well pleased.

12/18/16

You were not created to need the affirmation of man, you were created to receive the confirmation of God.

12/20/16

Don't allow the enemy to try and steal your heart. What has been placed inside you is precious and has much worth. The plan of the enemy is to be diligent in trying to steal and remove your identity, but you have been given a double portion of refreshing winds and grace. Your strength has been restored and your mindset renewed! Now go and walk in victory!

12/21/16

Don't let rejection determine your direction. Your path is always open and is not regulated by man.

12/22/16

There is a significant release of peace today. Situations and scenarios that are present in your life and causing quite a bit of havoc will suddenly cease. The peace that surpasses all understanding has paid you a visit today, simply because love prevails!

12/24/16— In D.C.

A Prophet shall be invited to the House called White, and will be used to speak over the President and share the words that will be given to him that focus on the next 12 years. Great mysteries will be released and divine visitation shall take place.

12/29/16

Don't be discouraged because you have not received everything you are hoping for. When the enemy tries to bring you down, I laugh at these plans because they have no power nor will they stop My path for you. I am renewing your strength today and you will experience a sudden increase of My presence.

Remember My words. My thoughts are not yours, and ways are not yours! Stop trying to figure out why specific things have not transpired the way you were expecting. For in this day, you shall see and hear directive words from Me that will encourage and give understanding. What is coming is bigger and will produce greater fruit in your life.

Part Five

Prophetic Words — 2017

John Natale

1/1/2017— For 2017

We would like to wish all of you a Happy New Year!! It has been a significant season that revealed the supernatural grace of God!

As with Moses, he came to the Red Sea, and a decision had to be made that would shape the generations to come. The many around him, some filled with faith and some not, made their words known. Just like today, many speak words to your ears that try to influence your decision making, but I have given you such a grace, such a comfort and such a confidence in your heart that will cause you to do what seems impossible.

The waters are about to open for you! I will say it again, My Child!

The waters are about to open for you! You have heard the chariots coming, you have heard the voices in the background. You have heard the sound of the enemy, but there is a roar that comes from Heaven that will part the very thing that has stood in your way!

You have walked and you have not grown weary! You have been steadfast in times of great adversity and you have been patient when there seemed no way to move forward.

The journey has been long and at times, filled with struggle and doubt. You have thought about going back to previous scenarios that brought comfort and at times, even tried to make these things come to pass, but all seemed empty when your eyes opened in the spirit.

There has been a stirring in your inner man throughout this season to keep contending even when you did not want to. Something very real inside of you that made you keep going! Something that would not be extinguished. That strength has always been inside of you. That power, never broken! You are an overcomer!

As you enter this new year, you shall see nothing but a clear path and the way made crystal clear. The ground shall be dry with no hindrance and there shall be no opposition in front of you or behind you. You shall see the Hand of God at work in this season on your behalf and you shall be glad!

Stand firm and hold your ground! As with Moses, raise your arms and declare these words over your life and family! "Watch and see the glory of God and how He has divided the enemy and cleared our path.

1/3/17

Your heart has been heavy with very specific pains that have caused you to reach out to others to fill that void. Today, you will see and experience a love that fills the holes in your heart. A very strong wind of confidence in who you are shall blow on you, and a fresh identity shall be given.

1/5/17

A very, very special door is about to open for you! What was not known, shall be known.

1/9/17

And yes, a very specific event will take place. One that will grab the attention of young and old alike. Heads will turn to the left and to the right and the voices will say, "What has just happened?"

They will look into each other's eyes and they will see something that has not been seen. They will melt with compassion and a new love that will orchestrate a new beginning, a new day! So lift up your heads, for you have not been defeated! The victory shall come forth swiftly and you shall see a mighty move of justice that reveals the glory! A new peace! A new joy! A new freedom is about to embrace you!

John Natale

1/11/17

The enemy has been trying diligently to remind you that you will not get off the ground and move forward, but these words are declared over your life today. Those who hope in the Lord will renew their strength. They will soar on wings like eagles; they will run and not grow weary, they will walk and not faint. It is time to rejoice, for your flight has been ordered today and you are clear for takeoff.

1/12/17

I want to remind you today that what you see as failure, I see as victory! I want to remind you today that what seems to be an endless effort in your pursuit and perseverance will bring such amazing fruit. You have condemned yourself and you have been overwhelmed, but a sudden burst of My presence shall give you a fresh wind of encouragement and confidence.

1/17/17— In D.C.

"How and why? How can this be? Who is watching over him?" *These are the words that shall be spoken! This man that is called Trump. As I slipped through the crowd, so will he. The plans, the plans. They conjure up and they seek the demise, but it shall not be so! For you shall see an increase of protection, an increase of authority! A hedge that surrounds completely shall not be visible to the eye, but shall be seen in the spirit. So watch and see, as that day approaches! The nations shall watch and they shall be in awe! I am confusing the plans of the enemy and the wind shall come, for it shall surely come and scatter the darkness. Watch! Watch!*

1/18/17

The stage is set and the battle is about to take place! Goliath has called out David. He has tried to intimidate, discredit, and manipulate, but there shall be a great surprise that unfolds! The mocking, the plans, the resistance is about to encounter an authority that is of a higher realm. My words and My hands shall produce such a sudden burst of glory that all darkness and oppression shall cease. So on that day, the power will be released by one and given to another, look up, for signs shall be given that shall bring great peace and great comfort.

1/19/17

Some very interesting events are about to take place. Watch people, watch! What the eye cannot see, the ear will hear; and what the ear cannot hear, the eye will see. The hearts of men and women alike will stir with a joy and a peace that surpasses all understanding. The voices will say, *"It has come! How can this be? From where? We have lost control. It's over!"*

1/20/17

And so it has come! This day that has caused so much bitterness and joy! What is the final decision? What is the outcome from all of this? You shall see, you shall surely see! For a sign is desired and a sign shall be given. For even before the silence comes, a roar shall be heard that shall cause a stirring and then the sound shall cease. It shall be heard no more and a freedom shall blow in with a mighty wind.

1/21/17

Woe to those who come against Me! Woe to those that bring a seed of discord! For I will come against this thing and I will allow the waters to come back to their place and swallow up the darkness! For they say, "We will disturb and we will not relent."

But they have a thing coming! Watch! For the sound shall come from the east and it shall come in when no eye is watching or ear is listening. Who is greater? Who is in control of all things? I Am that I Am! My hands cover the very thing that has been established and My angels surround with a battle sound that you cannot comprehend!

1/23/17— In D.C.

Over the next 13 days in the Trump administration, there will be a surge of favor and grace. Individuals waiting to be placed in their positions will not be hindered or delayed any longer. Watch how division tries to make its roar heard, but this will quickly fade away.

1/25/17

Help is on the way! New beginnings are right around the corner! February! Oh how you will come with many surprises! *"Look!"* they say! *"Look what has become of us!"*

Unprecedented favor! Yes, you shall receive! But watch, for one shall make her voice heard again! For she has another plan! But My plans shall crush those plans and peace shall come and frustration shall cease.

1/28/17— In D.C.

What was not established will be established! For eight days have come! For there is an increase of alertness in this land called United States! You shall see in the days ahead, a roar that will flood the nation and a wave that is not stoppable with human hands!

Watch, for a new connection will be made with one that wears white. For in this hour, the nations are being prepared and they shall come with open arms and say "We bring an offering of peace."

1/30/17— In D.C.

Now you will see that there will be a significant increase of My presence in the White House. A cloud of glory shall come over it and guard against the principalities that seek to defile and discredit. My glory shall shine in every window as a whirlwind of fire that shall be a symbol of My power and My authority. Watch, for in the next several days, an atmosphere will descend and all that enter it will not only see, but hear the sounds of heaven.

1/31/17

Allow Me to keep your heart pure and filled with peace. Do you not know that I am watching? Have you forgotten that I am in control of all things? Did I tell you to worry, or not to worry? My word says that out of the abundance of the heart, the mouth speaks. Place all your trust in Me and I will bring you a peace that surpasses all understanding. Lay your burden down and allow Me to give you this peace.

2/1/17

It is here! The month you call February. Watch, for a chain of events will take place and suddenly remove barriers that are causing hindrance. Freedom reigns, and justice has come to those that seek peace.

2/3/17

An increase of hearing and understanding has been made available to you today. Many different ways of discerning shall accompany this fresh wind of new revelation. Your season of understanding is upon you!

2/3/17— In D.C.

A great connection shall be made! A strength shall multiply, and those that discredit and plan shall be silenced. Watch, for Israel shall be embraced with a stronger heart and a relationship shall be joined at the hip. For two leaders shall develop a relationship that goes down in history. Watch as this unfolds quickly, significant blessing and favor shall increase in this nation that is called America!

2/3/17

Do not back down for righteousness sake. Stand firm and hold your ground. The enemy is a liar.

2/6/17

And the enemy once again has tried to convince you that progress will not come and victory will not be achieved. Now listen, I have set things in motion now and what was delayed, is now moving forward with great speed. Watch, as this day, and the days ahead reveal what was hindered and blessing comes forth.

2/8/17— In D.C.

And so it comes! Watch as the mysteries of Heaven are revealed. For the white shall come and it shall blanket and comfort. So they shall say, "What is it that we feel? Can you feel it?"

My glory is descending in ways that many do not expect, but watch, for in its course, and as it comes to an end, a sound shall be heard that has caused many sounds by one that dwells in the one that is surrounded by white as well.

2/12/17

In a dream this morning, I saw the spirit of deception operating and deceiving many to follow them. There is a strong attack on people right now in the atmosphere. They used kind words, music, and acts of love to cause the minds and hearts of many to be influenced. They will say they are one with you, but they are not!

For I am revealing the plans of the enemy this day, and what is not from Me shall be revealed and removed! For in this hour, not one, but three individuals have come to deceive you, but I have given you means of escape from the snare of the enemy. Freedom has once again knocked at your door.

2/8/17— In D.C.

The enemy is trying to not just discredit and dishonor this man called President Trump, but his whole family, but I have seen and I have heard! Enough! For you shall see and you shall hear. For a great restoration is coming that will cover like a wave! Is it you that controls all things? Is it you that knows all things? For I am in control, and it is I that restores all things. So now you will see the sudden increase of honor and the sudden increase of glory be released and established."

2/14/17— In D.C.

Out of the abundance of the heart, the mouth speaks. What you are seeing and what you are hearing in this nation is the very thing that words from the ancient of days has spoken of. A great division has come to divide. To call evil, good; and good, evil, but it is not time yet. For I shall show wonders in the skies above and the earth below. Who holds all the keys? For watch, as one heart melts that has the influence on many, so will the heart of many melt for that one, and bitterness and anger shall be replaced with love and understanding. Now watch, for this shall come quickly.

John Natale

2/18/17

There is a strong wave of justice being released right now on the earth. Watch, for those that have come against you shall not just be silenced, but have a change of heart and join you in the fight.

2/20/17

Today, in a vision, I saw a hand placed in the sand. A line was drawn and these words were spoken. *"I hold all things, I control all things. Enough of this! I have heard the cries of many! I have seen the tears! Oh America, what has become of you? Why have you hidden your heart? You shall see a glory and a sound that you have not heard before! There shall be a separating and there shall be a joining! For watch, a restoration is coming and it shall not be hindered any longer. For the appointed time has come, the time that you call Spring. For My hand has drawn not just a line in the sand, but My finger has pointed at this nation and help is on its way, and In this you can trust!"*

2/22/17

Oh how the enemy comes to kill, steal and destroy! But these plans are not My plans! Some of My Children have suffered sudden attacks that have come and tried to steal your joy and hope, but this was quickly defused and light conquered darkness. The enemy has been trying diligently to break up your family and focus on the sons, but this has not been allowed.

Disunity and discord was present, but this has come to an end. Very specific blessing is coming for those that have endured these sudden struggles. For in their faith, their heart did not grow weary, and in their mind, they carried a expectation that would not be removed. Now watch, for not only is restoration coming, but justice! For the enemy has been

98

swept away and his power is no longer. So rejoice! Great joy and great peace is here now for you and the prodigal has returned."

"BUT THOSE WHO HOPE IN THE LORD WILL RENEW THEIR STRENGTH. THEY WILL SOAR ON WINGS LIKE EAGLES; THEY WILL RUN AND NOT GROW WEARY, THEY WILL WALK AND NOT BE FAINT." Isaiah 40:31

2/24/17

There is a spirit of unity being released now! Mindset changes, heart changes. What was lost is now found. Watch, for the wind blows and sun shines, and in the days ahead, as you wonder and as you gaze, you will look up and you will look around and many will ask, "How did this happen? When did this happen?"

This is My glory and My presence. For this month that you call February will not end quietly, but will blossom like the wildflowers that show their colors.

2/24/17— In D.C.

NO WEAPON FORMED AGAINST ME SHALL PROSPER! *These are the words that come and crash like a wave! Woe to those who scheme and plan against this President. Do you not remember the words that he is protected around and within. Do not give the enemy credit, for he is the father of lies. There is a great hedge of protection around this man that is called Donald Trump, and you will see in many ways how My hands cover him.*

2/27/17

Today, as you persevere and endure for your breakthrough, a sudden revelation will come and cover you with understanding and peace. As with Thomas and Peter, both were overcome with discouragement because they thought I left them, but I am here to tell you I have never left you and will always be with you. Great peace and blessing is coming to you! Watch and listen, for the sound soon approaches!

2/28/17

So the month called February has come to a close and the new season fast approaches. Now listen, for many struggle with the cares of this world and time is moving ahead. It will not cease and it cannot be regained, but what I promise and what I desire is simple, that you would take every moment, every day and enjoy it to the full. Don't allow the enemy to burden you down and steal your joy.

For as the new season comes that you call Spring, not only will it show its colors and reveal what is hidden in the earth, but I will reveal what has been hidden, and the treasures that have been waiting for you shall come suddenly. So rejoice, you shall shine bright and your joy shall be once again overflowing for all to see.

2/28/17

The sound has been heard and the voice has triumphed. Watch, for the strength has begun and the momentum moves swiftly in historic speed.

3/1/17

In a vision I saw Angels being released on behalf of all Law Enforcement individuals. *"Enough is enough,"* says the Lord of hosts! *"Enough of this hatred! Enough of this anger! Your justice is coming in a way that is not comprehensible to mankind!"*

3/2/17

Oh so many want just to be loved. They try so hard, they toil, and they persevere without complaining. Many go unrecognized, their words unheard, their smiles unseen, but I have heard and I have seen. My love is sufficient for you, and My love shall embrace with such a comfort that words cannot express. So now, receive and know that you have been strengthened and restored. What you have been waiting for and what your heart needs, is here, and it is always available to you.

3/3/17— In D.C.

And so they plan and they hide behind closed doors seeking their revenge, but this shall not be so! For those that come against what has been established in the White House shall have all plans exposed and destroyed. For they forget easily that My voice reveals the hidden things. For there is one that is hidden, and that one is watched by Me. For in its time, the revealing shall come and honor shall be replaced with dishonor.

3/5/17— In D.C.

Watch how March exposes the one that hides behind closed doors. For that one shall fall and all that was gained will be lost. It shall unravel like grave clothes and expose all motives and intentions. The laughter shall be turned into weeping, and the proud shall be made humble. That House shall be a brilliant White, and those that come to taint its foundation shall have all plans swept away like the winds carries the dust."

3/6/17— In D.C.

What are they saying? What are they doing? That will all come to pass shortly! But in the moment that is now, the atmosphere stirs up, the ground shakes, and the people watch closely with wonder and curiosity as to what will be revealed. For there will be a shaking with some that have hidden agendas and it will be dealt with, but In this time, do not be concerned or have no worry, for such things must come to pass, but I say to you now, peace, glory, blessing and joy are here now for you. Your month called March is here and it shall make its voice very clear to you and rise up in your favor with such inspiration and breakthrough.

3/7/17

You are My Child! You shall comforted. Why are you so weary this day? You have overcome so much! So much perseverance, so much endurance! I am so proud of you! Stand up now and take My hand. Let's walk together. Let Me show you the new things that are about to be revealed. It is upon you, you just don't see it, but you shall! It is all around you, but you don't feel it, but you shall! For in this new season called March, you shall encounter a new freedom and glory that has not been present. For it shall come and it shall stay! For I say this again to you, it shall stay!

3/8/17

Do not get overwhelmed by what you see or intimidated by those around you. You are awesome and you are great! Never forget that! Too many of My Children are striving to know Me more and all it takes is to stop what you are doing and sit on My lap. Place your head on My chest and listen to my heartbeat. That encounter will change everything.

3/8/17— In D.C.

And the one that left that House that would not speak, but kept silent, for I watch him. For he smiles, he schemes and his hidden role shall be revealed. For his influence is great and he keeps his posture low, but I shall reveal that present place and reveal the secret plans that work behind closed doors and brick walls. For the curtain shall rise and the voices shall cease. For this Ahab shall see the justice and the glory of My hand.

3/13/17

Times are changing and you are changing as well. What is being established is far greater than you know. Your month called March is now in full bloom showing its colors. Now watch for what is revealed, for in the next few days ahead, very interesting things will be revealed and opportunities will make themselves known. Now, for what is happening in that place that is White, what is covered presently, will melt suddenly and what is saturated shall dry completely. For the skies are being used to restore and heal.

3/14/17

No matter how hard it looks or how difficult it has been, you must carry a mindset and belief that change is capable of knocking on your door. You must remember that faith is the substance of things hoped for and the evidence of things unseen.

3/15/17

A sudden turn shall come and your mourning shall turn to joy!

3/16/17— In D.C.

What is this? Why do they come against what is in place and forget who they dishonor? For a shaking is coming! For your fight is with words and they have no power! For your strength is nothing and can do no harm to whom I have positioned in this time. For I will show grace again and again, but this grace will not be taken advantage of.

For I hold all the keys and all the answers. For a sign shall be given and given it shall. For in the days ahead, you will see who holds all the stars in His hands and who sets all things in motion. A stirring shall come and a voice shall be heard that silences the arrogant and the proud! For they say, we shall conquer and divide, but I say, your plans shall come to nothing and be swept away and remembered no more.

3/19/17

Today starts a seven-day journey. For over the course of the next several days very specific scenarios that have created unusual levels of stress and discouragement shall be removed. Many will come to recognize they have been fighting in their own strength. But this is the week that strength is revived, hope is restored. There will be a sudden shift, a sudden spark that even the skies will show quick sudden changes. For this is not just happening to a few, but to many. There is a significant stirring by My spirit to bring comfort and confidence to know that you're not fighting alone, you're not walking alone. Rise up, take your mat and walk. As with the pool at Bethesda, rise above your situation. It's time to move.

3/20/17

It's beginning! You will start to see and hear the water flowing. What you are seeking and what you are in need of is in the beginning stages of manifesting. Watch how things unfold today.

3/21/17— In D.C.

For I have set in motion this Administration for such a time as this. For many play the game to discredit and to mock, but I will have the last laugh! For what you dishonor, I will release a double portion of favor and grace. For your tactics will only reveal your own unrighteousness and cause your heel to stumble. Your efforts are in vain and only cause columns to be strengthened. For My hands and My voice guard the House and all that are within.

3/22/17

As with Naaman, he had to do something that was not on his expected list in order to experience something great. You too will experience the unexpected as it comes in many ways. Job opportunities, homes, and relocation. New assignments are coming and will be revealed as April shines and introduces her blessing!

3/24/17

You are not alone! For the one that has lost hope and for the one that sees no future ahead, you are not only forgiven, but you are cherished. Your past is behind you and I am with you! What I see, is greatness and you will make it! In this you can be sure! It's not over yet, the race is not over yet, simply because you are victorious and I have destined you to overcome all that comes your way. Open your eyes, My Child. I am here.

3/26/17

When you seek righteousness and pursue justice, the road on which you travel must be followed by those that carry the eyes of revelation.

3/27/17

Your month called March is coming to an end, and it was shown again how I am in control of all things. Now as the month called April comes forth, you will find yourself sitting at the table in which at first did not seem possible. For your waiting and weariness has caused a release and breakthrough that shall not just bring significant increase, but unprecedented favor and honor. For a chair has been waiting for you and there are those that will bless you and surround you simply because you have been purposed for such a time as this. Now watch, for it is a very pivotal and interesting month and its name shall be called "Honor."

3/28/17— In D.C.

What is all of this? Will you spend every moment trying to undo all that has been established? It will not be so! For there is one that hides behind his smile that conspires behind closed doors, but I will reveal him in the days ahead. For this House that is White will not be defiled nor will it be dishonored.

3/31/17

You are loved and you are cherished. You have been so diligent and you try so hard! It is a joy to watch you! What you think is failing, is progressing and setting you up for a great blessing and surprise. So continue and keep going right where you are at! It is not in vain. Nothing you are doing is in vain. For there are great things that are happening behind the scenes that you do not see. You have finished this month called March! So prepare and watch! Did I not give you a glimpse about this Month that is upon you called April? For all things are subject to change!

4/3/17— In D.C.

So the table has been set once again. Oh how they look under every rock trying to find answers to questions that cannot be found. But certainly what they are looking for will be their own hidden mysteries that revolve around their own hidden agendas. For in this month that you call April, a great exposure shall be revealed. For I always rescue my friends from the enemy. For you have not learned as of yet that what you have tried to displace is held together by My hands. For this President that holds his place and holds his ground, shall be victorious and he shall see a great vindication and justice that will be remembered for generations.

4/5/17

Don't seek affirmation from man, receive confirmation from God. The imperfections that you see in your own life, God sees as the brilliance of colors that shine from the choicest of diamonds. It's your month of honor and it's your time to shine.

4/6/17

For there are many that have pulled away from the place that is called church and they have been judged unfairly. They have been seeking My presence that is free and pure. For they shall be comforted and directed for what is of Me. For they have waited patiently and they shall see their victory. For you must remember that you are the church. It is not a building or system. You carry everything you need and you carry the light in a dark place. Today, be reminded of what you carry and Who is always with you.

4/6/17— For D.C.

What do you see? Have I not told you before that My hand is upon this man that dwells in the House of White? You are seeing the beginning of days that resemble a King named David. My favor is upon him and the enemies shall bow their knee. For they shall see a confident warrior that is not intimidated by man, but one who pursues justice for the nations.

For there will be a continuation of favor and grace that flows like a river, and those that come against and resist this nation with their wickedness shall see the mighty hand that comes suddenly and fights for righteousness sake. For in its time, a great impact shall be made and a revealing shall be uncovered. You have seen the beginning of honor, and you shall see why this must come to pass.

4/7/17— For D.C.

The stage is set for very significant scenarios that will take place. This man that holds his place in the House that is White has made a choice to take a stand. Other nations will come and test his courage and his capacity. But you will see that I am with him and his strength comes from a higher source. Watch, for in the weeks ahead, one will speak out in wickedness with his declarations, but that sound shall have no impact, but only make this President that has been placed in authority, stronger, and this Nation shall be honored greatly.

4/9/17

High honor has been released upon your behalf today. The enemy has once again tried to silence you. Even shaking and disrupting the ground on which you stand. As with Haman, gallows were built to take you down, but he has lost and his plans exposed. Prepare, for your King is about to do some very special things in your life.

4/10/17— For D.C.

Who is this man that is called Putin? Does he not know that I know every plan that is hidden? For he is nothing! For he tries to intimidate, but he shall come to nothing! For I shall reveal his plans and expose the darkness as the sun rises and brings light to the day. Watch, for his hour comes quickly when truth is revealed and significant honor is restored to one that has been dishonored.

4/10/17— Regarding Syria And Egypt

Let us keep in prayer the people of Syria and Egypt in our prayers.

There shall be a great divine intervention that will take place in the land. Justice will be served and all those responsible for acts of injustice to mankind will be found from their place of hiding. There is one that is sneaky and he thinks he cannot be exposed because of his status, but this is not so! He will be hard pressed, not by man, but by Me! He will find torment in the days ahead and he shall lose all that he has gained! Watch, for in the days ahead, his smile shall turn to sorrow.

4/11/17— For D.C.

"Jericho is about to fall." In a word from Holy Spirit, these scriptures were given today.

Then the Lord said to Joshua, See, I have delivered Jericho into your hands, along with its king and its fighting men. The enemy is about to be delivered into the hands of righteousness. Whosoever comes against this nation called the United States, shall see the mighty hand of God sweep and remove all injustice and unrighteousness. A great wind of redemption and justice is about to be on display for all the nations to see and they will see the favor on this nation. This President called Trump is protected and carries favor that many do not understand, but in time, all will see the greater picture that is present.

4/13/17

You have come into a season that is testing your capacity and character. For this is being allowed now simply because of what shall take place in the days ahead. For there are doors that are open that you shall walk through. These shall be very pleasant and bring light to a greater level that is consistent with your destiny. It is a time to rejoice, for April has come, and it shall not leave you without displaying its love and its blessing.

4/13/17— For D.C.

So shall it be heard? There are rumblings in the land. For Putin thinks he has won a victory, but this is not so! There will be a stronger resentment against the United States, but this is not unusual. It is only for a time. For in its time, an announcement shall be made in the land that is occupied by that leader that thinks he is invincible, but he shall see who is in control, and his power is nothing. For I am orchestrating such a sound that cannot be conducted by men, but by Me. Now watch, for this Nation, called United States shall see an increase of favor and blessing in the Summer months that will come in very significant ways.

4/16/17

I say to you now, what has been prepared for you in this new season is at its point of release. A brand new thing that was not expected is coming to knock on your door. Watch how things unfold as a significant milestone and breakthrough comes and sweeps you off your feet. They will say that April 2017 was the turning point in your life. Yes, it shall be so!

4/20/17

Sudden things have turned in your favor. What was not expected has come and introduced itself to you, and for some, the knock is fast approaching. For these things will take diligence and perseverance, but do not be overwhelmed, you have been prepared all along for sweet breakthrough and victory.

4/20/17— In D.C.

So there is a bitterness that has come on the one that has left his office. For there will be many questions that go unanswered in the weeks ahead. There will be a stirring and there will be searching. For My eye is upon him and My grace is available. So watch, for in the days ahead, the heart softens.

4/22/17

Watch and see! You have been distracted and discouraged, simply because what you thought was supposed to come in the time you expected, did not. So today, watch! Justice has been released again on your behalf, and many will experience breakthrough today! You know, I must remind you of this. I am watching you closely. I laugh with such joy when I see you acting out. The funny thing is that the enemy thinks he has you, and that makes Me laugh that much more! So today, I speak and release My laughter upon you and your situation! Now watch what joy can bring and what breakthrough follows!

4/24/17— In D.C.

Oh how they are desperate to achieve their wickedness. They have finally understood that they cannot crack the pillar that is in place, in the House of White. So they seek other means to disrupt and to discredit. For they think they have found a weak link, but they do not see, it is My hands that holds al things together. I have My eye on them as well. For they will not gain victory in any way, but will only open a door that leads to exposure to wickedness. For their motives shall be used against them and justice shall be revealed.

4/25/17

Perfect love casts out all fear. You have been struggling with fear in the area of finances. What you see is causing great anxiety and doubt, but I am here to remind you that I Am your source. Don't allow this to dictate your future! I am bigger than your situation and I govern all things! Now watch, for breakthrough comes suddenly, and it will also bring new understanding. Learn from this and take authority over it. Once this takes place, a river will flow.

John Natale

4/27/17

There are times that what you seek and what you expect shows up in ways that are not what you imagined or considered. At this time, I have positioned you for something significant. It is more than you think and will touch many lives. What you carry inside of you is needed at this time for others. The blessing that comes from this shall reveal a greater assignment that unlocks significant promise to you and your family.

4/28/17

Get ready for a weekend of sudden bursts of breakthrough. Significant surprises will be revealed. Watch what takes place!

4/30/17

The April month is now closing and what is coming ahead is, as Ezekiel would say, "overwhelming". Watch, for very significant breakthroughs are preparing to make a surprise visit. The water shall start flowing as you approach the day of honor. These shall set the foundation for the month called June.

5/1/17— In D.C.

I have been watching this President that is called Trump. He is praying and he is listening. Many do not know his heart. They listen to a voice that is not Mine. For in the days to come, a compassion and understanding shall rise and will sweep through this nation. Watch, this month that is called May, holds a key that will unlock and reveal a beautiful mystery.

5/4/17

Sometimes you are asked to do the unthinkable, the unimaginable. What seems crazy to you, is perfect to Me! Perfect love casts out all fear. For this month, you will explore new territory that has been waiting just for you!

5/8/17

Many of you think you are failing, and some believe you are falling, but I am here to tell you, that is not so! The enemy is a liar, and I Am a good, good Father that will not allow you to fail or believe the lies of the enemy. You shall succeed and you shall overcome in this season. This month called May shall surprise you. In this you can be sure. It shall be good! It shall be very good!

5/10/17— In D.C.

A PROPHETIC SHIFT HAS TAKEN PLACE IN THE LAND CALLED D.C.

Authority has been taken away and new, greater authority shall be given. Watch, for in the days ahead, this change shall be used to complete an assignment that many have had their eyes on. A justice shall be served and gates that were once open, shall be closed. One will rise to defend, but this will only lead to darkness being exposed that much more.

5/11/17

Many of you keep looking back to regain what seems lost, but I Am here to tell you that greater days are ahead. You have not lost anything! You actually have gained much! Many additions shall come forth in this month called May, and you will see and experience an unplanned opportunity filled with a double portion of grace.

5/12/17

There are times that your strength feels as if it is gone and your faith is no longer upon you. But just one shift of perspective changes everything. Today, you will experience that shift and move forward with great progress and determination. Watch how sudden bursts of encouragement visit you today from unexpected sources.

5/16/17

Fear is the strongest tool that the enemy uses to hold you back. It was not meant to be a stronghold, but a key of revelation to open new and exciting doors of opportunity. Today, you will be given strength and understanding to overcome this adversity. Watch how things become easier as the week continues and grace is released.

5/17/17

Sudden opportunities shall spring up and come in like a fresh wind. Watch as specific details are released and movement occurs that you have been waiting for. The blessing has been waiting for you, it was actually caught in the thicket. Your faith, which at times seemed insignificant, has caused very special scenarios to be released

5/18/17— In D.C.

Have they not learned from all of this? They shall see what they are looking for, but it will not be from the one called Trump. For they look under rocks and they plan. There is one that is behind all of this and this one keeps silent. The mystery that comes forth is called fear. They are losing control quickly, but they do not realize they are not in control. For one shall speak soon, and many have their eyes on him, but what he reveals is not what they are expecting. For there is justice fast approaching. Watch and see!

5/22/17

Don't let your spiritual perspective be distracted by natural directives. Your ability to overcome adversity and conquer insecurity is valued by your self worth. You are being refined as gold. The fire seems hot presently, but the end result is purification and value that words cannot express.

5/23/17

Overcoming is not as hard as you perceive, My Child. What you have conquered in the past has become the building blocks that enable you to rise above any situation that comes your way. It's a bit hectic right now, and at times you just want to cave in, but My strength and My plan is greater than your situation. You will overcome! There will be a very important breakthrough that comes your way very soon. You have not been forgotten. It's closer than you think, and it comes with wind and a day that is filled with heat. The warm wind shall be your sign!

5/25/17— In D.C.

The one that dwells in the House of White is weary. He has prayed for strength, he has prayed for guidance. For in the days ahead, you shall see a renewed perspective and diligence that comes from within. The people will wonder how and where he gets his strength from, but that is just the mystery of the evidence. For an announcement shall be made shortly. One that puts focus on the accusers. Watch, for a very familiar name that is common to man shall be revealed. For his own agenda shall be spoiled and purposes unraveled.

5/30/17

A very significant healing is fast approaching. Depression...Where is your grip now? Cancer....You have no power! Anger...Your pain has been removed and thrown into the abyss. Michigan, Delaware, Iowa, your names have been spoken. Indiana, you have been called! Watch, for sudden divine intervention shall come and restore what the locust has stolen.

5/30/17

Your diligence and perseverance comes from a strength that is given during times of testing. You are seeing progress in others, and you are questioning yours. What you are about to see in your life will not only silence these negative thoughts, but create a revived heart and mindset, that your future, both near and far is awesome.

6/2/17

What you are experiencing now is the beginning of a great shift. What transpired in the month of May was the foundation for the walls to be built in June. Watch, the framing of something very special is about to be revealed. This month you shall see significant breakthrough and comfort. Just remember, that when a foundation is poured, it must set before the walls go up!

6/5/17

Today is a day of new beginnings! You have been wrestling and struggling with a situation that the enemy says there is no hope for restoration. In fact, you have seen yourself losing the battle. Many have actually started condemning themselves, but I have come to give you the help that is needed to overcome. What you have seen in your mind as defeat, I am showing you as victory, in the spirit and in the natural. You will experience a great breakthrough that comes quickly. For many families shall see this come to pass in the month called June.

6/7/17

So many people, they come and they go. Struggling, worrying and living as if there is no hope in sight. You were not created just to exist, you were created to thrive. Today, I remind you that if you believe and do not doubt, you will see great days, and you will see great victories. Just believe!

6/11/17— In D.C.

So as the word has been spoken, they will come out and reveal their own demise. But, watch, for everyday that this President that is called Trump is in office, darkness will be exposed and agendas will be revealed. Now listen closely, for the summer will reveal an even greater exposure, one that has not been spoken of. But for the significant one, he is fully aware that many watch him, but he is not aware that I watch him. The one that could not speak truth and spoke venom, he shall see a revealing so great that brings such a justice that has been long overdue.

6/13/17

When things are not moving in the way you expect, I am still working on your behalf. There has been a pause over the past several days for very significant reasons. What you see is different from what I see! It has been frustrating for you, but I still have been with you during this time. So now, there is good news, when a season of calm has completed, a fresh wind blows. The windows have opened and the wind shall come with such a peace and blessing that you cannot contain. This day that you call Tuesday, shall be your reminder, that all things work out for those that love God.

John Natale

6/17/17

At this moment I am showing you how much I love you. Many are being touched right now. Embrace what you feel and run with what you hear. I am with you!

6/20/17

Sudden distractions have come to try to keep you off the path you are on, and the focus you have been faithful to keep. Do not believe the lies of the enemy. I will silence the storm now and peace shall fill your heart and the atmosphere around you.

6/23/17

For the season has changed once again and a new mystery shall take its place. Watch, for the next several days shall be very interesting. What takes place shall be such a comfort to you and reveal some special breakthroughs.

6/25/17

Get ready for a summer of great restoration and reconciliation. For what has been stolen shall be returned. For you shall see your family brought into a place of peace and joy! The hearts of many have been melting and prepared for such a time as this, simply because you have prayed and not given up. Remember that love conquers all oppression and darkness, and it is My love that has authority over everything. In this, you will see the manifestation of supernatural healing in the months that are called summer.

6/27/17

Today is a reminder that there is someone in your life that you have to forgive. Remember these words, Father forgive them, for they know not what they do. People have problems with love simply because they were not loved properly, or not at all. The capacity they have is the capacity they give. Watch, how hearts are turned and relationships healed. It's the season of restoration!

6/30/17

There is nothing too difficult for Me to fix and heal. I will give many a revelation and understanding of just how capable I am to help and comfort those that are hurting. As the words have been spoken that restoration and reconciliation was approaching to those that have been crying out, you will see a sudden shift in the lives around you that you have been praying for. The enemy has been working so hard to defeat you, but I have prayed for you and you shall see victory!

7/4/17— In D.C.

For the Trump shall sound again! For a mighty establishment of relationship shall come together in the weeks ahead. An alliance shall be formed with several leaders in the Middle East. This shall come together to bring unity that has been waiting for years. Leaders that were once against each other will now work together for the common good of mankind. Watch for the summer holds a mystery that shall soon be revealed.

7/6/17

These little distractions that keep coming and stealing your joy and peace shall be no longer! I am setting things in motion now that will help bring you to a place of confidence and stability. The enemy hates your progress and is at work diligently simply because of the authority and calling that is on your life. July will be a month that brings great fruit and reveals great answers that have been sought after with great faith.

7/7/17

Today, prepare for an outpouring of blessing and opportunity. This date and time is very significant, and in time, you will understand the mystery. The windows of Heaven are open for you and shall flow like a river! Suddenlies, surprises, and unexpected events shall come your way, simply because you are loved!

7/9/17

As Jacob pressed though and overcame, he learned that fear cannot only cause you to doubt, but lose sight of your destiny. Allow Me to open your eyes to this spiritual stronghold that the enemy has used for generations. Today is a day of unprecedented freedom for you and your journey.

7/11/17

Take this summer and run with it, Child! You will have a very special opportunity come your way! Don't allow discouragement to steal your joy during these significant months. Shake the dust off your feet and look up with great expectation. You will look back as September draws near and see how I was with you all the time and preparing you for such a breakthrough!

7/13/17

There has been a release that has shifted in the atmosphere that will cause a shaking suddenly. Hidden agendas and motives that have been used to hold you back will all of a sudden be revealed, and justice shall come to you with great favor.

7/14/17

Deception is a tool that is used specifically to hide hidden agendas. Watch as these are exposed in the second half of the month that is called July. What held you back in secret will promote you forward in public with honor!

7/14/17— In D.C.

I have heard the cries and I have heard the voices that tarry throughout the night praying for this nation called America, and for this President that is called Trump. I will elevate him higher, and at the same time bring a strength to this Nation that has not been seen before. For in the summer, a decision will be made in the House of White that will stir this Nation and cause the weary to be strong and the angry to be joyful. What is coming is not what you have expected, but what is needed. There is a double portion of grace flowing upon him right now, and you will see as the summer increases, the voices of wrath shall decrease.

7/17/17

A sudden shift of events has been released in the spirit realm that will manifest in the natural. Watch and see how the justice of God moves swiftly on your behalf. For Haman has spoken enough of his lies, and now he has been given a sentence to be silenced. For in the spirit, righteousness has once again defeated unrighteousness! For your adversary has been plucked out and his voice removed from your ears! You will not be hindered any longer! The voices that you hear moving forward are ones of inspiration and comfort!

7/20/17

Above all things, above the sounds, the storms, the laughter and the tears, people just want to be loved! They cry out day and night for something they do not have control of. Their hearts ache with the sounds of neglect and rejection, but I am here to change all of that! As you think about those that are in your life that need this love, pray for them! Love them and pray that their hearts would be open to truth and life. For in the next several days ahead, you will understand why this word has come to you!

7/28/17

You will travel many roads and experience many things on this journey. What I desire for you is to understand the mystery that follows you. Look back and see what you have overcome! Look ahead and see what you shall conquer, and see now what needs to be mended and healed. You have the power and you have the ability! Do not give up on yourself and do not doubt for a minute that I am working on your behalf.

7/29/17

A great mystery that has been avoiding you shall suddenly meet you face-to-face. What was hidden in the garden shall quickly appear and bring great delight and comfort. You will understand why specific things are relevant in this season. Watch and see how things all work out for the good.

7/31/17— In D.C.

For the words come and they go, and the winds bring the warm summer air. But in this, there is a message that brings comfort. For an unusual occurrence shall come to this man called Trump in the days ahead. For he is praying with an open heart. For he prays for his enemies and he prays for his friends. This has caused My ears to be attentive. For in the month called August, there shall come a great revelation and it shall bring answers to very specific questions. For one shall speak by his side and the nation shall listen and understand what their ears would not embrace. So it shall come! So it has already begun!

8/1/17

You have continually come into a place of faith and pursuit. At this time, I ask you this simple mystery! What is it that you want? As I spoke these words to the man by the Pool of Bethesda, they have come again to you. I bring this again to you because many of you have lost your sight of very specific dreams and promises that you know I want to give. Time is still on your side. You must understand that I control time and with Me, there is no worry or doubt that these things will come to fruition. So today, this day, is your reminder that I am going to reveal the hidden things and you will see great blessings in the new season called August.

8/1/17

The decisions that you make today affect the generations of tomorrow. So in this, you have been strong and fought hard. I declare over you now that your Children and their Children will reap a harvest of blessing that came from a foundation of faith that you have chosen to follow.

8/3/17

The wind has once again arrived with the scent of change. What was in the past and carried a mindset of history has cycled back to your door. I have been at work on your behalf to prepare you for the assignment that calls you by name. In this season, you will understand the mystery and follow through with strength, confidence, and victory. What you thought was not significant, was very significant to Me. Now watch as the harvest is released as a reward of diligence and faithfulness!

8/4/17

A repositioning is coming now. Your path has been a bit off center, but I have realigned you in this season and have given you the tools to finish this part of the race. What is important is that you take captive these thoughts that carry discouragement. They try to sneak up on you and steal the joy that I have placed inside of you. So a settling shall occur now in your heart and in your mind. This will clear your thoughts and allow you to see very specific things that I would like to speak to you about in this month called August. This is the month that the exchange takes place, and the stepping into new things begins.

8/7/17

For a day has come to celebrate life. For the mystery goes unknown for so many, but I have come to give you life and give it to the full. A renewed understanding of My love and grace is being released now to you. Today, you shall experience a quickening of My spirit and it shall fill you with an overflow of peace and joy! Watch, as the mystery of love reveals itself to you and you become overwhelmed by My presence.

8/10/17— Prophetic Vision

What I saw in the spirit was a blue blanket being brought down to cover those that needed to be comforted. This meaning is symbolic to freedom. There are many that have placed their heads on the pillow of rest, but have not entered into that season as of yet. At this moment, the great Comforter is placing His hands on you and sitting with you as you fall into a deep place of isolation with His presence.

8/11/17

Don't take time for granted. It goes faster than you think. You can't go back, but you can enjoy the very moment that you're in right now to the fullest! What's even better, are the plans that I make for your tomorrow, and the expectation that they will be good. In fact, they will be very good! So keep your head up and do not be discouraged, I will be with you—and with Me, all things are good.

8/13/17— In D.C. & North Korea

What is this with this man from North Korea? Has he not learned his lesson? For the implosion has begun! This Nation that is called United States will not have to bring about justice to the one who has determined to destroy many. For he shall see a justice that comes not from the hands of man, but from the hand of God. For a quickening shall come and a wind shall blow to bring about a calm that ends the storm! Watch, for the season comes to an end and a new season shall arrive with healing in its wings!

8/13/17

Not only is your life precious to Me, it is a mystery that carries keys that can be unlocked by the very hands that have formed you before time began. The next several days ahead will show you just how these doors open and who is the one that opens them! Watch and see how the excitement begins and continues!

8/14/17— From The Grand Canyon

Never say, Never! You can do all things simply because I said you can! What I have created for you is for your joy and pleasure. Now it is time to understand the mystery...I have created it and it is good!

8/17/17— In D.C

Have I not told you already that the prophets are coming to the White House? And they are coming with a message. But watch, for what they reveal is not darkness within, for I am already doing that, but darkness and resistance that is outside the gates. For in the months that you call Fall, a revelation shall come forth and a mystery revealed. It shall shake the media and Jericho shall fall.

8/22/17

Oh how the change has come! Many are experiencing it now and many will see the curtain rise over the next few days ahead. This month called August will show you how things must be alignment. The big things, the little things, they are all important to Me. So you have just a fragment of days left in this month, and some believe that it will end the same way it started, but this is not so! What comes at the end is the very thing that was not expected. For a great celebration shall be heard from the voices of many! It will not end with disappointment, but in jubilee and victory.

8/24/17

Sudden experiences today that will cause you to look at your life and see that it is good. You will take a breath and see that the storm you just passed through set you up for divine favor and blessing. Watch, for today and tomorrow that exists in your mindset carries some very significant suddenlies and blessing that you will not forget.

8/24/17— In D.C.

A strange beginning has come! One that will grab the attention from nation to nation. Watch, for a discovery will be made and a source revealed. Who is the one that they say is not popular? Who is the one that they say cannot be? I have the last laugh! Indeed, I laugh at the mockers! For they have already seen what was not seen. For at this time, and a time again, you will see such a glory and demonstration of power in this land called D.C. For their plans to bring down are only causing strength and resilience to be brought up! For they have feared this day, and they have truly allowed panic to enter their hearts. For they will come undone and they will grow weary. Many will leave their posts simply because they have come to understand that the fight they have fought is against something that cannot be defeated. Now, watch, I say, watch, for this comes quickly and it shall bring a calm to this nation. Yes, the proud shall be humbled before their own kind and they will see with new eyes.

8/25/17

Doors will open today that carry unprecedented favor. Watch, for the hidden mysteries that you seek shall rise and be revealed. When you have been faithful with little, you shall be given much.

8/27/17— In D.C.

What is this? They come after the innocent? It shall not be so! For the woman and Child in the White House shall be protected all their days! For I have a special love for them. For this woman is stronger than you think. For she has waited to speak and she has held her tongue, but in a time that approaches quickly, you shall see a warrior that is not afraid to address the nation. She carries something very special. She has prayed for her family, her husband and her Nation. Now watch, for her time comes quickly, and it will shake nations to the core. The sound that is released will cut like a knife and penetrate the darkness and reveal a great light that illuminates the masses!

8/29/17

I am healing and restoring specific areas of your life that have been dormant. This day is very significant in your life. The enemy has tried to

John Natale

keep these places lifeless and hidden. The struggles and pain that you have been going through will no longer be able to keep you down. What once was will be no longer, and the history you carry will be removed by the glory of today.

9/1/17

A sudden calm shall take over and fill you with peace. What I desire to take place in your mind and heart is the trust that all things work together for the good for those that love God. I want you to spend more time living in freedom, peace, and joy! Do not allow things of this world to rob you of that. There will always be challenges, but My presence can override at any time. Our relationship is key to your peace and to your joy! Allow Me to show you how much better it can be! So today marks a new beginning with your perspective. You will see the difference when you believe!

9/2/17— In D.C.

This man that is called Mr. President will suddenly soar like an eagle! He has been given a double portion of grace and compassion. In this hour, he is learning some very specific mysteries that have been disregarded for many seasons. He will be known for the accomplishments on paper, but more importantly, he will be recognized for his heart for humanity. Now watch, for a season fast approaches that a certain individual that has fought against this man will surrender and relinquish the agenda and be humbled. The mountains shall melt like wax before the Lord. Light overwhelms darkness. So this man that dwells in that House has made Me significant in the heart and has prayed for unity. He has been rewarded. Now in the days ahead, watch, for it is relevant to understanding, as one comes forward to speak, a nation shall listen to the heart that has changed and surrendered their fight against righteousness.

9/5/17

Divine blessing shall overtake you and overwhelm you. The enemy tried to distract you from receiving this beautiful extension of the Father's love, but it would not be allowed. The celebration has already started for you and your family. Watch how faithful He is!

9/7/17

The undiscovered land of opportunity shall suddenly pay a visit and welcome you with open arms. Watch how specific details line up this week and release the big plan that has been waiting just for you and your family.

9/9/17— For September 2017

FOR THE WINDS BLOW AND THEY DO NOT KNOW WHAT DIRECTION IT TAKES.

For many have tried to understand the mystery and solve the questions. ***Why do you think that it is I that brings this on America?*** *It is not so! For there are those that speak of such lies and they deceive many, but I will not allow this! For in this month, there will be a gathering of people that will see the truth and what is actually taking place behind the veil that blinds the eyes of so many. An understanding and a revealing will suddenly come, and people of all nations in this nation called America will share a common ground of unity and compassion. You must remember, it is I that brings life and freedom, and it is I that can only bring good out of things that seem dark. Watch how this month suddenly shifts and reveals the promises that I have chosen for it!*

9/11/17— In D.C.

For this man that is called Trump is watching, and he is waiting. For he has heard My voice and he is discerning the sound. He has been given grace and he has been given a double portion of patience. For he has learned much over the time he has been entrusted with. Now watch, for he will act quickly over the next several days and he will cause the hearts of many to soften. He will direct a nation with a heart that is sincere and understanding. Even so, as this time ends, another scenario will arise and he will respond quickly. For there is a shaking that will come in the land called D.C., and a judgment shall be made. For there is one that opposes the Administration and this one tries to hide beneath the cracks, but he will be exposed in the days ahead. For this dishonor will not be tolerated. For in this new season, I will bring everything into light, and I will bring a justice to this land, and I will restore what was stolen! Nothing is hidden, and wickedness is exposed once again!

9/13/17

For a turn shall take place for you and your family. What once was, shall no longer be. The wait has been long and at times, has caused your strength and faith to be tested. But in this, there is a new beginning that has come. Watch and see, for significant blessing arrives shortly.

9/14/17

You will see others in ways that you have not seen before. An understanding will suddenly come and fill you with a heart of compassion. It is critical in this time, simply because there are specific people that are about to be placed in your circle of friends. This new beginning will help with progress, destiny, and blessing.

9/15/17

I am with you through every storm. At times you feel as though I am not listening, but I am. There are moments when you feel as if I am not with you, but I am holding you. Today, I am giving you a double portion of grace and comfort. For it is My desire for you to be confident in My plans for you. So the sign shall be given. I will remove the doubt and frustration that has caused this to be a thorn in your heart. You will overcome!

9/15/17

You have thought long and hard about your past and those that were in it. Some are no longer and some remain. Some have come home to Me, and some are still fighting the good fight. What is needed in this time of your life is to know that I hold all things in the palm of My hands. There were days that were hard and you could not change the circumstances, but I was with you. You will come to understand in the moments ahead that every step that you have taken, I have been with you and have walked alongside of you. Don't look back any longer and ponder what could have been. You have much life inside of you, and your journey ahead is good! You will receive a new perspective on your life and how significant it actually is.

9/18/17

An open Heaven is upon you right now to release supernatural grace and peace. Angels ascending and descending are bringing messages of comfort and hope. Watch how your week increases with the power, favor and blessing of God. FOR HE IS A REWARDER OF THOSE THAT DILIGENTLY SEEK HIM.

9/18/17— In D.C. & North Korea

This President that is called Trump shall suddenly meet the man that has caused trouble in the land called North Korea. For a decision shall be made quickly. For he again shall stir the waters and test the character of the President of the United States. For many shall have their eyes on this conflict. For I have been speaking to the man that dwells in the White House, and he will know exactly what to do. Watch, for the world waits, for they know not the answer to the issue at hand, but I do and I have the last word!

9/19/17— In D.C.

As in the days of Moses, the water was held in place for the righteous to pass through. Suddenly, as they prepared to finish their crossing, the enemy tried to stop their forward progress and pass through as well, not knowing that I would not tolerate wickedness to violate righteousness. So it shall be also in the land called D.C. I will unfold all the plans that target this President and his administration, and expose once again the arrogant and proud that think they cannot be stopped. For they have already lost strength in their fight and clarity in their thoughts.

9/22/17

Do not allow the enemy to discredit you or stop your forward progress. Your identity has been targeted for what you stand for. But this will not come to pass, but only strengthen. Watch for the sign that you will be given. What came against you will suddenly be like the dust that is removed by the wind. A new assignment with new direction shall be revealed that builds off of what you are doing presently and the voices behind closed doors will suddenly cease.

9/24/17

Unexpected open doors will be revealed this week as you press in and seek clarity and direction. Watch how discouragement and doubt fades away and renewed hope breaks in.

9/25/17— For Baltimore

The oil will run down through the streets and be directed to Baltimore. There a city will be revived and a love will be reborn that penetrates the very hearts of men, women, and children. They will remember and they will be satisfied. For they have waited and they have cried. Their tears have been captured by the hands that hold all things. For in the days that come, watch, for a city that has been forgotten shall open its eyes and see the glory of the one that brings life and heals the broken.

9/25/17

As one comes, the other will go. As one door opens, one will close. You have come into a time where you will reap and I will prune. For it shall benefit not just you, but those around you.

9/27/17— In D.C.

For out of the abundance of the heart, the mouth speaks. For they have tried once again to bring the distraction that causes influence and changes hearts. Shall it be so? No it shall not! For they have no understanding that their words only destroy the foundation and walls they have built with their own hands. For every time this man called Trump is persecuted with words, his authority increases and his voice becomes that much louder. Now watch, for what is desired is peace and unity, and that shall come. I desire peace for all. So in the days ahead that come quickly, a specific voice that came against shall lock arms and reconcile. For he has been hurt and his trust is weak, but I have been speaking to him and at times, he has listened. He will experience a grace and a reconciliation that only I can bring. For his voice has been loud, but My grace and pursuit shall overcome his pain. His eyes shall open to truth and opportunity shall knock at his door. For a new relationship shall be made in the land called D.C. and is shall impact a nation and it shall be good!

9/28/17

Within yourself is the inner man saying that you can make it. You have been tested this week and your patience and motivation has been challenged. Do not give up. For what you are presently doing will suddenly soar and opportunity shall come forth like a roaring lion!

9/29/17

Something very significant will take place in your life suddenly. This comes from a situation that took place recently that you thought was not in your best interest. It actually was used to benefit you both physically and spiritually.

10/1/17— In D.C. & North Korea

For this President that is called Trump is sweeping through a nation. For a victory that has not been seen in many years shall come forth suddenly. Now watch, for the people of North Korea shall suddenly be a voice that has not been heard. Their government shall experience a pressure they have not seen before and the collapse shall begin. Their leader does not understand the mystery, nor will he have the strength to stop the momentum of change that is focused on peace and justice.

10/2/17

And so the mystery continues. You are cherished and you are loved. On a path walking, waiting, watching. You look to the left and to the right, but the answer is not there. Your feet are tired and your strength is almost gone, but inside of you there is a voice that reminds you that you will make it. You will suddenly see ahead of you a great sight that has been waiting for you! Your diligence and determination has brought you into a season and place that will facilitate great growth and unexpected blessing that most have said would not come. Now watch, for the beginning of the month called October has many surprises that you have not seen. It will release its blessing as each tree gives up a leaf to the ground to prepare for the next season of life.

10/2/17— For America

You have lost sight of those that watch you. For the Children are watching and what do they see? They see a divided nation. They do not understand and they will not be forgotten. Their hearts are so pure and they have not let the cares of this world dictate their joy. You fight and you speak about things you cannot change. It is only love that changes the heart. This has been the mystery that has been established before the foundation of the world. For I will shake things again and I will show you how the innocence and beauty of a Child can restore this nation. For when you take your eyes off of yourself and see the joy and hear the laughter of a Child and allow it to melt your bitter heart, you will humble yourself and recognize that love exists for one reason and one reason alone, and that is to restore and reconcile that which has been orphaned.

10/3/17

In the adversity, I am there. In the storm, I am there. Many hope and pray that I can stop the pain and hardships that take place throughout the nations. Some believe and some ask, "Why did You not intervene?" But

135

throughout history, through all the battles, all the struggles, I have never left, nor forsaken. I Am that I Am. Through the darkness, light appears and brings hope to the hopeless. So in this time, many will come to understand the mystery that love never leaves nor does it abandon. It is always available and always positioned to give.

10/4/17

Get ready for some interesting opportunities to be revealed over the next several days as the week draws to a close. Some doors are about to close, but this is in the plans for this season. Unexpected requests shall come your way and bring in new means of resources.

10/5/17

As Joseph stepped into his destiny and experienced blessing that he was not able to create, he never looked back, he kept looking forward. You have been chosen for that same measure. There is no limit to what you can dream or obtain.

10/6/17

Don't let little distractions hinder big blessing. These things are used to keep your expectation removed and your joy silenced. Today, watch how suddenlies show up and joy is restored. You have been faithful and you didn't even know it!

10/7/17

Don't underestimate your ability to overcome and receive the blessing with inheritance. Even though many will try to discourage and intimidate you, the plans I have for you will not be stopped. I am speaking to many people right now to help with your destiny, and you will experience significant breakthrough in the moments ahead.

10/8/17

In this life, you can get caught up with everything that is around you. The enemy will cause your mind to be convinced that the more important things are external, but actually what is most important, is internal. What takes place in your heart and how you see yourself, is more important to Me than anything you can comprehend.

10/8/17

The next several days ahead will be peaceful and carry a level of joy that has been avoiding you. Simply put, the enemy has been exposed ,and the attacks have been stopped. You have been fighting so hard and at times lost hope, but now you shall see great peace and blessing. October! Your month of new colors has come!!

10/10/17

There will be times that you will be asked to shift your path and step to the right or to the left. You will not understand why, and feel as if you missed something. But at this time, I have a reason and a plan that will carry out very soon and show you why this had to happen. It is actually bigger than you think, and as this week increases, opportunity comes.

10/12/17— For D.C.

And so the story continues with its foolishness. So there shall be a trumpet that sounds again, but this time it shall be a sound of sweet victory and justice. For this President is taking back ground that has been stolen. For one in the media that smiles and grins shall be called out. For this one has been watched closely. So in the days ahead, watch and see how the curtain rises and the unrighteousness and lack of integrity is exposed.

10/12/17

A sudden breakthrough will arrive today and dismiss a mindset of discouragement. As Naaman dipped his hand in the Jordan for the last time, what came forth was not expected, but more than he imagined.

10/15/17

Your character is being tested to distract you from blessing and opportunity this week. It has been released to steal your joy and cause your mindset to be filled with frustration instead of expectation. Now grace and peace has been given to restore your faith and you shall overcome again!

10/16/17

There are times that you feel as if you are not good enough or do not measure up. Today is a reminder that you have been created perfectly, and there is no one that can change that. You see, the enemy diligently tries to bring self-condemnation on you, and works day and night to steal your identity, but My glory brings all things together and gives you beautiful peace. So right now, for those of you that have been struggling with who you are, there is an In-filling of strength, comfort, and confidence that will change how you see yourself and ultimately how you see Me.

10/17/17— Prophetic Dream

The enemy came to intimidate and was ready for a fight, but what came forward was sound of strength and confidence. The gloves were shown and your response was this; You will be knocked out in the first round or the latest second. There was such a confidence in the response to the enemy that he left before the fight began.

This mindset will cause a sudden surge of blessing to come forth as the windows of Heaven are opened.

10/18/17— In D.C.

Watch how this President that is called Trump is rewarded with a victory in the month known as November. For the one that was against, suddenly shall have a change of heart and speaks truth. For in this month, the enemy shall be defeated, humbled, and purified. The restoration of the heart shall become an armor-bearer in well-doing.

10/20/17

Watch how sudden blessing and promotion comes your way today. A great surge of victory shall present itself to you as the spirit of justice leads the way!

10/21/17

Get ready for the supernatural to be natural. Sudden opportunities will come that reveal the heart of people and how they seek truth! For divine appointments will be present all weekend long and show the glory of God! They are coming simply because you have been faithful with your pursuit of truth, and your capacity to show love.

10/23/17

As in the days of Noah, a word came forth to prepare for a flood. This was a directive to watch and wait. Today, a word in season has come to you. Watch and wait, for the flood waters have been released to bring blessing that is overwhelming! It shall bring you above your situation when you thought there was no hope and cause you to land on new soil that facilitates a new beginning and a clean slate.

John Natale

10/24/17

At the end of the day, those that you believe are pouring into you will show their true colors by how they not only push you, but how they value you. Anything else is a misrepresentation of love and carries a smokescreen of hidden agendas.

10/24/17

Behold, as the year called 2017 comes to an end, a new sound shall be heard. It will be the cries of the people seeking truth. For they have hungered, for they shall be filled. For in the south and in the west, two significant movements will be brought up and accusation and justice will come forth. For the hidden things shall be revealed and righteousness will come and occupy what has been tainted. For I do not tolerate deception, and in its time, honor shall be restored and arrogance removed. In this time, it is critical, for a fresh outpouring shall be released and it will occupy places that have been unnoticed. These places will be houses of rescue and restoration. In these places, you will find a river that has not been tainted or defiled, but pure living water to drink from. So watch and do not grow weary, for in its time, the enemy shall try to steal your hope, but I will be with you and I will strengthen you.

10/26/17

As in the days of Elijah, he was one that carried a great faith that caused hearts to tremble. In this hour, I am releasing that same measure. What he carried was given by Me and what was established, changed nations and revived hearts. This day, listen to these words; Faith reveals confidence that produces expectation and opens the door to justice. These words, guard in your heart. For the mystery comes to be a light, but the enemy waits at the door to steal what has been given.

10/29/17

The waters have been extremely rough and the wind significantly strong of late. This will all come to a sudden calm as you enter a new season of promotion and peace. November shall be a month that stands out in 2017, and be remembered as THE MONTH OF REVELATION that brought understanding to why you had to walk though such a storm and carry trust to the end.

10/31/17

Sudden surprises of blessing shall meet you today and remind you that you are not to give up on some of the things you were expecting. A Dad and loving Father at times wants to surprise you, rather than you always knowing when something is coming! Just ask Ezekiel that!

11/2/17

What you gave up on, I was preparing before the foundations of the world! You see, I never give up on you, and I'm always working on your behalf to bless you and bring you such joy and peace. Don't let the things of this world steal your expectation. November is a significant month in your life, your family, and your destiny. Over the next several days, you will come to understand the mystery, and your faith will be renewed.

11/3/17

Today you are reminded how valuable you are to Me and how amazing your life is! Many have become tired and worn out through living everyday life, but I wanted to let you know that I am always here to refresh you and strengthen you. As you approach this weekend and shake the dust off of

John Natale

your feet, you will not only feel My presence, but you will see how I can shift things in your life suddenly!

11/5/17— For Sutherland Springs, TX

OUR HEARTS ARE BROKEN TODAY AS WE'VE HEARD THE NEWS OF THE SHOOTING AT THE FIRST BAPTIST CHURCH IN SUTHERLAND SPRINGS, TEXAS. We speak a double portion of peace and grace to everyone that was affected by this tragedy. We declare over the community that they will rebound and be restored to a greater level of camaraderie and unity. That their hearts will join as one and hope and expectation will fill the atmosphere and be a source of strength and inspiration to people nationwide.

11/6/17

Watch how the justice of God manifests on your behalf! A double portion of grace is about to be released and you shall overcome. The enemy thought he had won a battle, but he had no understanding that God was setting you up for one of the greatest victories in your life!

11/7/17

Get ready to take a big leap forward as a door has opened that will not just bring significant blessing, but remove the burden you have been carrying for several years.

11/9/17

Understanding the mystery doesn't have to be as difficult as it seems! Your revelation will come quicker if you let go of the baggage and burdens you are carrying. There is a great storehouse of blessing that is waiting to be released. Just let go and let the river flow!

11/11/17

Specific words that were spoken regarding the restoration of family have already manifested in the spirit and are now taking shape in the natural. Watch how sudden shifts take place. My timing is perfect and understanding the mystery is critical in how you see things come to fruition.

11/12/17

Understanding the mystery will soon come to pass. The time has come again to dip your hand in the Jordan one last time. Timing was everything. Season of restoration is upon you. Time that was lost will be replaced with a double-portion blessing.

11/14/17

Peter stepped out of the boat and walked on water that night! As he approached Me, did I not know that he would eventually sink? Of course I did, but during that brief encounter and journey, laughter, joy and encouragement could be heard as each step was taken. You see, even when you fall short and think you have failed Me, My joy in you never ceases, and My laughter can be heard throughout the ages, simply because you are loved beyond your understanding.

11/17/17

Sudden scenarios will be brought to your attention today to let you know that what is in process for your breakthrough will soon come to pass and double honor shall be given.

John Natale

11/19/17

Diligence and perseverance is key to overcoming obstacles that affect your blessing. Over the next several days you will see things come to pass simply because you have been given a double portion of tenacity to facilitate the breakthroughs needed in this current season.

11/21/17

A sudden increase of unity will take place over the next several weeks simply because a great presence will be felt throughout the Nation. From the streets, to the media and onward to the Capital that is called D.C. Watch very closely, listen to the sound, for glory shall come in like a cloud and surround the masses. Even the atmosphere shall be affected and make its voice heard. So watch! It is the season, and the season has come!

11/23/17— Thanksgiving

FIRST WE WANTED TO WISH YOU A VERY HAPPY THANKSGIVING TO ALL OF YOU AND YOUR FAMILIES.

Your season has come and shall bring an understanding to a mystery that has avoided you for some time now. The top of the mountain that never seemed to be reached is now not only in front of you, but beneath you. What comes next is the door that is open for you that provides an abundance of blessing. Watch as the door opens and more than enough is waiting for you and your family!

11/27/17

Increase has been released in the spirit realm that will soon manifest in the natural. What was not expected has been ordered to pour out in this season. Watch, for the windows have opened and the blessing has become more than enough. For December is coming and it will reveal a mystery that has been waiting to show its face for sometime now. When it does, you will remember, and generations will learn from its history.

11/29/17

Your perseverance and tenacity has caused the enemy to flee, and a double portion of blessing is arriving at the perfect time!

11/30/17

Even though the season comes with its own frustrations, these do not have to affect your expectation. Stay focused, be alert and watch how the month called December brings a delivery of multiplication in your life.

12/1/17

Many of you look ahead and hope for a better future because you're not satisfied with your present life and what you see. Today, you are reminded that there is great promise for you right now where you're at, and all things are subject to change. Never give up on yourself and never give up believing anything can happen at any time. You just have to believe!

12/1/17— For D.C. 12/1/16

And yes, you shall see in the years to come, a Trump that shall sound for the next eight years! And they will say, how do we remove this Trump? And they will say, we must come together and dismantle this power, but it shall not be so! For not only will the sound carry for eight years, but will carry eight more. A new day has come and you will see great transition come forth as the House called White is filled with righteousness and power.

12/3/17

Many things are established in the spirit realm and prepared to be released for some serious soaring to take place in your life. Get ready for significant new doors that you will pass through in 2018. December is the month that sets all things in motion.

12/4/17

Even though your thoughts are not Mine, and your ways are not Mine, My presence is more than enough. What matters to Me is that you understand that you are loved unconditionally. You don't have to try so hard to please Me. All I want is for you to understand that with Me, there are no levels of expectation that you need to meet. Just live and love. It's that simple, and everything will fall into place just right.

12/7/17

Unusual occurrences that come shall reveal its true identity in the moments ahead. Watch, for wonder and amazement shall be of epic proportions, and release a sweet peace and joy that lasts for seasons ahead!

12/8/17— In D.C.

For this Leader called Netanyahu and this President called Trump will align themselves strategically and cause a great stirring in the land. For a strength shall be given to both that cannot be shaken. For in the months ahead, a new power shall come forth that has not been witnessed in decades. It shall send a message to the opposition that a wall cannot be breached, and bring a newfound freedom that cannot be silenced.

12/8/17

The sacrifices you have made have not gone unnoticed. What is coming is fast approaching. So prepare your jars, for more than enough shall be given, and it shall take you into many seasons.

12/11/17

In the moments ahead, you will have an encounter with destiny that has been waiting for several seasons to come to fruition. Not only will perspective change, but joy will fill your heart and your resources will double. Simply because faith has unlocked doors of abundance!

12/13/17

During the course of this year, you have endured much, persevered and held your ground through all adversity and battles. What you did not know during those times was the preparation of a glorious outcome that was to come in its time. You will look back at 2017 and see how all things positioned you for one of your greatest victories called; THE INHERITANCE OF 2018.

12/15/17

As this year comes to a close, the sound of ringing shall be heard and display its warmth that brings the heart pure joy. What was undiscovered in the year of 2017 shall be seen and revealed in its entirety in the season called 2018. You shall enter a door called promise, and it shall be well with you. What was considered forgotten shall suddenly become established.

12/16/17

One of the most significant seasons is upon you! 1/2018 reveals specific mysteries

12/18/17

A wind of peace has been released to bring you the comfort that you have been seeking for you and your family. Watch, for in the days ahead, a very specific person is coming back to your knock on your door. This individual was not expected to return, but I had other plans to complete the mystery that surrounds you.

12/21/17

A fresh anointing has been released, and significant peace given. You will experience a great shift in the atmosphere of your home, your mind, and heart.

12/22/17

Do not make yourself vulnerable to the enemy, but choose to be vulnerable before God, and all things will fall into place, and the plans that are prepared for you will come to fruition.

12/24/17

A quick, sudden unexpected attack of the enemy tried to disrupt the Christmas season, but to no prevail. What comes after is a burst of peace and blessing that silences the darkness.

12/27/17

You shall enter a new season ahead with strength, peace, and prosperity. Your battle has been won, and your honor shall be present among many.

12/28/17— The Lion is roaring again

In a vision I saw the Lion of Judah walking along a path and releasing a sound that caused all the demonic forces coming against you to flee. Your path has been cleared, now walk and stay focused, because the enemy will come back and seek to find you distracted.

12/30/17

As the mysteries line up, and wisdom and discernment is revealed, watch, for the sparrow flies to its own to feed the mouths that are open. The season has come to give what has been portioned.

Part Six
Prophetic Words — 2018

1/1/18

The season has come upon you to inherit what has been waiting in the balance. Words of direction shall come suddenly as you seek wisdom. Watch, for the month called January aligns and positions itself to unlock very specific opportunities that have been waiting for generations to be released.

1/3/18

Some unfinished business shall return and knock on your door. You thought that a door was closed, but it actually was opening wider for you. A hidden mystery that could not be revealed at one time is now ready to be brought into focus. At this time, stay alert and do not allow the enemy to distract you. It will take diligence and perseverance to carry through.

1/6/18

The enemy has just learned that you have reinforcements coming to your aid. A swift retreat shall soon be seen, and significant advancement shall be made in the spirit realm that releases promotion in the natural.

1/8/18

It's time to take it to another level. You will experience both spiritual and natural promotion as you continue your steadfast journey in this new season. Watch how January reveals new mysteries that accelerate your growth in many areas of your life.

1/9/18— In D.C.

Watch how South Korea silences the storm and is taken to a new level of authority and influence. This land will have new prominence with the nations as a new voice comes forth, is heard, and honored.

1/10/18

What seems to be a delay is in fact a plan to discourage and frustrate your momentum. Watch, for your progress will surge suddenly and what was expected shall come with victory and celebration.

1/11/18

As the wind blows, so do the mysteries that surround you. All it takes is to reach out your hand and allow the breeze to gently touch you and fill you with refreshing fragrances from Heaven. There is coming now a wind that shall be accompanied with grace. For a double portion shall blow in suddenly and be so sweet and peaceful that you will find rest and comfort in a time where you have sowed diligently.

1/12/18— In D.C.

Oh how they seek and they search for clues that will never be found. For in the days ahead, an unexpected turn of events shall come and disrupt the plans that continually try to bring down a President called Trump. For have you not heard the words before, this man shall hold his office for eight years. For what has been put in place spiritually cannot be removed naturally.

1/16/18

You will experience breakthrough today that carries a spirit of justice. The enemy is a liar and his plans have been broken and shattered. Expect more than enough.

1/19/18

There is a double portion of blessing coming your way for the warfare you have just experienced. This last week had much on the table of resistance, but your faith has not failed you and your diligence will be that much stronger. Watch, for a special door opens suddenly that will bring a supernatural grace to you and your family.

1/22/18

For a great comfort is coming to you now. Do not give up and do not allow the enemy to influence you any longer. Shut the door to it! For he has been whispering in your ear relentlessly that it is not possible, so just throw in the towel. But there is good news, for in the week ahead, you will see a victory so great that those around you will be amazed how great the favor actually is.

1/23/18

Be encouraged My people, for your pain and anguish has been seen. My justice is upon you, and I will make the crooked places straight in your life. Do not hesitate to make the changes necessary in your life that will bring you into new rivers of freedom. You have been waiting and desiring these things to take place, and at times relied on the affirmation or release of man to move you forward, but this is not so. Your opportunity will come, and it will come suddenly. You will be victorious in this new year. Stay focused and expect. My desire for you now is to enlarge your capacity to receive fresh revelation that will uplift, encourage, and promote you to new and rewarding benefits. As with the woman of Shunem, you too will find yourself blessed with the promises that were spoken over you that you gave up on and lost hope. These promises will come forth in a double-portion, and your life will be a testimony of the goodness of God in the land of the living.

1/26/18

The enemy has plans to steal your joy this weekend, but God has different plans! You will experience a great time of rest, blessings, and open doors!

1/28/18

Get ready for a week of significant increase. For a promotion and upgrade has been established in the spirit realm that will manifest in the natural shortly.

1/29/18

I want you to watch closely to the things that take place this week. For they will set in motion very important plans that I have for you. For the month called February will be one that is close to your heart. It will be like a soft cool wind on a hot day that soothes and brings sweet comfort.

1/31/18

Today, look at your life and reflect on all the things that you have persevered through and overcame. See how you are truly blessed. Now, what is critical to understand is this simple mystery. Whether you believe or not, your future has been planned with greatness in mind and My plans are good. There are so many open doors that wait for you, and opportunities to be revealed. Never give up on these! Never agree with the enemy that time has been lost. It has just begun!

2/1/18— In D.C.

Keep your eyes on the land called D.C. For there is one that has positioned oneself in a posture of dishonor and disunity and has caught the attention of the nations. It is a plan to be a thorn in the side, but this plan shall come crashing down as the walls of Jericho fell on that day when the people shouted. For you have been told, a shout has been released in the atmosphere. One door is about to close suddenly and another open. This is the mystery that only I know, and the manifestation

John Natale

shall come suddenly. A house divided cannot stand, but in the days ahead, you shall see unity come to fruition.

2/3/18

As you move forward this weekend and upcoming week, you shall be brought back to something very important that is needed to reach your destination. Something that is critical, but not burdensome. You will see in its time what was spoken of on this day and you will rejoice simply because all things work out for those who put their trust in Me.

2/5/18

You are about to experience a great season of prosperity that comes from perseverance and faith. Well done! For your season comes suddenly and it will not end until all that is planned for you is completed with a significant outpouring.

THAT PERSON IS LIKE A TREE PLANTED BY STREAMS OF WATER, WHICH YIELDS ITS FRUIT IN SEASON AND WHOSE LEAF DOES NOT WITHER— WHATEVER THEY DO PROSPERS. Psalm 1:3.

2/8/18

I was with you when you were a child and I am with you now! Do not have any regrets from the past or those things that have not been accomplished, for in its time you will understand the mystery and see why certain things did not come to pass then, but are about to come to pass now!

2/10/18

A time that comes and goes! It passes like the wind and it cannot be followed, but it can be remembered. In the next several days ahead, you will brought back to such a time that had significant influence in your life. This encounter will inspire and encourage you in the now to implement and complete a very important decision that must be made. Watch, for the outcome brings much joy!

2/11/18

Showing people that you have a valuable interest in their lives will not only change a life, but restore a generation.

2/14/18

Preparations have been made for a brand new significant door that is about to open for you and your family. Watch closely, for the next several days reveal hidden mysteries that will facilitate new beginnings.

2/15/18

"Over the course of the next several days, Trust Me," says the Lord!

"I am making the path clear for you to walk. Obstacles and hindrances are removed now and your mind will be at peace. Decisions that need to be made will come swiftly and with ease. There is no worry in My Kingdom! Use this time wisely and seek ME. For I am a rewarder for those that diligently seek Me, and those that seek ME find ME!"

2/16/18

During the month of March, you will experience a great shift in favor, protection, and grace. During the time of Nehemiah, a wall was restored that signified favor and the presence of a mighty God on the side of those that have suffered greatly. You are about to experience a great restoration as your God shows the multitude of enemies that have tried to hold you back who is on your side, and how triumphant you have become. Not only will they see great progress, but they will flee in every direction and you shall move forward with significant speed and progress.

2/19/18

At times, the road you have traveled seemed endless and tiresome. The heat, the bumps, and the distance between exits all took a toll on your hopes and dreams. But then, as you travelled throughout the night, all of a sudden the sun began to rise, and a peace came that could not be quenched. A refreshing mindset and renewed strength began to manifest and bring a spirit of expectation that your journey has in fact purpose and meaning. So today, you are reminded that even though you have been going through some tough situations and at times your willingness to continue fading, you are about to finish and finish well. The light of a new day fast approaches, and the end is near. A chapter coming to a close. So watch and see, you will not be disappointed in what transpires as this part of your journey comes to an end. For I am with you and you shall see victory in this season.

2/21/18

Thank you, Billy Graham for all the years of service you have given to advance the Kingdom!

There has been a major shift in the spirit realm. For the time has come for a new chapter in this nation. Watch and see what transpires as many things have shifted in the spirit, and soon to be revealed in the natural. For a new voice shall be heard and be seen with open arms, and it will be one that is not expected, but I have chosen this vessel to shake this nation again!

2/23/18

The eagle soars as the wind lifts and gently passes through the wings that have been created to bring flight to one that was called to fly. Today, I am reminding you that you were created to fly! In this time and season of your life, you will feel the wind lift you above your situation and bring you to new territory. The higher you go, the greater perspective and revelation you will get as you soar and see the very thing that tried to hold you back. Enjoy the journey, for the flight will be most pleasant.

2/21/18

Thank you Billy Graham for all the years of service you have given to advance the Kingdom!

There has been a major shift in the spirit realm. For the time has come for a new chapter in this nation. Watch and see what transpires as many things have shifted in the spirit and soon to be revealed in the natural. For a new voice shall be heard and be seen with open arms and it will be one that is not expected, but I have chosen this vessel to shake this nation again!

2/23/18

The eagle soars as the wind lifts and gently passes through the wings that have been created to bring flight to one that was called to fly. Today, I am reminding you that you were created to fly! In this time and season of your life, you will feel the wind lift you above your situation and bring you to new territory. The higher you go, the greater perspective and revelation you will get as you soar and see the very thing that tried to hold you back. Enjoy the journey, for the flight will be most pleasant.

2/23/18— Trump & Graham

A new clue to the mystery of the ages. Elisha asked for a double portion of the mantle of Elijah, and it was given on a day that reshaped the prophetic for generations to come. Now, this day you are told that a double portion has been given again, but in ways that you do not understand. One has come forth and the other has been taken. One has been placed and holds the authority over this nation, and the one who has been taken influenced this nation with integrity and honor. These two individuals are your sign that a great shaking and outpouring have been released in the spirit that will manifest in the natural in the days to come. The mystery of the ages that has avoided the minds and hearts of men and women alike shall shine like the sun as a new day has come to bring freedom to the captives, sight to the blind, and freedom to the oppressed.

2/26/18

A promotion in the spirit has been granted that will manifest in the natural very soon. March is your month! You have been waiting for justice to come and bring vindication. This has been granted, but not just justice, but favor and joy accompanies this release on your family as well.

2/28/18

March is your month of great transition. You will experience a great shift in the spirit that will cause your passion to soar. This change will reveal a sudden new realm of authority and ownership. Keys have been released and will be placed in your hands in the days ahead. Your time has come to take your place and be the voice!

3/5/18

Expect a very significant outpouring of a double portion of grace and peace. You are in a season of abundance that will bring more than enough! The widows' oil has manifested, so watch the multiplication begin.

3/9/18

The mysteries surround you this month as the atmosphere was shaken to display power and might. There will be a sudden shift again, and a sign in the skies in the upcoming days that points to the north. Watch, for things shall turn for the good and bring in a such a peace and hope that causes the season called Spring to be remembered for generations to come!

3/11/18— In D.C.

A great double portion of blessing and the miraculous is about to come to this Nation called The United States. An open window and portal that releases the mysteries of Heaven shall be available to the people that cry out for understanding and revelation. So many are searching and longing for truth. They shall be comforted. Now watch, for there shall be a quickening of peace in the nations abroad, and a wind that calms the storm. For there is one that shall have his heart softened and suddenly change his mindset. For he will see through different eyes and understand the mystery that has stirred in his heart for years. For he shall come to this nation and will not be judged, for he comes in peace, and peace he shall find.

3/13/18

The skies continue to reveal the mysteries that come forth shortly. In its time, you will understand why specific things took place in the month called March. Keep your eyes fixed above, for more is coming and what is displayed is not what is expected, but necessary in this season.

3/14/18

Your journey in this season is coming to an end. The top of the mountain is now visible. There will be a closure that takes place and an open door that suddenly Is revealed. Walk through and watch what unfolds quickly. For this will facilitate the next phase of your destiny.

3/16/18

A wind shall fast approach that shall take you to that new place that you thought would not come. Keep alert and stay focused with eyes wide open. For the keys and opportunity come quickly.

3/19/18

In a time and season that you are presently in, it has been both bitter and sweet. You have been diligent in your determination to keep strong, but at times, have grown weary because it has used up all your strength and caused some questions to arise of uncertainty. You have had your ups and your downs and you still keep pressing in. Today, I am here to remind you that your strength shall be renewed and your blessing released in a double portion simply because you are loved more than you can imagine. My steadfast love never ceases and My mercies will never come to an end. They are new every morning. Great is My faithfulness.

3/22/18

Your journey does not end without finishing well. The season has come and gone and your questions shall be answered. It is a time to rejoice simply because you have overcome much. Now it's your time to reap what you have sowed.

3/24/18

Do not be intimidated by the sound or the presence of the enemy. He is fully aware of your strength in this season. The enemy will use the tactics of affecting others around you to get to your faith. Stay focused and strong. Your season shall not be disrupted in anyway.

3/25/18

Your days of redemption are fast approaching and your restoration just over the hill. Watch, for your Summer will be one that changes everything. For a very special occurrence shall come and bring the healing that you have been seeking.

3/26/18

The way you see others, reveal the condition of your heart. It is My desire for you to see people through My eyes and not your own. The choices you make to judge or label them, will not only affect their future but hinder your destiny. Compassion and grace will allow the curtain of uncertainty to rise and showcase the mystery of unity.

3/29/18

As the word was spoken regarding restoration in the Summer, watch how the mystery is revealed and the reconciliation sweet as honey. For in the days ahead, your relationships shall be mended and years stolen shall be returned. For it shall be a Summer that will be remembered by what was healed and how scars were removed.

3/31/18

The atmosphere is ready for a fresh outpouring. An open window of revelation is about to be released. Watch, for a unusual sign shall be witnessed over the weekend with many hearts restored and questions answered.

4/4/18

The time has come now! In this present season, the enemy has tried and tried to bring you to a place of defeat, but I would not allow it. There has been many things that have been taking place behind the scenes for your good. Your time to shine and experience a great restoration has come! You thought it would never come, but is has! Watch, for you will not only walk in a place of restoration, but of peace and joy! For in the month of April, it shall be remembered by laughter. For these special days have come to replace tears. You will see very important relationships restored and years returned.

4/9/18

A mountain that has been in your season is coming to a close. The journey you thought would never end has come to welcome you home. In the next few days ahead, you will understand why you had to leave specific people behind and walk alone. What will be seen next is the view of a valley that has never been present in your life. You will walk down the hill refreshed and revived as you prepare for a new assignment and connections that help you establish yourself in a season of grace.

4/10/18

Judas lost his ability to understand the mystery of grace. He was convinced that he could not be forgiven. Today, you are reminded that in your imperfections and in your failures, there is much grace simply because forgiveness was purchased on the cross. Don't allow the enemy to steal your sight. Judas was called to follow Me, but his heart turned cold and he went to a tree and failed. I went to a tree and the power of darkness in your life was broken. Never forget and never give up!

4/12/18

The cool wind of grace fast approaches as it flows over the mountain of adversity. As you continue your journey, the relevance of the mist it carries will not only comfort you, but give you the strength needed to complete the assignment at hand. And this too shall pass and you will rejoice for you have overcome once again!

4/13/18

Sometimes what is visible becomes invisible simply because you are overwhelmed by your current circumstances. This weekend, watch, for the veil of discouragement and weariness will be lifted and your joy shall be restored!

4/15/18

What was taken will be replaced. What was hidden will be exposed, and what was dishonored shall be vindicated. Get ready for some serious justice coming to you and your family in the days ahead.

4/19/18— From 4/18/16

Beware of false teachers that deceive and misguide you. Self-promotion does not bring Me glory and only exhorts oneself. My gospel is not to be entertaining. It is in place to be a source of strength, hope, trust, and guidance. My gospel is to direct all to Me and in this you must use wisdom and discernment, as many have come and will come in My name like wolves in sheep's clothing.

4/20/18

Expect a very significant surge of grace as you prepare for the weekend ahead. Some unexpected setbacks and scenarios are about to leave and not return. The enemy has tried to discredit you, but all voices have been silenced.

4/22/18

A sudden burst of grace and My presence shall overtake you as you seek the beauty of My fullness. Many have been dissatisfied with their current position and spirituality, crying out for more, but unable to enter into the heart of worship. But today is a new day and a new day it shall be! You will be overwhelmed and recharged as your day continues and My presence strengthens you. You will be brought back to a time when your joy was so strong and your hope expectant! Even though you have thought your fire was gone, it was I that was cleaning the ashes to make room for more wood to add to the fire. It will be a day that comes and it will go, but it will not pass without releasing what you need from Me.

4/25/18

Time to walk down the mountain. The waters of refreshing are just ahead. You did not give up, nor did you fail. As this week continues, the water shall renew your strength and perspective. For a new path has been chosen, one that will bring significant opportunity. There will be fruit that is visible from the branches that you have not tasted as of yet, and in its time you will come to understand the mystery that remains.

4/29/18

Joseph experienced many setbacks on a journey that he was not expecting. The key for today is that he never gave up and still kept his faith and trust. Many of you are on this same journey, and the word for today is; *You too will arise and come forth in victory and favor.* It might not look good right now, and in the natural make no sense, but great opportunity and blessing awaits you and soon will be part of your life.

4/30/18

Your life is beyond precious to Me and those around you. Do not believe for one minute that your existence has no value or worth. Even when you think you have hit rock bottom, there is still room enough for Me to work in your life and show you the glorious days ahead. So now, watch as many things unfold and change in your life. For the season that you are in has come to make the way for light to shine brighter than ever before. It shall not only brighten your day, but make your path clear and visible for the journey at hand.

5/3/18

Some challenges have come to test the waters, but once again grace is sufficient for you. May will bring unexpected breakthrough and peace that has felt overdue, but actually is right on time!

5/6/18

Some interesting turn of events are prepared to manifest for you. What was dormant for several seasons is now ready to be restored in your life. What is coming is more than expected simply because you are worthy of a double portion, and I enjoy blessing My Children.

John Natale

5/9/18

You will see a great peace come and victory in your family as you contend for justice and reconciliation. For the enemy will use simple tactics to create complex chaos, but I have given you strength and diligence to overcome the assault on your joy. Watch how all things come back into place this week and joy comes in the morning!

5/10/18— In D.C. & North Korea

So the mystery continues with this man that is called Trump. For he has established himself with the nations and has created a common bond that will not be broken by the voices of those who hide behind their smiles. Watch, for North Korea will make an announcement that will stir those who have come against this Administration. For a great advancement of trust and economic breakthrough shall come as the two unite and reconcile the differences from two Nations that are pivotal in the Summer months. Now pay close attention, for there is one that shall try to be a thorn in the side of this President that is called Trump, and he will travel this nation to bring the people together to resist the very thing that I have put in place. But it shall not succeed, but be dismantled suddenly, and his popularity shall decrease because the heart has become cold. For as one weakens, one strengthens. For it shall be so!

5/12/18

Many will cheapen the very essence of My sovereignty and not even know that their actions do so. One must remember that My love and My authority is perfect and by no means should anyone change or add to that consistency.

5/13/18— Mother's Day

It might be a little late but wanted to wish all the Moms a super Mother's Day and release:

As Esther was prepared with oil for a promotion in the natural, you too will experience a sudden elevation in the spirit as you have been prepared for a new season of honor.

5/15/18— In D.C. & Israel

So the times and seasons have come! For a man in an office that has changed the face of this nation called United States, has taken a risk that many were afraid to facilitate. For he has recognized a nation that has persevered through much adversity and has overcome. Yes this is true. Your nation will soar like eagles as natural honor is released and intertwined with spiritual foundations of justice. For Israel and The United States shall be joined at the hip, and a man call Netanyahu and another called Trump will plan strategically, and their support from within and from nations near and far shall partner and they shall be used mightily for the increase of justice on the earth, and together their relationship shall stick closer than a brother. For Israel will show its strong arm and silence those that come to oppress her voice. For what once was, will be no longer. For what has been put together from My hand shall rise above all things and will be displayed for years to come!

5/17/18

A quick sudden shift of grace and favor shall supernaturally be released and handed to you. In the moment of despair and hopelessness, the timing is once again perfect for you and your family. For what I see is far different from what you see. All things are subject to change even when your thoughts say different. So rejoice, for the release comes like wind, and will not go without giving a blanket of peace that comforts your weary heart.

5/18/18

As with Samson, he used a simple jaw bone to wipe out his enemies. Now this same tool will be used as well for your victory. The jaw bone represents the mouth piece, and what is symbolized was the voice of God! So today, your victory comes from what you say to the enemy! He will flee when the voice comes forth and it come from a foundation of the throne room of Heaven. Your words have the power of life and death, they can bring life to you and bring death to darkness, so speak My words and watch as your enemy bows in defeat and runs from My presence that is spoken from your heart and released from your mouth!

5/23/18— In D.C.

As his heart was molded and shaped by My hands, he once again shall have a voice in this nation. For a spirit of redemption shall come and walk beside him. For this man that is called George Bush, Jr. shall speak a word in season, and it shall be good to the ears and hearts of many. For he is being prepared for such a time and time again!

5/23/18

Expect a new level of authority to be revealed in your life in this new season. What was once the tail, shall now be the head. There will be a new directive and achievement fulfilled, and the alliances that the enemy used to strike your joy and progress have been dismantled. Your forward progress now will be smooth, and your transition sweet as honey.

5/24/18

A supernatural grace and open door is about to come and pay a visit to you and your family. The windows of Heaven have surely opened.

5/25/18

Do not despair, My Child. All things work for the good for those that love and trust Me. You have chosen to be faithful, and you have shown the enemy that you are a Warrior that does not back down. Certain battles have come and gone, and in your eyes you have determined that these were lost. I am here to tell you that nothing has been lost. You have been victorious in your battles, and great blessing is about to accompany you and your family. The unseen is about to be seen in great ways.

5/29/18

For a sign shall be given in the days ahead that draw near. For in the skies above, it shall be clearly visible that I hold all the stars in My hands. What was asked for shall be given, and My glory shall be seen across the nation. For your Summer comes and it will be one that draws the attention of those that question My existence and they will understand the mystery.

5/30/18

A breath of fresh air and a refreshing drink awaits you as you press in to a day that brings more than expected. Watch what unfolds as hidden secrets from Heaven manifest on your behalf.

John Natale

6/1/18

When the enemy tries to convince you that you are trapped, remind him of the prison that is prepared for him, and the Heaven that is open for you. The lies of the enemy are smokescreens that are produced to block the spiritual and natural flow of blessing. Now watch as June comes in with open arms and wind that is unhindered. You will experience a great freedom as the storehouses of Heaven have been opened for you and your family.

6/1/18— For California

California, My eyes are on you! You are watched closely and a plan is in place to reconcile the foundations that have been disturbed. For a voice shall be heard and it shall shake the very ground that occupies the west coast. It will not come from familiar voices, but from a voice that has been prepared and seasoned for such a time as this. In fact, one familiar voice will enter into its rest and be called home. For as one leaves, another appears.

6/3/18

Your victory is right around the corner. It's time for you to experience brand new growth and opportunity. June will be filled with new and exciting scenarios that reinstate your place in peace and favor.

6/6/18

Don't let your lack of experience fill you with fear or doubt. Your ability to overcome any obstacle comes from your level of confidence in yourself. Today, that is all changing and you will see some serious shifting take place in your life and the circumstances you are currently in. The season is now for some crazy life-changing steps of confidence, and nothing will stop that progress.

6/8/18

Inspiration, encouragement, and restoration are your three words for this weekend. You will see some interesting events and scenarios unfold as the weekend comes upon you. Get ready for some serious fun with the Son!

6/11/18

It's now time to take some serious initiatives that will move you and your family forward. Watch and listen as new directives come your way to start the process of new beginnings.

6/17/18

You must continue to be strong and not look back. The top of the hill is closer than you think. People give up just before the breakthrough comes. The season is here. Great breakthrough! Do not give up now. You have come so far and the reward is moments away! June is a month that will test your faith to see what you really believe and what you really expect. Stay strong and go deep, the harvest of blessing shall come!

6/22/18— For The Summer Of 2018

The time has come for change. The transfer from one to another. The mantle that was given to you is now ready to receive increase. What was operating in lack, shall now shift into abundance. The enemy has tried for generations to stop what was spoken of and planned for you and your family in this season that has come. Now, as the Summer draws near, you shall suddenly see the wave of blessing begin its collision course towards you. In its time, as the Summer increases, the waves shall crash over you and toss you to and fro, but do not worry, for what is taking place is a dramatic shift that is shaking off all the junk that the enemy used against you. It shall be completely removed, and as the water recedes, you will find yourself refreshed, reinvigorated, and restored to full capacity as you enter a season of unexpected, unprecedented favor!

6/28/18

It's your season to shine! It doesn't matter what comes your way. Even though you are dealing with some pretty significant drama right now, over the next several hours you will experience a dramatic shift that will remove the junk and create an atmosphere of peace and joy! Watch, for the weekend comes with an increase of hope and blessing that will cause your faith to rise and sustain you in the days to come.

7/3/18

Pressing in at times means that you have to be diligent in scenarios that are uncomfortable. You will be given grace to get through this circumstance and your perspective will change as you come to understand the mystery that is at hand. Just ask for strength and it shall be given!

7/5/18

A relationship that has been broken and pain that is present shall be healed and restored suddenly. Your forgiveness is key to this reinstatement, and your ability to love unconditionally will be increased as you persevere in a difficult season.

7/10/18

Your course of action is correct! Not only will you experience a sudden breakthrough today, but a very interesting confirmation will arise and make its face present. Expect some significant peace and rest to come and help you through a difficult time. Even though you feel as if the tanks are empty, you will be refueled and recharged today with hope and joy!

7/12/18— In D.C.

A strong wind of occurrence shall suddenly come and stir the waters once again. For a familiar voice is planning on making some noise in the August month. For the sign shall be revealed in the latter part of July. Watch and observe how plans that are not in the best interest of this Nation and President are uncovered, and unrighteousness is exposed once again. For they shall see again how light penetrates darkness.

7/15/18

What the enemy has planned for destruction, the Lord has used for victory! Haman had gallows built for Mordecai for one specific reason. To stop the advancement of freedom and liberty to the captives! The Lord vindicated him and brought JUSTICE through the destiny of Esther. This word is spoken over you today to declare that the JUSTICE of the Lord is about to be revealed and brought to fruition in your life and in your home!

7/16/18

The enemy is trying to get in between you and a very significant other. Relentless attack to divide and conquer, but these plans will be destroyed, and your relationship is already healed. The fruit of healing shall be seen shortly, and your heart shall be renewed and restored completely.

7/17/18

A swift change of events are coming to establish a new foundation in your life. Many of the cracks in the floor shall be filled, and once again give you stronger ground to walk on. Even though you have been presently shaken up and discouraged, you will be rejuvenated with hope and expectation to carry you into the new season that is waiting to bring you some very interesting new surprises.

7/23/18— In D.C.

"Plans, plans, and more plans! What is this? Did you not hear the sound of My voice already? What are you scheming behind the walls that you hide from? For you use your smile to win over the people? But I will have the last laugh," says the Lord! *"For what is being thought about against what I have put in place shall not come to fruition, but reverse its course and come to you! This is not a time for darkness nor will it be allowed! In this hour you shall see a great exposure in the land called D.C. and it shall cause many to tremble. For righteousness shall once again echo throughout the skies and the sound of peace shall fill the atmosphere. Enough of this! For dishonor shall not strengthen, but only weaken and a voice that once was loud shall fade and not be heard."*

7/27/18

Increase is on the way! Even though a sudden delay and barrenness showed its face and has made its presence known, the doors are open and windows have been lifted to the top. The wind shall come in and the blessing shall be at the doorstep in the moments ahead.

7/29/18— From Arizona

Unexpected people will be used to open the door for you when others kept it closed and have tried to keep it locked. Watch how suddenly the circumstances change and you walk in. It's time for freedom and refreshing winds to grab your sails and give you the momentum needed to continue moving forward. Over the course of the next several days, you will find liberty from some chains that were being stubborn and would not fall off, but that is now over and the steel has become dust. Take that step and walk. You're free!

7/30/18

The enemy will try everything and anything to disrupt your progress and blessing, but these plans have been destroyed, and nothing will stop the season of breakthrough you are in right now!

8/1/18

Not just a word in due season, but a word many have needed to hear ASAP in their life right now!

There is nothing to fear, not only will you make it, but you will succeed beyond your expectations!

HAVE I NOT COMMANDED YOU? BE STRONG AND OF GOOD COURAGE; DO NOT BE AFRAID, NOR BE DISMAYED, FOR THE LORD YOUR GOD IS WITH YOU WHEREVER YOU GO.

8/3/18— In AZ.

BEFORE WE RELEASE THIS WORD, IT HAS BEEN A VERY INTERESTING TIME HERE IN AZ. WE HAVE DEFINITIVELY STIRRED THE SPIRITUAL POT AND THE ACTIVITY JUST KEPT COMING. FROM A MONSOON STORM THE OTHER NIGHT THAT LEFT US WITHOUT POWER, TO A DUST STORM THAT WE OUTRAN YESTERDAY IN OUR TRUCK. GOD IS GOOD ALL THE TIME.

For in this time, you have not just finished a critical portion of your journey, but an establishment has taken place in the spirit realm that will manifest in the natural very soon. You have advanced in your authority and the enemy has now recognized an increase in your authority and your armor. Watch, for the storm that followed you will suddenly exist no longer, and open heavens shall bring light upon your situation and clear access to your victory.

8/7/18

Keep your heart tender and never lose focus of the life you have been given. No matter how hard things can get, everything is subject to change. Today, reflect on the things you have overcome and how victories were won in the battles of life. A new grace shall be given and a perspective renewed that focuses on you and your life. It's time to shake off all the dust that has lingered on your feet, and prepare for a new walk that is unhindered and delayed no longer. The season has begun that will generate the passion and hope that has been avoiding you for sometime now, and replace the struggle that kept you positioned with doubt. Your time has come to enjoy many things that you thought were not obtainable, and this will not avoid you any longer.

8/9/18

Watch as a sudden burst of favor comes your way and brings you to a new level of greatness. Something very significant is about to be restored in your life.

8/20/18

This day is very significant with inner healing. Every stronghold and torment that has come from the accuser is broken off and destroyed. The weight that you have been carrying is lifted, and now, as you move forward, you will suddenly have a peace and grace that covers you as the day progresses and the night shows its face. You will remember this day for seasons to come. For in this day, healing came when you thought nothing was possible, but all things are possible if you believe!

8/21/18— In D.C.

Watch as new plans have again come together to bring down this President called Trump. The one that smiles, plotting and scheming. A strong resistance made known to this Nation with arrogance and pride, but this will not be so! For this one shall be humbled before man, and what is intended to bring destruction shall be exposed and defeated. Now listen, for as August comes to a close, the heat shall intensify. For September shall be filled with warfare that is strong and great, but do not be concerned. For in this time, one will come to set the mark of discouragement and accusation against this Administration and stir up a turbulence that is significant to change the heart, but these plans will not come to fruition. Watch, for the winds shall come and the ground will shake as it cries out for justice! Supernatural favor will come as the 21st day of September arrives and the curtain closes on a plan that did not come to pass. Watch, for a great peace shall flood this Nation and a calm that causes the eyes of many to open wide and see justice that only can come from the throne room of God. For in this storm, I am there not only to bring peace, but to show this Nation who holds all things in the palm of the hand.

8/25/18

An unexpected breakthrough that has been avoiding you for some time shall pay a visit this weekend. The timing is very significant in your life and your family.

8/26/18

The enemy has tried to disrupt your breakthrough, but this weekend was critical in your season of restoration. Nothing shall stand in the way of this outpouring of grace.

8/27/18

Don't let fear stop you from your advancement and what is destined to be yours. You are positioned for a significant and strategic placement of promotion.

John Natale

8/31/18

As the wind blows and carries the seed from one place to another, there shall be an arrival of the seed you have been longing for. There shall be a planting in the ground, and the roots shall form and you shall be watered and prosper for many days ahead.

9/2/18

So the restoration has begun. What was spoken over the families, that healing would take place, has manifested and made its debut. The spirit realm has authorized the natural to begin its course. Watch, as the weeks ahead that have been spoken about regarding this nation take shape and form, there will be a significant grace over those that have eyes to see and ears to hear. Don't take these weeks for granted as you approach the day called September 21st. For there is much to be in tune with, and this Nation is in need of the prayers of those that are standing in the gap for justice and restoration.

9/4/18— In D.C.

For a very peculiar situation will arise. There is one that will get the attention of this President and expose a hidden darkness that has lingered for a time and time again. For in this month called September, every rock shall be turned over and every hidden thing revealed. Light will penetrate once again and illuminate the dark place that has tried to go unnoticed. They were foolish in thinking that this would not be found. For My eyes are fixed and My gaze cannot be moved. Then you will see a realignment again in this House, and one positioned as a watchman on the wall to guard that which has been set for many days to come.

9/5/18

Secret doors closed for seasons have been directed to open and share its mysteries with you. Your faithfulness has been strengthened and your resilience sharpened. Now is the time to watch what comes forth!

9/10/18— In D.C.

For the clouds shall roll in and share their mystery. For grace and mercy has been given because one has prayed. Watch, as a sign is revealed and the display shall be known. Unusual activity in the atmosphere that stirs the heart and troubles the mind, but peace given in its time. Peace that surpasses all understanding simply because I AM.

9/10/18

An outpouring of wind and rain is coming! Look to the skies, for they hold mysteries that have not yet been revealed. For what comes, exposes hidden treasure and reveals clues to a mystery that has been avoided for some time. The direction shall suddenly change course and focus its attention on a region that has caught the attention of My gaze. Keep watch and see how all things are held in place and cannot be moved. For glory shall be revealed and nothing can change that or remove its presence.

9/12/18

Keep your eyes open during the next seven days. For mysteries will be revealed and questions answered. A time of uncertainty that will be followed by a storm, but not to worry, for it fades quickly. The calm will begin, as the day called "21" approaches.

9/16/18

Keep pressing into the word that was released regarding family restoration. For what I am about to do, shall bring an outpouring of joy and justice that replaces pain and frustration that has been established for years. It is a time to carry a mindset of expectation. Many of you that have been suffering will suddenly be renewed, restored, and act like little children when your reconciliation comes. The enemy has had too much influence in your mind, that this will not come to pass, but watch as this month comes to a close and October arrives with freedom in its wings!

9/18/18

Expect a sudden outpouring of blessing to come and bring sudden surprises. It's at the point now where it's going to burst through the walls that have held it back. It will come and it will go, prepare your jars and wait. Do not allow patience to slip through the cracks. For there is more than enough to go around this time!

9/19/18— In D.C.

That man named Kavanaugh, who comes against him? It shall not be so! For what I have allowed shall not expose him, but shall expose a certain few that have hidden agendas and hidden mysteries. So watch, the days come and they go, but shall not pass without a victory. Hands shall be raised and smiles known, and in this, many will see again that light conquers darkness.

9/21/18— D.C.

So this day has come, September 21. Many have waited, watched, and listened to the sound that comes forth from a voice that is not orchestrated by man, but of God. The curtain falls today on a storm that was present, and the blessing and harvest comes and replaces that which was planned for destruction. Light conquers darkness and now you will see the benefits of faith, diligence, and perseverance. Watch how very important decisions are made and new puzzle pieces are put in place to help facilitate justice!

9/24/18— In D.C.

Have I not told you before that darkness cannot overcome light? In the days ahead, not only will you see one leave, but two. For a great stirring has come, and an army of Angels have been summoned to march around the House called White. For there is not only protection in the spirit realm, but a new source of protection in the natural that will be seen shortly. The plans to remove and replace cause Me to laugh, and this will only bring chaos among those that scheme against what I have chosen. So watch, for another shall come forth, and two will leave their posts and so it shall be so.

9/26/18

What I brought you through in your past is now shaping your future. Take time to reflect and remember, those days were more important than you know.

10/1/18

Your significance is not based on what others think, but what I have planned and purposed. How you see yourself is about to take on a very significant change that will bring confidence, perseverance, and expectation. Watch, for this month called October is more than you expected, and it will not leave without epic proportions of greatness.

10/4/18— In D.C.

Don't be alarmed for what is about to happen suddenly. For this must come to pass. What is hindering shall be removed, and what is missing shall be placed into position. October is a transitioning month, and in it you will see much that is required to change in order for progress to keep moving forward. Very serious scenarios will take place in this Nation, and unexpected step downs will suddenly appear. Arrogance has no place in this Nation, and as the skies open up and manifest in this month called October, you will understand the mystery of grace and know that what is held together is not by you, but by Me!

10/7/18— In D.C.

Prepare for a very unusual event to take place shortly. For a sudden breakthrough comes and establishes a new seat for an unexpected guest that will help create opportunity and promotion.

10/8/18

In a time when uncertainty is all around you, a strength comes and a hope is restored to a time that once was. Today, your mindset will change and the weight that is felt will lift and give you the freedom to press on towards the mark. It's time to live and enjoy the fruits of your labor. Nothing you do is in vain, and you will come to know that very soon!

10/11/18

Oh, how it gets pretty interesting over the next several days. But you will not be disappointed at all. For very exciting times of refreshing winds have come to pay a visit, and in this you will be rejuvenated and restored.

10/12/18

Watch, for a very significant breakthrough comes and knocks on the door and brings the prodigal home and the relationships that were stolen back into place. November is your month, and will not end without this manifesting significantly.

10/14/18— 2019 is the year called Ownership.

What has eluded you for some time will suddenly make its way into your possession and fulfill a promise that was spoken many seasons ago. Get ready for a very significant door to open and cause your influence and boundaries to expand greatly. The tent posts are about to be removed and placed in new soil, and this will establish you in a greater capacity of influence and inheritance.

10/17/18

Your ability to discern accurately, will be sharpened suddenly, because what is coming is a strong wave of deception that will try to manipulate and control your path. Stay focused and surround yourself with seers and watchmen on the wall.

10/19/18

There are many natural shifts and changes taking place in the atmosphere right now that are a reflection of warfare in this nation. Many are confused and concerned about what is taking place, but watch, for November not only holds clues to a significant calm, but a dramatic occurrence of favor in the land called **The United States**!

John Natale

10/21/18

As the rain falls, so does the blessing. The season called Fall has been showing its colors in different ways than you were expecting. Get ready for a burst of blessing as it prepares to enter the November month. For there will be much to be thankful for, both individually and in this Nation. For many surprises wait in the balance to show who is really in control.

10/22/18

Nothing will stop your destiny! Even though a barrage of distractions and setbacks came this month and tried to steal all the ground that was made up, you will see a great momentum and victory before October comes to a close. The sound of rejoicing at the finish line can be heard throughout eternity, simply because you have been given everything you need to finish well in this season!

10/23/18— In D.C.

There is nothing to be concerned with. Another November to remember that will shadow that which was! What was started will be finished and nothing can change that. Do not be discouraged for what you see. For truth sets the captive free. Spiritual keys open natural doors, and I hold all the keys in My hands!

10/24/18

As the weather patterns have caused a bit of concern and have patterned their gusts to the drama of National issues at hand, watch. For what is actually happening is the clearing of distractions, blockage, and deception. For the wind will blow once again, this time much stronger. But what comes from it is clean, clear air that displays the skies that have a hidden mystery to reveal. November....Watch!

10/25/18— For America

Such a strong stirring to release this word this morning about the Gettysburg Address for America.

Your nation called the United States will see a new release of freedom and unity. What is present is not acceptable, nor is it allowed. The disunity and the lack of compassion for others has tainted this land for generations to come. The only cause for restoration is when the heart of man reconciles and turns towards a direction of unconditional love and carries the mindset that all people are created equal and carry purpose, and without unity, nothing can be truly accomplished. A man named Lincoln gave a speech seasons ago that spoke of these very words. He also spoke about a Nation that must remember where it came from, and how to achieve the ultimate goal of freedom. He had no idea that his words would keep moving through the atmosphere for generations upon generations to come. So watch, for the heart is stirring in a nation that is crying for peace. Over the next few months and into 2019 you will see a dramatic shift take place, and a softening of the heart as a nation starts to reconcile and be restored to what was once beautiful and glorious! His last words,

> *"...that this nation under God, shall have a new birth of freedom, and that government of the people, by the people, for the people, shall not perish from the earth."* [1]

You will see a great unity in Washington, D. C. as the years unfold, and how men and women alike turn from their wicked ways and lay their agendas down to promote peace and justice. For this you can be sure!

10/29/18

Windows have opened, doors have opened and bells are ringing with the sound of Jubilee. In a time when weariness is all around you, a wind comes and lifts your arms and gives you flight to see things in a new

187

perspective. The only thing you need to do is allow Me to lift you, and restore hope and expectation. Yes, the enemy has been working hard to keep you down, but My breath has come to raise you up and provide all that is needed in this season. So watch, the view will surprise you and give you a new sense of freedom as you soar like the eagle!

11/2/18— In America

So he becomes relevant again! This man named Lincoln, his story continues and his legacy lives on. For a mystery has eluded the generations upon generations, and the blood that was shed cries out for justice once again. For such a time that it was, a nation lived in the midst of a civil war that could not comprehend the beginning from the end. Lives shattered, families destroyed, and a nation that had no idea of what tomorrow would bring, except for one individual that could see through the eyeglasses of eternity. This man named Lincoln, his diligence and his ability to see what others could not see and hear what others could not hear brought a nation together, but also knew the cost that it would take to see freedom come and free the captives. Through a civil war and the strategy to keep the enemy at bay, wisdom and revelation was used to confuse the enemy, and the glory of a righteous King came in and changed the hearts of men to see into the portals of time that would inevitably shake the nation and change the course of history.

Yes, this nation is now again in a civil war; anger, bitterness, resentment, and lack of honor rise in the hearts of many, but in a moments time and time again, you will see a house that was divided come back into unity, because a man named Lincoln shall have his heart and passion recognized once again in a land called Washington, D.C. His understanding and revelation of reason and compassion for people shall be brought to attention once again, and the life he laid down for the sake of others shall not be in vain, but for a time that has been designed now for a new awakening in a land that so needs reformation and healing.

In these next few months and in the year called 2019, he will be remembered for the spirit that he carried and the passion for the common good of mankind. It shall hover over a nation and blanket people with a new sense of peace and unconditional love for one another. You must remember those before you that laid down their lives for the sake of justice, that never saw freedom. You must never forget those that answered the call to help facilitate freedom, and you must never forget that nothing comes without a price. It is a time now that this nation called America comes back to her first love and remembers. Freedom comes from a change of heart, and in the months ahead you will see a great change of the heart in this nation, and unity will once again occupy My house and the House that is called White.

11/5/18

A new level of understanding is about to be released. A key will be given to unlock a door of mystery, and what walks in will literally change everything as the year called 2018 comes to a close.

John Natale

11/7/18

A sudden attack has ceased and the enemy has fled. Watch, for what seemed broken and shattered has been restored and put back into place. The strength from this now cannot be affected anymore and will bring sudden blessing from lost time.

11/9/18— In D.C.

Prepare, for a great shaking shall take place in this nation. For one shall come again from the land called Israel and shake the hand of a man called Trump. The two shall go and speak, and one that resisted shall join, and what was expected shall shift and surprise the people. So watch, for they watch and stand ready.

11/12/18

As your spiritual authority expands, natural opportunity increases and the windows of Heaven open to release an overflow of blessing to you and your family.

11/14/18

Your perseverance and diligence placed you in such a wonderful place. Throughout time, many good things were being positioned to surprise you, and in this season they come to you. It is through My strength that your testimony has become your story. Never forget what you have come from because your life is a hope for someone else that needs that inspiration. So rejoice, for you have done well. Now go and tell others of how a living hope kept you moving forward!

11/16/18

The windows of Heaven are open and what is given is more than you can imagine. A season has come that carries the redemption of lost time and starts a cycle of blessing that has been promised before it was envisioned. Watch, for many good things shall come and introduce itself to you and your family. Now run with God and don't let anyone distract you from this outpouring. It is your time, and you have fought long and hard. Now enjoy the fruit of your faithfulness.

11/20/18

Increase comes in a way of a mystery that surrounds the family and reinstates honor. Watch, for as the day approaches that completes a table, a reconciliation comes and takes its place in a vacant chair that has carried its dust for many a season. Now it is a time to rejoice and be glad.

11/22/18

How can it be? Can these windows of Heaven be open so much that blessing is more than enough? Yes, it shall be so and your new year called 2019 will be just that! Watch, for the fullness thereof shall knock on your door and pay a visit and sit at a table that has been waiting for this seat to be occupied for many a season.

11/26/18

2018 does not end without very significant restoration in your family. Before the month called December ends, the things that the enemy tried to keep hidden will be revealed and healed. January 2019 will come and your pain shall be no longer. Laughter will fill your heart and tears of joy shall fall and saturate the ground you stand on as a sign to the enemy that your victory has come and darkness has been defeated.

John Natale

11/29/18

There are times that your weakness will be your greatest strength and will spark the faith that can move mountains.

12/3/18

Your revelation increases when your natural expectation decreases. Codependency was never meant to inhabit the natural realm, but occupy the spirit realm.

12/4/18

December is your month and you shall not be disappointed. As the month progresses, the spirit realm will shake the natural realm and the atmosphere will change course suddenly. Watch, for what is above reveals secrets to what the season holds. So the outpouring of blessing shall shine like the sun over you and your family. For there will be much to be thankful for when it comes to a close.

12/6/18— In D.C.

So the mystery continues as does the pursuit of peace and the common good of mankind. As one President left an office and another occupied an office, a stirring is preparing to take place. A mutual understanding between the two, and a pursuit of a dream that once was, and always will be. Many will say, *"How can this be? What has changed?"* So in time, the establishment of grace and the softening of the hearts shall take place and ideas will be shared, and two voices shall agree and one shall be heard. For in the months ahead, the revealing will come and the attention that it brings will be felt across a Nation, that when unity is present, peace is felt and joy is heard. The grace and peace that this Nation needs shall be seen in the place called White, and it shall be so and it will not go unnoticed.

12/9/18

Expect breakthrough to come suddenly. Specific doors that have been open and caused frustration, anger, and fatigue shall close, never to open again. The season of freedom is upon of you. Watch, for the signs come soon and will give a hint to the healing and restoration.

12/12/18

There are many that have not received the mystery of revelation. Some have not understood grace, and there are some that abuse the grace. And then there are some that want to cast their stones, but now, I ask this question; He who is without sin, cast that stone. Why do you spend so much time concerned about others and their relationship with Me when My Word specifically says to be more concerned with your own heart? You must let go of the conditions you place on others and pray for them. Encourage, inspire and help those that have not yet understood the mystery. For their day comes, just as your day did. Now go, be a light in a dark place and remember, they will know you by your love!

12/16/18

A new season of rest has come that will facilitate an increase of your revelation and awareness. The fruit of your labor that is positioned in the spirit realm manifests shortly in the natural. Over the next several days, watch what takes place, as a very important opportunity and breakthrough becomes present.

12/19/18

Get ready for a blast from the past, as an old friend pays a visit and brings a breath of fresh air! Now watch, for what comes is more than you think is possible.

12/23/18

Prepare for a sudden shift of positioning and the increase in the storehouse. December does not end without you finishing well. The unexpected turn of events that you thought could not happen will not only arrive, but will stay positioned for several seasons!

12/25/18

The enemy has lost a very serious battle, and now, victory is at hand. What was prophesied days ago regarding how you will finish well in December is now in motion. Watch and prepare, for a very significant change comes to the family.

12/27/18

As the year of 2019, that is called Ownership, draws closer and closer, direction and activation is revealed, and facilitation is achieved. Now prepare, watch, and stay sensitive to My voice. For the time comes when the hourglass shows that the sand has almost finished its journey downward, and the things positioned for blessing are released.

12/28/18

Your ability to overcome any obstacle or hindrance in your life is not based on any man's words, but how your heart and mindset see and act. It's a new season, and this is where your perspective suddenly changes, and nothing will stop your forward progress.

1. Abraham Lincoln. Gettysburg address delivered at Gettysburg Pa. Nov. 19th. 1863. https://www.loc.gov/resource/rbpe.24404500/?st=text

Part Seven
Prophetic Words — 2019

John Natale

1/1/2019-Happy New Year Everyone!

Your word for today is **VISION**.

2019— The Year of Ownership is all about how you see what is ahead. Now it is time to lift your vision higher and set your sight on the goal. Don't be afraid to take the step, I will be with you. A religious spirit will try to hinder a spiritual blessing that is destined to manifest in the natural. It's your time, you will overcome!

1/7/19

Watch, as a door opens and gives opportunity for an increase in the storehouse. Don't be afraid to take a very serious step, and do not allow your natural expectations to convince you that this is not from Me. It will challenge you and test your courage. In its time, it will not only meet the needs of your current situation, but also help facilitate plans that are in the making for the rest of the year called 2019.

1/10/19— In D.C.

There is an unexpected visitor coming to meet with the President. Where two would not agree, one will. It will set in motion an alliance that at first will not react favorably, but then turn suddenly and share each other's interest in the common good of mankind.

1/12/19

What is destined to come, shall not come without a fight. The resistance the enemy uses shall actually cause the smoke to clear and enable you to make the decision necessary to obtain what is yours. Watch, for January is the month that creates the opportunity to reign and rule!

1/14/19

An obstacle that caused hindrance has been removed and gives way to some necessary freedom and opportunity for you. It's not time yet to act, but soon enough will come. The key is to be patient and wait. As you stay sensitive to My voice, you will be given the go ahead to move forward and obtain what is yours.

1/22/19

As the days progress, there is a valuable decision that needs to be made. In this season called Ownership, you must resist the temptation to settle and continue your pursuit of the greater plan that has been established for you. Now watch, for a mystery shall be revealed this week, and a puzzle piece placed in position to show you exactly what needs to happen in order for a promise to come to fruition.

1/24/19

For as the Summer draws closer and closer, so does the transfer that will take place. For a season shall come upon you that will be accompanied by honor and remembrance. For you will look back at the days gone by and reflect on the memories that both encouraged you and challenged you. Do not be mistaken, it is not a time to mourn, but a time to rejoice, for an inheritance shall come and rest upon your lap. The season shall bring an unprecedented grace and favor that will cause your individual life and the life of your family to progress and soar like an eagle. The warmth of the sun during that Summer of 2019 will be an unusual sign that the heat has increased and removed the cold that surrounded you in the winter months. Again, I say rejoice, for what comes, has been destined before the hourglass has been given its name.

John Natale

1/28/19

As unexpected turbulence came your way to disrupt your journey. The calm has been released to remind you again who is in control of all things. Always remember that the rough scenarios that take place in your life are and will be used to focus your gaze on Me.

1/30/19

An increased level of faith is being released right now as you prepare for a new beginning this week. The enemy will try to influence you with fear and anxiety, but you will overcome and take hold of the blessing that is moments ahead. Settling is not an option for you or your family. The land of milk and honey has open space with your name on it. Now go and put stakes in the ground.

2/2/19— For The United States

So in this day and a day, how can this be? What do they think? What do they say? For My anger arises now, and the ones that smile and laugh at life and hold no value to its origin shall see the song that comes from a Throne of Justice. For in the day of Pharaoh, there was one that stood and spoke a warning of what would come. Now I say this again, do not tempt the Lord thy God with your petty thoughts and decrees! For in the spiritual realm, the enemy has once again considered himself victorious in the realm of life, but this is not so! For in the months ahead, an overturning shall take place and a voice heard. It shall echo throughout the Nation and a sound once again shall rise and take its place. For these Pharaohs that think they can rule without humility, and not hold to the sacred value of what I have spoken into existence before mankind was even thought of, shall see how just I really Am! For life and death have its power from the very tongue that speaks and declares. I have come to give life and give it to the full. Now watch, and fix your gaze on the skies above, for they will send the sign of what comes in the Summer months. For your heat shall be great, and you shall seek water to quench your thirst, but that will not give you peace, but repentance will. One will find comfort, but another will not. Even your shade will be disrupted. Remember Jonah, for he could not find the comfort he so desired until he surrendered his heart and allowed Me to give him the revelation of how I see every life! So in this Summer of 2019, you will see a great change, and many will see the glory of the Lord, and many will turn and yield to Me!

2/4/19— For The United States

The signs have already started to show their faces. Keep watch, for as in the day of Moses, many opportunities will come and many will go for those called to change the heart. But this will not stop the progress made for the many that are held in bondage. For in the days ahead, what was unexpected shall find its way into mainstream media, and a voice shall cry in the wilderness and be heard. A voice never thought of or considered, but raised up supernaturally for such a time as this. Focus your attention to the part of the nation that was the catalyst for freedom. For in the moments ahead, he comes forth and gives a shout that will echo and penetrate darkness. That platform comes quickly and justice that you seek, is heard loud and clear.

2/7/19

Don't be worried about what you see or hear, an amazing victory has been won in the spirit that will manifest in the natural before the month of February ends!

2/7/19— Prophetic Vision in America

In a vision I saw a baby in the womb. Its head was down and there was no movement. It showed no life, and as I was watching, I could feel the heart

201

of compassion that God has for all life. I knew that this vision represented life and also the spiritual condition of this nation.

Suddenly, the Child's head moved upwards, the hands started to raise and then I saw the heart beating with a sound of freedom and everlasting joy that could be heard throughout the ages. What seemed impossible BECAME THE POSSIBLE. The child then looked up, and you could see a smile that caused the greatest of pains to be washed away and a release of peace that surpassed all understanding.

Then the voice came and said these words, *"Oh, My Children, for many have tried to silence your voice in the womb and outside the womb, and many think they have defeated My plans, My ways, and My heart for all people, young and old. Today, is your reminder, that what has been hindered by man will be overturned by Me, and nothing will stop the heartbeat of Heaven that comes from a Throne of Grace and a Throne of Justice. For watch, in the days ahead that you call 2019, there will be such a shaking and stirring, that the hearts of men will tremble in fear and understand the mystery that the One who sits at the right hand of the Father holds all things in place by His mighty hand, and nothing can come against what has been established and set in place by Me. For I Am, and again I say, I Am!"*

2/11/19

Samson knew his Creator and he heard My voice. His sacrifices, his pain, and his laughter can be heard throughout eternity. He knew that at the end, he was created for such a time, and his very purpose was to be a light in a dark place. This day, this very hour, the strength that he carried in his heart and soul can be yours as well. All it takes is to stay in a place of intimacy and allow Me to guard your heart from the deceptive plans of the enemy. For those that need this reassuring grace, know that it is available right now! You will see the walls come down that the enemy has placed around you, and you will see the glory and the blessing that is yours to comfort you and raise you up from your pain and bring you to a place of freedom and supernatural joy!

2/14/19

The door in the spirit realm has opened so wide, that a natural manifestation of significant opportunity shall make its way and give you what you have been praying and waiting for. The patience in which you have showed has been of epic proportions. Watch closely, for it comes suddenly!

2/15/19

There might be a bit of confusion going on right now with you and your decisions. But God is about to change everything and make it real clear what you need to do to establish the blessing that is present to overwhelm you and your family.

2/17/19

There seems to be some giants in the land that will try to distract you from moving forward. Some on the ground and some in the air. Stand your ground, for the ones on the ground make much noise, and their bark is greater than their bite. The ones in the air are only to cause your attention to come off what is ahead. Stay focused. All are spiritual attacks that will manifest in the natural, but My grace is sufficient for you, and you will continue walking to the promise. Remember, that promise is ownership!

2/18/19

Open doors, new opportunities and breakthrough that will change your life forever! Get ready, get ready! Spring is coming and what springs up is more than imagined!

2/19/19

As you sit and stare out the window pondering if things will ever change, watch, for the opportunity comes suddenly. I want you to remember that a wonderful plan is set in motion to change everything. What is purposed for you is designed by My hand, and it's important that your future plays out according to My desire. Don't allow anything to change that!

2/20/19

The question is simple. What is your heart saying about your current situation? Are you being led by the right voice? It's time to shake the dust off the boots and press in. It's time for change!

2/21/19

As you walk today, stop and take a look back at what you have come from and what you have overcome. Now imagine what's ahead and the glorious future you have! You have been through so much, yet it has just begun! Now, go and contend for your breakthrough, for there is much to be accomplished and much to be given!

2/22/19— In D.C.

Yet another release of angels again being sent as a covering and a protection that surrounds this President called Trump. For he is asking Me how to plan for the next season! Now watch, April comes and goes, but not without showing the colors of the spirit realm and how powerful it really is! For a mystery is revealed and the strength of this man will not go unnoticed. For preparations are being positioned for 2020.

2/23/19— In D.C. *The Joseph Inheritance*

So how can this be? A man that took a risk on a dream! His passion for Me was more important than anything that this world could offer. He didn't despair in trouble, he didn't give up in time of need. In fact, he held onto a dream that was brought to him by Me. He could see the future, even though he didn't quite fully understand it. He had no idea what was ahead, nor did he ever imagine the price he would pay for the very thing he contended for. At one point, it seemed he lost everything, but it still didn't stop him from becoming what he was destined to be!

This Joseph, this man of honor! What can be said of him? Why is he so important to mankind? Now I tell you that his legacy, his heart, his mindset continues this day, and now, in this season, I am imparting the same thing that I gave this great man of God, to this President called Donald Trump. He shall walk the walk as Joseph did. Many will dishonor him, discredit him, and disown him, I will give him the strength he needs to continue his journey and finish well. But woe to them that try to stop My plans for him. They do not understand the mysteries at hand. For he will enter into the next term, not only with strength, but with My grace and peace. For he will lead again! Over the next 12 months, he will have accomplished more than what was expected and will gain the favor of a Nation.

For many do not see through the veil that covers their eyes. As with Joseph, his own brothers did not understand the mystery that was formed in My hands before time began. They only acted out simply because of their own weaknesses that controlled their hearts. Joseph was raised up to change the heart! What he accomplished in the natural was already completed in the spirit. You see My Children, what is taking place in this Nation that you call the United States, is not about any one person, it is about a people that have been crying out for help and they didn't even know it! I have given the platform to one that has the ability to speak what is spoken, and do what is done. In the short time ahead, a reconciliation shall be seen throughout a land. A peace shall come and gently sooth the broken-hearted. The bitter shall become sweet, and the angry shall

205

become joyful. In its time, the veil that was on Joseph's face shall come down, and the restoration of a Nation shall come forth! Do not be mistaken, for it shall come and a wonderful wind shall blow freely without opposition across the land. It will have the fragrance of healing in its wings, and rest will come to those that have been weary. It is a time now to rejoice, for this Joseph is about to be revealed.

2/24/19

Sometimes all it takes is to let go of the things you are holding onto and let Me guide you. It's that simple. Today, surrender everything that is holding you back and the things that might be getting in the way. You will not be disappointed in the outcome that has been waiting for you! Abraham was challenged and his love was tested. He passed the test because I set him up to be victorious, and you as well have been positioned in the same manner. Don't be afraid, for I am here!

3/1/19

March has come! Now your word for today is **ADVANCEMENT!** You gained ground, and it's time for a magnificent new beginning to be released as a double portion of grace is given. Your opportunity for what you never thought would come is at the door. Listen for the knock, take the step, and open the door. You will not be disappointed!

3/3/19

Watch, for today brings surprises! Expect more than enough, see what hasn't been revealed, and hear what hasn't been spoken. It will not end without going unnoticed! In this you can be sure!

3/5/19

An intense week of warfare has come down like a descending cloud and created some very interesting chaos. But watch, for the week will not end without a massive breakthrough that facilities celebration and justification.

3/7/19— In D.C.

Pharaoh thought he could stop Moses from bringing a new day to those that were in bondage. He guessed wrong! As with this President that is called Trump, he too will find a great freedom as he completes one term and starts a second. Thus completing a journey of what was considered unimaginable and unachievable. It will spearhead a new movement of freedom that has been crying out for generations upon generations, and a silence shall come quickly to the ones that have been a voice of darkness. But one must remember that light always conquers darkness. For in the fight, natural weapons cannot defeat spiritual authority.

3/10/19

I will establish you in a realm of grace and peace. For your cry has been heard and help has been sent. You will have a great victory today, and before the sun sets in its place, peace will have come, a peace that surpasses all understanding. Do not worry, for all things work together for those that love Me!

3/11/19

As with this journey called life, your ability to overcome the very obstacles and adversities you face will require you to press in each and every day. I did not promise you that it will be easy, in fact, serving Me will be a hard and challenging road ahead. There will be times that you will think it is too much, or it will not be worth going on with the everyday struggles of pain or suffering. But in the midst of trouble, there is a reminder that I overcame the world, and even though trouble lingers all around you, you can rejoice, simply because My joy is your strength, and in this you can be sure. I am releasing a new joy in your heart and mind, and you will understand that My very presence in your life will grow and grow in this season. Allow Me to remind you of what you have overcome and what you will experience in that day that has waited for generations to come! The day when our eyes meet and arms are opened wide and that long awaited embrace finally happens. The day that declares, welcome home good and faithful servant. You see, when you understand the mystery of what is ahead and how real it truly is, your perspective changes and your mindset shifts to supernatural thinking. So let Me in, and let me show you how good life is! For I am with you always!

3/13/19

The door is open for a very significant breakthrough! Even before this week comes to a close, there will be a shift that comes your way and reveals a hidden mystery. Pay close attention, for what comes requires decisions, and in this comes blessing!

3/14/19

Your ability to make the very important decision that needs to be made presently will require you to step back and take a breath. Take your hands off and allow Me to complete this blessing in your life.

3/17/19

You are getting very close to what will be a very dramatic and cheerful breakthrough! A fast approaching wind shall overtake you and sweep you off your feet as one day closes and another begins! Watch for the mystery is at hand and speaks in a still, soft voice!

3/18/19

In a world that so desperately needs the light that illuminates a dark place, it can be found and it can be placed in your heart. In this hour, one thing that I desire is for you to have an unquenchable passion for those who have no candle to light their way. There is a groaning and an aching for the very ones who still wander the path of uncertainty and blindness. You have been given an ability and an attraction that will help set the captives free and cause their steps to find the path that leads to freedom. There are some that I have placed on your mind recently that have been heavy on your heart. But there is good news. Before the season that you call Spring comes and shares its beauty, there will be a wind that comes and blows on the heart and soul, thus bringing a restoration to a first love. So now, watch and wait, for the unveiling of truth comes, and in this, you will not be disappointed.

3/23/19— In D.C.

So the mysteries are about to be revealed. What is next? How can this be? As for what I Am going to do, nothing can stop the forward movement and positions that will be kept in place and moved out of place. For a very great change is coming to the land called Washington, D.C., and to the soil that is represented by the name called the United States. For this man that is called Trump has been listening to My voice, and he has been responding to My leading. He has answered the call to honor the land, that which is Mine! The land called Israel.

He continues to honor that which needs to be honored, and in this your land is prospering and will continue to prosper. Now listen and watch, for in the next several months ahead and in the completion of this first term, an awakening shall come and be revealed in the land called D.C. For many will think that an end will come and a new beginning shall proceed with a new voice, but this will not be so! For I have the last say, and the people of this nation have had their hearts already softened. A second term shall follow from a first and what comes in those next four years will be more than possibly imagined. For it will be remembered for a time and a time again.

Even when this man leaves his office, there will be historic scenarios that the people will embrace in their heart. They will say that we judged unnecessarily, and we did not see the heart that was formed before the foundations of the world to help people and a land gain their freedom and strength to be positioned for what is to come. Now again, I say as was spoken before, the man called Netanyahu will be strengthened and his relationship with the man called Trump will go down in history as one that formed the Nations into a place of peace and prosperity. For nothing can touch this alliance and nothing can touch the land called Israel. For she will gain in numbers and she will gain in such a strength, that even the giants that come to try to intimidate will be put down like the Philistine champion called Goliath. Now again, In this term that this President is completing and in the term that he will begin again, the heavens will remain open and pour out such blessing and opportunity for the people to receive and be filled with plenty.

For this will bring such advancement and will facilitate what has been promised. But listen again, for when the second term is complete, the windows will be shut and a famine shall come in ways that was not thought of. Man will say that this wasn't possible, but it must come. But there will be no alarm for those who put their trust in Me. For things will come and cause confusion and disruption in the land, but it is necessary for the carrying out of very specific plans that wait in the balance. A humbling will come and for those that have heeded the words and trusted in Me, their storehouse will not run dry, but will be kept for a time and time again.

Keep your eyes on the people that represent specific offices in D.C. For many new faces will come and be placed into new seats, and they will be ones that bring peace and comfort to many. Many voices that have come against Me will be removed suddenly and some over time, and the unjust shall become witnesses from the sidelines as their power was removed and not to be restored. Watch and pray, for we are in the times of times that bring many signs from above to show a supernatural power and also a comforting grace.

3/28/19

Prepare and watch for a unique opportunity to arise that will come from a source that was not expected. A bit of vindication is about to accompany you, as specific progress is being made behind the scenes to bring what is needed and what is due. Over the past three years, this has been in the making to bring blessing, honor, and position.

3/30/19— In D.C.

This President that is called Trump shall be given a double portion of grace and power in the moments ahead, as specific individuals that have been testing the waters of dishonor come forth again and speak with bitterness and anger from their lips. His words shall penetrate the darkness simply because it is I that speaks and silences the voices of adversity once again. So watch, for the two come with hidden agendas and plan their demise. But this shall not be so! For what is revealed is completely exposed. For the plan that comes to dishonor only brings more honor to that which has been positioned by My hands.

3/31/19

You're about to see some very serious increase take place as the next quarter of this year starts. April is an important month as it prepares for one of the greatest months of the season, and that would be May. Deuteronomy 1:11 is about to manifest significantly so watch and collect your jars!

4/1/19

In a time where uncertainty is all around you, there is a hope that changes everything. Today's word is all about faith and expecting the unexpected. You see, My desire is to give more than you can imagine. I want to give you what you thought was not obtainable. What I am going to release to you and your family in this season will cause the hearts of men and women alike to put their eyes on Me! They will be in awe of what has transferred into your possession, and they will question everything! Their hearts will burn simply because My hand was directing everything that needed to be established. In this, the great step of faith that caused the spirit realm to manifest in the natural will be a catalyst for others to pursue their forgotten dreams and cause what was once lost to be brought into the now. So take that step, for the season of ownership is upon you!

4/3/19

Extended grace and a warm welcome to the calm today, as the warfare that has been tormenting you finally comes to an end. There will be much to celebrate as the week continues, for what is revealed over the weekend brings about unexpected blessing.

4/5/19

The warfare is raging, but My grace is stronger. Help is on the way! The calm is coming and will conquer the resistance that was experienced from this week. Don't be surprised by the events that take place this weekend. For they are full of surprises and blessing.

4/7/19— In D.C.

So a mystery is about to be revealed, as the man called President Trump brings about another change, and is used as an instrumental voice of negotiations for freedom and liberty. A sudden breakthrough will come, and an end to hostility that has been present and causing much turmoil. I have given him a strategy that will cause the hardened heart to soften, and this will enable the eyes to see what could not be seen. Keep watch and prepare, for tears of joy shall be released, and what comes from the land that's off your eastern shores shall be something that men and women alike said could not be done.

4/8/19

In a time where chaos seems to be all around and hearts are hardened by the systems that are in place, I Am here! There's confusion, but I Am here! Doubt, I Am here! Bitterness, I Am here! So in the days ahead, many hearts shall be softened to understand the mystery of grace. It is time for My bride to understand that I work through many people in many ways, ways that you do not understand. You see, people just want to be loved, accepted and shown that they are valuable and significant in a world that judges and condemns.

The enemy has come to harden the very thing that I have come to soften. Over the course of time, the enemy has won many victories and has influenced many lives and caused much division, but it is declared now, that as the Spring shows its colors once again, an outpouring of love, peace, and joy shall fill your cities, your communities, your families. Your month called April is very significant to Me, to you, and to many! Watch, for My joy comes and removes the hindrance that has caused a wall between you and I. You will be filled to overflowing as My presence once again conquers darkness.

4/10/19

Supernatural open doors and a sudden opportunity awaits you in the moments ahead. As the enemy has been bringing some doubt and worry about a very specific situation that you are holding onto, and nothing has been happening as of yet. Not to worry, for the confirmation shall come all of a sudden when your hands come off the situation and you fully yield and contend with expectancy. April does not end without showing its colors, and in this, you can find rest.

4/12/19— In D.C.

Who has the last word? Who exposes what many thought could not be revealed? Watch, for the time is coming sooner than expected. For the sounds of justice shall ring in the air as two that have kept silent for a season are all of a sudden brought into the light. For a very unusual occurrence shall come as a great unfolding and revealing takes place and brings popularity and praise to an end. For the two who have conspired as one are subject to a swift justice. They will cry out and declare they are untouchable, but I have given a strategy to silence darkness and it shall not be hindered by natural power. For the great change in a great Nation that is called the United States has begun.

4/14/19

In the season that you are in, I am guiding you to that very special open door. Do not be discouraged about what has not opened as of yet. In its time, the one that has the wow factor will suddenly come to your attention and bring about the very thing that has been promised for you and your family. I am making it very clear what is Me and what is not. I do not want you to settle, I want you to lift your vision higher and expect more than enough! What is coming will establish you in the promised land, and the year of ownership is your key to victory. Hold onto the word, contend and expect! It comes when the Spring is fully established and shows all the colors needed to highlight My favor!

4/15/19

There are many times that everything you have poured into seems to not work out, or not go your way. Working so hard, trying to keep the faith and the motivation to stay strong, stay focused—time goes by, still waiting patiently for your turn, your opportunity. How can this be? Why so much waiting? Will it ever happen? The answer is yes! It certainly will. In this season, the warfare has escalated to an all time high, but you have been given a strength that kept you fighting even though there was nothing in you left. Thoughts of abandoning everything, leaving, giving up! But then a voice speaks, a simple sign, a tug on the heart, a remembrance of who you are, what you have been through, what has been overcome, gives you the resilience to keep going. Guess who that was?

You guessed it! It was Me giving you what you needed at that moment. Now, a shift has come, something that is generated in the spirit realm that will manifest in your natural. So just watch how healing comes, restoration comes, vindication comes, and opportunity says hello to your situation. For you have not been forgotten, but have been prepared as Esther was for such a time as this. You will see the fruition of a very serious and significant breakthrough for you and your family. It is time now, the enemy could not finish what he started, but I have completed what I began in you! In this, you can find your rest now.

4/18/19— In D.C.

For a very significant occurrence shall take place in the city called NYC. For the President shall pay a visit and a signing shall take place. A supernatural favor shall accompany him and great momentum shall be seen in the realm of freedom and unity. Watch, for those that were against shall all of a sudden be in favor of the movement that lasts for several more years.

4/24/19

As David experienced a supernatural boldness to approach his adversary, you too will all of a sudden receive this same authority. Watch, for the giant is going to fall and the warfare is at its end. The enemy shall flee and a calm shall come that brings very significant breakthrough. Your tenacity and fearlessness will cause the windows of Heaven to open up and pour out more than enough in the season called Spring!

4/26/19— In D.C.

In a season where many question everything and come against what is established, you must understand the mystery at hand. But for those that do not have eyes to see, the mystery never becomes revealed. So they fight and they fight with natural words, accusations, and carry a mindset and belief that what is in the now shall not be in the future. So it shall not be so, for this man that is called Trump shall see victory again, and over the next several years ahead, the nation shall see a dramatic change in the land called DC. For it shall increase in favor throughout the house and throughout the courts. For a great momentum shall come and blanket the land with a changing of the guards.

4/27/19

Very significant opportunities come over the next several days. Use wisdom and do not allow concern to distract you from the open doors that are available for you and your future.

4/29/19

Stay diligent in pursuit of your breakthrough. The enemy is trying very hard to keep you distracted and discouraged, but your tenacity will cause your blessing to come to pass sooner than later.

5/2/19

Don't be disheartened by what you are seeing or hearing presently. New opportunities and blessing have been released, but it will take some patience and some activation that will test your faith and character. These open doors are active and will not be closed until you have entered in. The end result will be very rewarding for you and your family. Take a breath and move according to the directives I give. Everything will fall into place perfectly.

5/4/19— In D.C.

So this man that is called Trump is guarded by what is unseen. Where there is no gap or cracks in the wall. A hedge of protection that cannot be breached. So why do you continue your assault on the one that cannot and will not be replaced? You have considered and positioned someone else to come against him, but this has already crumbled. Confusion has come in your camp and confidence cannot be found. A plan and strategy to remove what has been positioned by Me cannot be established, nor will anything come to fruition, simply because I will not allow it. It shall not be so!

For there is one who thinks he will dethrone the one who holds the highest authority in the land, but I laugh at your plans and your schemes. For you mock now, but In its time, your agendas and your motives shall be put to shame as the trumpet shall be heard again in the land and echo throughout the nation. He shall have a greater voice that rumbles like the sounds of thunder and he shall have the eyes of an eagle. For nothing shall go unseen. For darkness shall be exposed once again and one very important person who hides behind brick walls shall be brought to justice. Have you not learned, have you not seen? Your fight in the natural is no match to what has been placed in office by spiritual authority. But you will see again who holds the keys and who opens and closes the doors without any hesitation or hindrance. So now I tell you these things, your resistance only causes more strength and your mocking only causes grace to decrease. For the window is open for grace, so choose wisely. Open your eyes so you can see and open your hearts so you can feel. The next several years will reveal the mysteries of ancient days and in this you can trust.

5/6/19

WE HAVE A TEACHING COMING UP THIS WEEK ON THE MEMORIAL STONES SPOKEN ABOUT IN THE BOOK OF JOSHUA. IT WILL CHANGE YOUR PERSPECTIVE AND GIVE YOU THE HOPE NEEDED, AS WE ALL PRESS IN TO THE SIGNIFICANT TIMES WE ARE IN. OUR PRAYER IS THAT THIS BRINGS COMFORT, PEACE, AND HOPE FOR YOU AND YOUR FAMILY.

The eagle soars, effortlessly gliding on the wind and watching what takes place below. Uncertainty, restlessness, worry, but what has become of all of this? There are so many that tremble as the ground shakes and the rocks cry out! They contend, cry out, they war in the spirit, and they intercede for a nation. Even when there is so much darkness all around, a wind stays present and allows the wings of the eagle to continue its flight without hindrance or delay.

In this hour, I am releasing that same wind to you, so your wings can catch the air and cause you to rise and fly! I will cause you to rise high above your situation and give you the ability to see how the eagle sees! You will be allowed to see not only the stronghold that has been hindering you, but you will see the victory that is just ahead of you. All it takes is to extend your wings and allow the wind of My lungs to lift you up! Be prepared, for in the moments ahead, the eagle takes flight and the season of rest and enjoyment come to fruition. Time to fly!

5/6/19— Israel And The Gaza Strip

The blood speaks and the ground shakes! The rocks cry out! I have not forgotten, nor have I abandoned you. I stand and I watch, and My hand is extended across the land, so keep your eye on the Gaza Strip! For a swift victory comes and the giants flee the land. For a strategy created before time began has been released to the one who knows My heart. For he will govern wisely and a transfer shall come and restore what has been stolen. For the skies shall show their colors soon as a sign for what is to come. For what they said will never happen shall not only take place, but never to be surrendered again. The completion of what is mine soon comes to pass.

5/11/19— In D.C.

Trump, where are you? Come to Me, let me show you the way! For a very unusual occurrence shall come. A great shift to the heart, compassion, understanding, and wisdom. For I am giving him the words to speak, and the ears to hear. A new sound shall come forth from the trumpet that will resonate across the land and bring a swift change to the heart. For they say it cannot be so, but mysteries will be revealed in the midnight hour, and one very young significant person, who is welcomed to the platforms of America shall be a voice that is heard loud and clear. There will be a great surge of power and favor in the Summer months of 2019 as the Leader that is called Netanyahu comes for a visit and breaks bread with the man called Trump. For they shall share and reflect upon the past and how the adversities shaped and formed their future. So let it be so, for one shall comfort the other and raise the arms of weariness to once again be given the strength to carry on. Their friendship is pivotal for peace in the Mideast, and the strategy they are given shall defeat an army that suddenly seeks revenge. So watch, light conquers darkness, and what takes place in the Summer solidifies and grants several more years of favor, and in this you can trust.

Mother's Day 2019

Not only will this year be a milestone for you and your family, but a pivotal occurrence comes by June and sets new things in motion. Watch, for the breakthrough comes and reveals the puzzle piece that has been hiding for sometime now. What is revealed in the big picture brings great comfort that has been asked for, but not forgotten.

5/14/19

Now that there is a calm on the home front, watch how the oil runs down Aaron's beard and brings sudden breakthrough and blessing. The week carries much opportunity as favor has been increased for your storehouse.

5/17/19

The enemy has been scheming all week to bring you down and steal what you have left in your tanks, but joy comes in the morning and you will be refreshed! Strength! Strength! This day does not end without the greatness of God on display in your life!

5/19/19

The enemy is trying to keep you distracted with external sources, and the target is your character and confidence. Stand firm in what you have been given and what you have been created to be. You have come so far and have overcome so much, and nothing is going to change or stop this. The warfare will stop suddenly and rest shall be given. Keep looking forward, for there is a calm that will last for a significant amount of time, and as the week begins, the peace comes.

5/21/19

The windows of favor and grace are available. The storms have come to an end and the manifestation of grace is revealed shortly. During this time, unexpected scenarios will take place for the good on your behalf, and what seemed sluggish will take shape and move swiftly. Watch, for what comes, is revealed with compensation and restitution and does not end without significant purpose. For a new assignment is coming together, just be patient.

5/22/19— In D.C.

What are you saying now, Iran? What are your thoughts? Have you considered the cost? Eyes are upon you! Israel, United States, these two that you will deal with. For they are joined at the hip, and your words have no power, and your threats are meaningless to what has been positioned by hands that you do not see. For one called Trump, and the other called Netanyahu, are placed for such a time as this. You will deal with both, and your arrogance shall be humbled. Watch, in the Summer months ahead, the dust shall settle and your threats shall be removed and your voice of hardship silenced.

5/27/19— In D.C.

Who is this? Why do you think you have power? You have nothing! What has been wronged, shall be made right. This woman, she says she has a plan, she is scheming and working day and night to bring about change in this Nation. She stands close and her position is strong, but this soon comes to an end and the authority changes guard in the months ahead. She thinks she is close to a victory. Will this come to pass? Absolutely not! It shall not be so! The thorn in the side of the Man called Trump, the President, how he deals with the distraction. He shall have yet another victory. For in this season and the season ahead, the one who speaks and defiles authority openly and uses My name without understanding shall be exposed regarding the hidden agendas. So watch, June is pivotal and releases a new mystery in the land called D.C.!

OVER THE COURSE OF THE LAST 24 HOURS, ALL I KEPT HEARING AND SEEING IN THE SPIRIT WAS THIS SIMPLE WORD; **WISDOM.** IN A DREAM, I SAW TEETH THAT HAD FILLINGS BEING REPLACED WITH NEW TEETH.

John Natale

THIS IS A DIRECT SIGN THAT IN THE NEXT SEVERAL DAYS, THE DECISIONS THAT NEED TO BE MADE MUST BE CARRIED OUT WITH WISDOM, AND NOT FACILITATED PREMATURELY OR ADVICE GIVEN BY ANYONE THAT DOES NOT OPERATE IN THE SPIRIT. FOLLOW THESE KEYS AND FRUIT WILL COME FORTH IN ABUNDANCE.

5/31/19

FAITH IS THE SUBSTANCE OF THINGS HOPED FOR, THE EVIDENCE OF THINGS UNSEEN. *Just know that all things are subject to change. I give you the wisdom and the keys to make wise choices to unlock doors filled with opportunity and blessing. June is the month that sets very specific things in motion. You will have the opportunity again, even though it has presented itself before and fear caused you to delay in your decision. It is coming around the mountain one more time for you to choose wisely and reap the blessing of what is positioned for you. Do not be afraid or let the enemy fill you with anxiety. You know what to do! It's time to do it! I am with you, always!*

6/2/19

Delays in your destiny doesn't mean that what you are pursuing isn't achievable, it's an opportunity to prove to the enemy that you have tenacity and diligence. Rise up and be the overcomer that you are! The victory is waiting for you just ahead. Just keep moving, and I will keep giving you the grace that you need.

6/4/19

Watch closely and carefully. For a sudden turn of events takes place again. Where there was worry, there will be peace. Where there was doubt, there will be confidence. There is no need to be concerned for those around

222

you, I have a plan that will bless you and your family. You see, the enemy has had an inside source to your mindset and has influenced you to believe that you should just delay and not pursue any longer. But I have exposed those plans once again! I will bring everything back into focus so you can see what is ahead. Do not worry, for what I have planned for you and your family shall come and you will be overjoyed by what the Summer reveals!

6/6/19— Prophetic Warning

Be careful what you read and hear. Not everything that is released prophetically is from the Throne room of God. Many will come and release words that have already been released and take ownership of them. That is an antichrist spirit. You must be discerning and wise. Many use the platform of others to elevate their ministry. That is a deceptive spirit and eventually will come crashing down. Seek wisdom and choose wisely.

6/7/19

Now is the time to take advantage of the direction I have given you regarding your family's long term future goals. I have caused the enemy to flee and give you the opportunity to explore all that is within reach. Take a breath, get settled, and move forward. It's waiting for you. It's time to get your inheritance!

6/10/19

Stay focused and watch closely. It's your time now! As the week moves forward, some very interesting opportunities shall come and be revealed. What has been asked for shall be presented, what has been presented, shall be completed.

John Natale

6/13/19— Summer 2019

Some significant struggles that have tested your character and motivation have caused you to become quite weary. The enemy's plan was to drain the life out you emotionally. June has been a very difficult month, but I Am with you! It will not end without you getting the victory. There will be some sudden changes that come as July is revealed. You need not worry, for these plans must come to pass, and they will. You will have peace and you will he comforted. Seasons come and seasons go. It's time now to focus on the new chapter that is waiting for you. Watch, for something long awaited comes and fulfills a dream that has been yours that I can only bring to pass. Your strength shall be renewed and your mindset regarding your future shall be filled with confidence and expectation. The change is coming, the change for all.

6/14/19— In D.C.

Do not question what has happened with a voice that was significant and true. For this is part of My plan. They think they have won a victory, for it's not so! Watch who comes and is positioned into place. For a Lion has been prepared and will be established soon enough. For a concrete pillar is being placed into authority by My hands and will bring confusion for those seeking to dishonor and intimidate. This one will not be shaken, but will cause many to tremble and their corrupt motives exposed. For a move has been made on the chess board of life and one important move is about to come. Watch, for yet another is about to step down, one that was not expected at all.

6/18/19

The visions and dreams I have placed inside of you shall all of a sudden become more of a reality than ever before. You have been questioning and doubting because time has slipped by, but a simple sign and confirmation shall come and bring the expectation that has been eluding you. Watch, for this week shall bring what has been missing and reveal some very interesting mysteries to the future that is very bright for you and your family.

6/18/19

Why are you afraid? Have I not walked with you through every valley? Every path? You're not alone! Don't ever think you are. You're never alone! There has been an open door in your life and the enemy has caused quite a bit of chaos, but that all changes now! You will never go back to what once was! Everything changes now! You will never be the same! The shift in your life takes place now! Right now!

6/20/19

As I am waiting on the Lord for your comfort, this is what has been released: *"You will be given a double portion of grace as you have entered into a new season of multiplication. With much given, much is required. Your strength will increase, both physically and spiritually. Expect more than enough. It shall come, it most certainly will!"*

6/23/19

The God of breakthrough is here now! Warfare is ending and victory is at hand. Your peace has come! Watch what is revealed in the next several days!

7/3/19

The atmosphere is moving swiftly, and with the help of angelic activity, watch as the channel is cleared and the warfare silenced. Things will take shape again suddenly and peace will come in like a flood. The enemy is trying to steal your joy and progress, but this will not happen. What does take place is victory for you and your family. The week does not end without breakthrough.

7/6/19— National

Watch as the month called August reveals some very interesting events and scenarios. Significant shifts take place in your life and family. Don't hesitate to activate what is needed to take you to the next level. Pay close attention to President Trump, Benjamin Netanyahu, and Kim Jong-un. For they will be the subject of attention.

7/9/19

I know you have questions, and I know you have concerns why things happen in the way they do. You must remember that I do not pick and choose what to heal, what to touch, and what to restore. My plan is for everyone, and that means you too! I want you to have a greater understanding and revelation of the authority that you have been given. You see, the enemy only has opportunity to come in if you give him a key. Right now, close the door and take away the key that has been used for weakness in your life. Take authority over the very thing that has been a thorn in your side. You can do it, and you will. I Am here to help you overcome and put the enemy under your feet. It's time now! Victory is here!

7/11/19— America

Watch closely, California, Washington D.C., there is another shaking coming. For the ground speaks! From coast to coast, who said they cannot be exposed? Who said they are hidden from the courts of America? For two shall be brought to justice and one shall have a voice no more! Watch closely, for in its time the one who holds the keys to all things shall reveal once again what and who hides behind iron gates!

7/13/19

It's not strange when the unexpected shower of blessing comes and gives you a pleasant surprise. I actually want to do this more often with you! It's time for a new thing to come and give you that wow moment! There's nothing like when a Father surprises His kids! So watch and listen, it comes suddenly!

7/14/19

Don't condemn yourself, don't speak negative words over your life, and don't give up on your future! You're about to see some very interesting changes take place because you are valuable to Me and others. Don't ever forget that. Your Summer is your season of success!

7/16/19

I know that you are struggling and tired. It can be so hard at times to follow Me, this I know. It was never going to be easy, and at times, it doesn't seem it will get any better, but it does, and you get through. At times, you don't even know how you got through, but you did. Today, I want to refresh you, restore your strength, and reinvigorate you with joy that comes in the morning! Watch, for My grace is sufficient for you, and today, you will get that refreshing drink you need. I'm watching you! Don't worry, I'm here and I'm not going anywhere. You got this, and I got you!

7/20/19— In D.C.

For a significant celebration shall take place in the month called October in the spirit realm. Watch and fix your gaze on the House called White. For the sounds of jubilee shall fill the atmosphere. For a great victory takes place and brings yet another defeat to the adversary. For confusion has come again to a camp that only seeks manipulation and destruction. For they know nothing and their plans have already been dismantled. For the one who seeks to replace the President shall suddenly withdraw. For that will be your sign. Watch, for very significant events to take place as November draws near. November will not come to a close until you see the chaos that accompanies a party that does not have the best interest of this Nation called the United States.

And then there comes again the one to make his presence felt again. To encourage and motivate the masses. They will insist that he is the answer to the defeat of this President called Trump. His ability to motivate and tip the scale, for this will not be so! For his time is over and his power is no more. He has been stripped of his ability to empower. For I am dictating the next several years and nothing can stop that. For My voice shall be greater in the people because what will be experienced during these years ahead will cause them to cry out for mercy.

For I will hear their cries just as I did when My people cried out from the bondage of Egypt. Pharaoh also believed he was invincible, but that all changed when a voice came out of the wilderness and declared the freedom that only I can bring to the captives. So as November closes, and December begins, a great freedom shall come and reside in this Nation and to the House called White. You will be satisfied and know that I am always watching, always listening, and always in control.

8/2/19

A sudden burst of peace, favor, and grace comes as a door is opened and the windows of Heaven raised. Watch and see, declares the Lord of Hosts! My presence and power is more than enough! The clouds dissipate and the sun breaks in on a new day! It's time, it is surely time!

8/9/19

I have not set you up to fail or be defeated. As with Joseph, a sudden change came, and the door was opened to walk up and out! It's been hard, at times, more than you can handle, but the light is shining now upon you. Look up and reflect on the signs that were given. They confirmed your next steps and in this, you can trust.

8/16/19

As you contend for your breakthrough, continue to pray and expect the answer to come suddenly. Even though you might not see anything happening now in the natural, things are taking place in the spirit for you! Trust my word and declare this over your situation. THE EFFECTIVE FERVENT PRAYER OF A RIGHTEOUS MAN OR WOMAN AVAILS MUCH. So stand, for the battle belongs to Me says the Lord!

8/20/19

Take charge of your tomorrow by having an increased expectation for today. My plans are not on delay, they are ready and in place to bring you more than enough. Watch your sorrows turn into joy! I am walking now, things are moving. I have seen the tears and what you have sown, you will now reap with joy, the wonderful joy that comes in the morning! I have not forgotten and I have not overlooked you. It was a timing thing, that in time you will understand.

8/27/19

The plan of the enemy is about to be defeated. Not on your time table, but Mine. There is a fading taking place and a reversal in the making. Keep your eyes fixed on Me and watch closely. All I desire from you is faith. Simple faith. Don't give up, it's closer than you think. My disciples learned that when we were in the boat together. They lost sight of the understanding that I was with them in the storm. But they soon found out that defeat was not an option, and victory was moments away. The storm strengthens you, and the times that I am quiet, sharpens you to listen more attentively. BE STRONG AND OF GOOD COURAGE, DO NOT FEAR NOR BE AFRAID OF THEM; FOR THE LORD YOUR GOD, HE IS THE ONE WHO GOES WITH YOU. HE WILL NOT LEAVE YOU NOR FORSAKE YOU.

8/30/19

As with Elijah, you have been hidden in a cave waiting on the voice of reason to come and speak to you. Prepare your heart, says the Lord of Hosts. The sound of My whisper shall penetrate your heart and strengthen you. It is time now to hear My voice. Jezebel shall soon be silenced and the stronghold removed. Help has been released and is positioned for you. Your battle is not for you to fight, but for Me, and in this you can trust. In the time that is ahead, you shall see sweet victory knock on your door.

9/3/19

The season is over and the enemy has lost yet again. The battle was Mine all along, you just didn't believe it at times, but that is okay, I knew you would have your doubts. In My grace, there is understanding and unconditional love. All I wanted you to do was to keep looking at Me, and you have done just that. Now it's time to reap what you have sown. Your tears have been collected, it's time to water the ground and watch the beauty come forth. Well done, Child. You were never going to be defeated anyhow, simply because I would not allow it.

9/9/19

For those of you that are battling fear, He is with you, and He will never leave you. At times, it can be so heavy that you just want to cave in, but today, Holy Spirit has told me to remind you of His wonderful presence that is always there. You will make it! In this you can trust and nothing will stop that. Nothing!

9/12/19

The Lion of Judah roars for you today. I fight your battles, I give you the strength that you need. It's just a matter of time when all the backlash ends and the atmosphere is completely clear. My roar clears the paths and shakes everything that can be shaken. Watch, you will overcome, and you are covered and filled with favor and grace. Be of good courage, I am with you!

9/14/19

I will tell you who I Am. What I control, what I see, what I feel. Who do you say that I Am? What do you really believe? I Am conquerer? Deliverer? Do I hold all the stars in My hands? What is your answer? You long for a touch, that is what you ask for, but I long for an embrace. Such as Jacob received during a night of constant demand of My presence. He received just that, and I want you to know that what he received, you can as well.

Don't settle for the crumbs that fall from the table, I have so much more to give, more than you can fully understand. You have waited, yes you have, and I have seen every second of that wait, but now it's time for your encounter, your hug, your embrace. You see, there are times that what you seek from Me is not what I choose to give you. I want to give more than expected, simply because I have a storehouse of love that is far greater and deeper than the eyes can see when you look to the heavens! What is desired is a relationship and expectation, that what I have is fully available, at any time, and what is prepared is always positioned to be poured out suddenly.

It is time now that all the hindrances be removed, and you receive the strength, love, and authority to not just overcome, but to be restored and refreshed. You have been plagued for way too long, My Child. It is time now to receive your inheritance and be completely reinstated with restoration, justice, and position. So watch, your vindication comes quickly, in this you can trust, and in this, you will see Me move on your behalf, because I Am love, and you are truly loved.

9/19/19

The water has receded and the land is visible once again. The season was rough and tiresome, but you have overcome the storm. Now it's time to look ahead and not back, simply because there is new growth, new opportunity, and a clean slate. I also want you to know this very important detail. What the enemy meant for evil, I have reversed and made all things work out for the good for those that love Me and put their trust in Me. In the midst of what looked like oppression, I was establishing dominion. Watch, victory is here!

9/22/19

Increased awareness and sensitivity is fast approaching, as a sudden change of events come and catch your attention. New oil in your jar and fresh bread in the basket. It's time to sit and rest, you have battled long enough and I have made it known to the enemy. Time to back off and flee!

9/23/19— In D.C.

Oh how the tables have turned, and in the natural realm, you will surely see the manifestations in the upcoming days ahead. For a voice comes to speak, one that is embraced, one that is rejected. But this does not change the plan that has been crafted by My hands. Fearlessness, diligence, and determination is its name! For a very strong word shall come from the mouth of the one that occupies an office in the House called White. A sudden stirring comes, a change of heart, perspective and reception that leads to justice. Eyes shall be opened and ears shall ring with a sound not heard before.

Now listen, His name is Benjamin. He is fearless, and he is honorable. For alliance and friendship sets the stage for glory and freedom. A new standard, a new freedom! Watch, listen, Israel calls, Israel visits, Israel locks arms and defends. United we stand, for a sweeping victory can be heard in the Heavenly realm and what manifests on the earth and in the land called D.C. is your sign for the next several years. Freedom, justice, alignment. Watch, watch, for it comes quickly.

9/26/19

A sudden spring of fresh oil is about to fill your jars. What you thought was empty was nothing but a jar being cleaned and prepared for more than enough. This is a reflection of your current situation, which is about to change dramatically. Don't worry about the spillage, there is plenty from the storehouse of Heaven that is coming your way.

10/6/19

It's time to rest now. You have battled long enough! Take My hand and let me lead you to still waters and cool winds. Don't worry, I have everything under control, and in this you can trust. You will not be disappointed. Your rest is important to Me and critical for you. For the next season that comes brings about great work and great victories. For many changes in this season ahead, and there is much to be excited about. I want you to know that a time has come for you to be refreshed, and refreshed you shall be!

10/8/19

October, November, and December are your months of restoration. What the enemy stole will be restored in many ways. Things are already working on your behalf and will manifest shortly. Just remember, you have been called to rest. Take this time to unwind, get the comfort you need, and linger in My presence. This is very important in this hour. For in the weeks ahead, you will be fascinated by what I am doing and what I am positioning you for! Good news is about to blanket you and bring more comfort than imagined. I have not left you and have not forsaken you. I am here, and I moving mightily in your life right now!

10/18/19

The veil has been torn in two, and the walls created to bring division, broken and never to be established again. What took place many seasons ago are your reminder today that what the enemy tried to keep in place was not only conquered, but dismantled for eternity. A separation has been established for you now that was causing injustice, frustration, and pain. Walls are tumbling down now and freedom is replacing bondage. The sounds of Angels are rejoicing, for a mighty victory has been won! There was a great war taking place in the spirit realm for you and your family, and at times, you did not see the signs of victory that hung in the balance, nor did you hear the Angels singing, "Worthy is the Lamb!" Child, the battle comes to end now, the retreat of the enemy will be seen momentarily, and you will rejoice, cry with tears of joy, and sing a hallelujah, for your God rules and reigns. For I have never stopped working for the good of your life, for you love Me and I love you more than you know! Walk now, you are free!

10/21/19— Dream

In a vision I saw Jesus walking along the banks of a stream. The sound of water rushing, crashing over rocks, the wind rustling the leaves of trees filled with so much color. You could hear His steps, each one taken, each one placed perfectly. He then looked up, He caught the eye of His Father and smiled with a joy that was beyond anything that words could describe. The peace that accompanied this walk was more than anything known to man. It carried hope, love, and the fragrance of Heaven.

He then turned and looked towards me. Eyes filled with fire and burning with an everlasting love. He spoke these words, even through his mouth never opened. "COME TO ME, FOR YOU ARE CARRYING A HEAVY BURDEN AND I AM HERE TO REFRESH YOUR LIFE, AND GIVE YOU THE REST THAT YOU NEED." At that moment, He reached out His hand and pulled mine into His. There was no effort on my part, His love pulled on my heart and filled me with an everlasting peace and hope. The burden that was carried by our own strength was now released into His hands. Today, this very encounter is for you to receive. KNOW THAT IN YOUR PLACE OF HEAVINESS, HE IS THERE TO LIFT YOU UP AND CAUSE YOU TO FEEL LIGHT AGAIN!

10/24/19

Embrace the moment today when a positive shift takes place and causes unexpected breakthrough to arrive. A calm to a storm that gives you exactly what you need.

10/26/19— In D.C.

So what have they learned? What have they seen? Enough is enough. Their foolish ways come undone quickly, and their unrighteousness dealt with. I cannot stand dishonor and what is honorable shall be honored. Watch closely, for one speaks out against the very one who has been the instigator of ridicule. Now you will see the dismantling begin that includes not two, but three individuals that have dishonored this President, and the Nation as well. Truth revealed, and lies exposed once again. They are afraid of November, but it will come with great victory. For the heart of

Pharaoh has been hardened once again, and in its time, the door will be completely open to freedom and blessing. Wickedness is about to be swallowed up and silenced. What was thought to be inevitable by many, will now be revealed that justice prevails once again and nothing can stop destiny and history that will be made in the 2nd term.

10/31/19

Your miracle is coming! You have waited patiently, trusting, watching and at times suffering. I want you to know this, it will end, and that time is coming sooner than you think. I will give you a sign and that will be your hope that the end is near. Focus on Me and all that is good. There are many things that are moving forward for you and your family, things you see, and things you do not see. November is to remember! So never forget that which was done for you. A harvest month that reveals the table of peace!

11/4/19

Increased sensitivity and awareness has been released to help you in a critical time of decision-making. Watch for specific signs to lead you on your path and cause blessing to flow that facilitates promotion and opportunity. Habakkuk 2:2-3

11/9/19— In D.C.

So there is one who speaks against what I have placed in position. A voice that believes she is above the highest authority in the land. But this is not so! She mocks and she schemes, but the plans will never come to fruition, simply because I will not allow it, and I Am God! The dishonor that has been brought on this President only causes him to gain strength and favor. As with Meshach, Shadrach, and Abednego, they were sent in a fire because they would not bow down to a false god. What was seen by a ruler was freedom and not bondage. He could not keep in place what I have ordained. So it is the same in the land called Washington, D.C., for a certain one who speaks loudly believes that this President will be shut down, but it is not so! For he will proceed and November will not end without a very interesting scenario that takes place and sudden turn of events. They will reveal hidden agendas for 2020, but watch closely, for the one that speaks will be the one who listens, and listen she will.

11/11/19

If you could only see what I see! What I see in you! A path that I have carved out just for you. Your family, a beautiful family! Everyone in the palm of My hands. All taken care of, and all loved beyond description. You need not worry about anything. It's all taken care of. You will finish well in this year called 2019. The door is open and you will walk through with rejoicing. Significant signs will be given that you are proceeding properly. Don't be afraid to take faith steps. I will give you what you need. I will send messengers your way to help and guide you. You are not alone, and in this you can put your trust in Me. It might look too big, or not achievable, but what is needed to position you has already been released by My words. To facilitate My plan in this season for you and your family.

11/14/19

In your weakness, I am strong! In your doubt, I give you My confidence. In your pain, I give you healing. I want you to know this, I Am here to give you exactly what you need today. Let Me fill you up today and rejuvenate your spirit. As I have said before, signs will be given to show I Am with you and taking care of matters that are at hand. These days are significant and ordained. Your season is better than you think, and only will get better as the month draws to a close. I have a plan that will come to fruition, just believe and receive!

John Natale

11/19/19

Looking back at your situation, you might not of thought I was in it, nor was I doing anything to help you overcome, but I was there all the time, and a new beginning has begun. I told you that you would finish well in 2019, and it will be so! 2020 is a completing year. You will find out soon enough! Watch, receive!

11/20/19

Resist the enemy and he will flee. Stand on My word and believe, don't allow the enemy to disrupt your thinking. Stay focused, stay strong, and be confident. Overcoming is not an option, it's the only answer. And you will overcome!

11/22/19

Unusual circumstances are coming your way with unexpected timelines. These surprises are part of the plan in this season that will help you understand that I Am watching and helping you in this hour.

11/26/19

I Am renewing your mind and restoring your confidence. Your ability to overcome your mountains shall not be as hard as it once was, simply because your sight is being sharpened to see how I see, and that is good news. The enemy likes to play games with you during your time of rest, but I have rebuked him in this hour, and peace that surpasses all understanding has been activated once again. Watch and see what unfolds in the days ahead!

12/1/19

Joseph reached a pivotal point in his destiny as he was appointed second in command of Egypt. Even though his burden of pain was not restored, he still continued to stay focused and put his trust in Me. Then a suddenly came, and the scenario started to shift for his good. Finally coming to a full restoration that changed everything. Today, I want you to have the confidence knowing that in your situation, many things are working behind the scenes. You just don't see them, but they are coming together very nicely, and you will see it come to fruition shortly.

12/5/19— In D.C.

Learning to discern the times and understanding the condition of the present doesn't come from natural means. Pay close attention to My leading and watch very closely. For a radical shift is coming before the year ends, and in this you can trust. Keep your eye on Washington, D.C. and those that govern wisely and foolishly. For an inward dismantling is occurring and chaos is visible. My name shall not be mocked and used for validation as one chooses to do so. Watch, again I say watch, for the stage is set, and one very familiar voice will call out another and address this dishonoring. I will not be mocked, for I am Justice, and I Am Honor!

12/16/19

A crossroad is approaching that will bring a great joy, and place you on a path to open heavens. It has been part of the plan for a long time. Don't worry about what direction you will take. Both choices have been positioned with favor and grace.

12/18/19— In D.C.

There will be justice and favor granted that will be of epic proportions. The mystery is simple. The more you dishonor authority, the ramifications of injustice become monumental. Watch, the curtain closes soon and the ground rumbles. History to be made once again, this time, on a much higher scale that will be remembered for years to come.

12/23/19

Sometimes delays are not so bad! They work on your behalf when the enemy is trying to speed up things that will only cause chaos and destruction. Trust Me now in this time of perseverance, it will all work out soon enough, and in this you can trust.

12/31/19— 2020

I am walking toward you! Step by step, each moment passing by as the wind gently passes through the cool of the grass. I can see you, waiting, watching for the hidden mystery that you feel has been avoiding you for some time. That man sat at a pool waiting for his miracle. He even looked in My eyes and said he was awaiting for someone else to help facilitate his breakthrough, not knowing that he was staring at the King of the universe. Oh how time went by for him, his blind eyes that could not see, and his dependency on others to fix his problems.

I have good news though. In this year that is called 2020, it's time for eyes to open in ways that have never seen. Clarity, revelation, and understanding. I want you to know that I have been right alongside of you at every moment of your life. So many years have come and gone, does this mean that My plans are not still active in your life? Of course not! They are working every moment, every second of your life. It's time now, it's your time now! Look at your situation, and look directly into My eyes.

The mat gets picked up now and rolled up! It's time to move on and move forward. You have been positioned in the same spot long enough. No need to stress anymore! I have given the command! Rise and walk! Some of you, it will be your healing, some, their finances, and others, their homes. Repositioned for strategic plans that only I can put together. Now, the only thing you need to do is this, fix your gaze on Me, and as you focus on My eyes you will be comforted to know that the future is at hand. It always has been! It has never been disrupted, simply because I have hold of it, and nothing can take that away! Now go! Don't look back, and spread your wings. It's time to fly!

Part Eight
Prophetic Words — 2020

1/6/20

My presence is with you. My comfort, all around you. Watch, it comes quickly! For specific signs to be given, they will come suddenly and they will lead the way to very special new beginnings. Don't worry, and don't be concerned in natural things that try to steal your hope. It's your time, your family's time!

1/9/20

What was experienced in the past is now being used to bring an overflow in the present. Your struggles, tears, and frustrations did not hinder the future, it set you up for one of the greatest seasons of your life. January is a very serious month of restoration and multiplication.

1/13/20

Many seek My words to have an understanding of present situations and future scenarios, but there are many times that I speak words just to fill your heart with peace, love, and joy. To Me, it's most important that you understand how special, wonderful, and amazing you truly are! Today, I will show you just how I see you, and how nothing in this world compares to the love between a Heavenly Father and His Child! You are wonderfully and fearfully made, and nothing can change that!

1/16/20

Many will choose to remember you and many will choose not to. In this world there will be trouble, but rejoice, for I have overcome the world. Keep being who you are, what I created you to be, and the mark that you leave, will be the legacy that they all eventually receive.

1/17/20

With a storm of anxiety coming in that is trying to steal your joy, watch what takes place before the weekend comes to an end. Sudden blessings and confirmation will be brought to your attention and calm the waves raging around you.

1/20/20

Things are all subject to change. Never forget this, never doubt this. I am connecting you in this season to the right people, the right stream. You have been searching, seeking, and now, as the sun rises and reaches its peak, fresh sight has come to bring new revelation, that there is hope, there is help! Watch, for the new beginning that you have sought after has come. Confirmation will bring the confidence you need to set you up strategically in the new season that you and your family are in.

1/24/20

The scripture says in My word, CALL UNTO ME AND I WILL SHOW YOU GREAT AND UNSEARCHABLE THINGS THAT YOU DO NOT KNOW. *This was spoken for a reason, not to be taken lightly. You must remember that My word does not come back void. I do not lie! You have been given an opportunity and an ability to access resources far greater than you can imagine. The mind of Christ. What I carry is yours! Many do not pursue this, nor do they even believe. Today, allow Me to show you what truly is inside of you. It's the most wonderful heavenly boundary that has no limits. Just get your spiritual eyes and ears on the One who controls everything, and who is waiting to release good news to you and your family. Just believe, truly believe!*

John Natale

1/26/20

Increased favor, increased opportunity and joy beyond your wildest expectations! You will be loved and honored more than words can describe. In a season that has passed, for many, it represented pain and suffering. But you will be rewarded with a grace that will literally cause you to be speechless. Watch, for what comes blows in like the wind and will carry you to greater heights, and the most refreshing air that has been distant for some time.

1/27/20— In D.C.

Keep your eye on the one called Trump. For a sound comes again, and again I say, keep your eye on him. For he watches and he is protected. They will speak what they choose to say, and they will try to accomplish what is not achievable. For in a time, and time again, you shall hear his voice resonate throughout the Nation that is called United States, and it shall echo across the waters and bring justice to the oppressed. For the veil that has been created to bring division to a Nation is about to be torn to shreds, and freedom will once again reign over the people that are united and stand as one Nation.

How can this be? How is he not movable? Who is guarding him? These are the questions to the mysteries that will be answered soon enough from the highest courts that rule the atmosphere. You shall see the signs, the water, the wind, the shaking. Fear not, for what comes is needed and will be a source of hope and comfort for those that have eyes to see and ears to hear. For an Angel of justice comes to strike the land and bring unity, harmony, and peace to many that have raised their voice, and to the many that have been silent.

The season soon comes to an end, and it already has shown its colors and hidden clues. But watch and wait, for as the Spring comes closer and the ground prepares for growth and springs forth life, you will see the display and demonstration of power and honor that will be granted to him with a double portion that will last until I say it is complete.

1/31/20

The devil is a liar, and the roadblock in front of you is about to be destroyed! Don't be discouraged. It will end very well for you and your family in the moments ahead!

2/1/20— In D.C.

Very serious plans being established in 2020 between these two friends. It will literally shake the Middle East to the core. Keep your eye on the month called June.

2/5/20— In D.C.

For are you not surprised? Why did you think otherwise? Have I not told you that this man called Trump is positioned and placed by My hands? For it is so! Now I tell you this. For there was one called Mephibosheth, he waited outside the gate dishonored, but he never gave in. He knew is name, his lineage, and his identity. Even though honor was not present, in My eyes, honor never left him. Then suddenly a time came, a voice spoke, and he was positioned at a table in the presence of his enemies. A seat that a king restored and returned back to its rightful place.

A place of honor, never to be disrupted again. So this man called Trump shall be now given a double portion of honor in the presence of his enemies, and it shall last for years to come! Woe to those that have come against what I have positioned for such a time as this. For he will move swiftly and you will see very significant changes come in the land called Washington, D.C.

John Natale

For the Prophets spoke and gave clues to the mysteries. Some listened, some did not. They revealed what would not take place, and what would come. Open your eyes and your ears, for more shall come and give insight to the next several years. Discern and listen. Keep watch, for where they sought justice, justice shall come, but it will expose a greater evil that was hiding behind a veil. But this veil is torn now, and the heart has already been exposed. For My word says, your sin will find you out, and out of the mouth, the heart speaks. For one has spoken long enough and tried to move the masses, but natural means have no power over spiritual authority. Watch, for in its time, one enters again, and two exit.

2/7/20

The enemy loves to bring back to attention the past. It's pain, history, and struggles. Today is a reminder in the spirit realm, many things are happening for you and your family! Watch as the manifestations take place over the next several days. The enemy is a liar, what you experienced and what you were exposed to, was not truth, was not part of your destiny. It was part of a plan to destroy the rebuilding of family, future, and promised blessing. I have prayed for you, guided you, comforted you. Through many storms, I was with you, always with you. You have come so far, and through My grace, My love, you have conquered the enemy! Rejoice, for your reward is full of wonderful surprises, and I love to surprise My kids!

2/10/20

Yes, worthy of it all. I Am worthy! For such a price paid for you, but there is one thing you must know, you must understand. You are worthy! You are most worthy! For I came for you! For some of you today, you are feeling not significant, not confident, and doubting your decisions. Not to worry! For a sign shall be given in the hours ahead that will show you that the path you are on is correct. Favor, grace, and peace that surpasses all understanding. So today, I will give your mind peace and comfort. You are not alone, I am with you in this journey!

2/15/20— In D.C.

Keep your eyes on her! For she is reflecting on everything in her past and questioning her own thinking. There is a stirring that is taking place! For what was wounded a time ago shall be healed in the time present. Something unique is about to come and bring some significant surprises in the land called D.C. They say, "Who can this be? How can it be?"

For this man called Trump prays for her, and his prayers have reached My ears. For My word goes forth like an arrow and separates the darkness. Light comes to bring clarity and understanding. For this one, this significant one has exposed the past from the sounds of her heart, but I have not forgotten her. She calls for help, and help she will be given.

2/16/20

Don't underestimate your decision making. You made the right choice, and the benefits from that choice are now at hand. Special confirmations are on the way to bring the peace that you need.

2/17/20

THIS CAME TO ME AS A VOICE THIS AFTERNOON AS I WAS WAITING ON HOLY SPIRIT. THE PEACE THAT SURPASSES ALL UNDERSTANDING AND THE JOY THAT I FELT THAT HELP WAS HERE TO BRING YOU OUT OF THE FIRE! GOD IS GOOD! IT'S GONNA BE ALL RIGHT FRIEND! HE'S GOT YOU! READ HIS WORD AND TAKE COMFORT! HE IS WITH YOU!

"Don't be afraid, I've redeemed you. I've called your name. You're mine. When you're in over your head, I'll be there with you. When you're in rough waters, you will not go down. When you're between a rock and a hard place, it won't be a dead end— Because I am GOD, your personal God, The Holy one of Israel." Isaiah 41:1-3

2/19/20

A controlling spirit has made its way into the camp. Stay alert, use wisdom in your decisions and reject what is not from Me. In the moments ahead, complete freedom will come and the enemy will be exposed.

2/20/20

As the gold is dipped into the fire and purified, what comes out has more value and worth. Today, your trials have not just tested you, but have presented you to be honorable and significant in the sight of your enemies. They will look to you as a source of hope, reconciliation, and reinstatement.

2/24/20

I am with you right now! In that place where you are, there I Am. You have cried out to Me, you have sought out others to help you. Even though they were not able to meet your need, don't be discouraged, I Am here. There are times that I use others to help facilitate the breakthrough, the healing, the comfort, but this time, it's all Me. Just Me. You and Me, that's all that is needed at this time.

You will be comforted, you will be made whole, and this is My promise. I will hold your hand in this time of transition, and I will guide you on this path. So let go of what you hold onto, and trust in Me, for the walk you take with Me has begun, and the finish line is just ahead.

2/29/20— In D.C.

Keep your eyes on the one who smiles and thinks she is untouchable. For she is scheming once again. This time, she has brought reinforcements. For she thinks she has won a battle, for this is not so! She is seeking a position, no matter the cost, no matter the price. For injustice she seeks, but what she will find, is justice that knocks on her door. For I will expose the wickedness once again, and bring light to what the plan was created for, and what was intended to carry out.

For she is bitter, her heart has been hardened once again, and she prowls secretly to bring down this man called Trump. For it not so! He will continue his tenure, because I need him there, to carry out My plans for this nation. Watch, behold, it comes like a flood and sweeps across a nation and travels into the Middle East. Israel, the U.S. — unstoppable, epic proportions. Intense friendship, historic accomplishments, and a peace that surpasses all understanding. For the plan shall crumble before it comes to fruition, and I will reveal the source that carries weight in D.C. that sits silently and watches.

Believing that no one notices, but I notice, and I will reveal. They are trembling, they are stirring, simply because the inevitable is coming that will change the course of history once again. So now, the enemy stirs up a plan and calls it Coronavirus. To deceive, to mock, to discredit once again. Who is in control? For it shall not take root in this nation called the United States. For fear is trying to establish itself among the people, but I will not let it be so. For in the days ahead, you will see the signs in the skies above to reveal the mystery that My mighty right hand is raised high!

For there will be no chaos, no destruction, for My protection is upon this land. For the people have prayed, for they have closed the door to the enemy. They have chosen to not live in fear, but to put their trust in Me. In this, you can trust. The enemy only has access where authority is given. My church has sacrificed, worshiped, cried out, and I have heard their cry. I am the God that carries all things in the palm of My hands, who is to test that? Who is to question it? This nation has persevered, sought after Me, and prays day and night, night and day!

For I will have the last say regarding this virus that has no power, no authority. Everything that has a name bows to Me, submits to Me. So watch, behold, the heavens will reveal the signs that prayer has been heard, and prayer has been answered. I say again, the plans once again to dishonor authority are crushed and dismantled, to never be heard of again.

3/7/20

Great strides of accomplishment and success are beginning to reveal its colors. What you thought was impossible is now preparing to be on display for you and your family. Behind the scenes, in the spirit realm, many great things are in position to come to you and your family. In time, they are released according to My plans. In this way, they have the full benefit of not just blessing you, but many around you.

You will see soon enough, as the nearing of the season called Spring comes, that there is a quickening that will take place. Once started, layers of oppression, pain, and years stolen by the enemy will be removed and replaced with peace, joy, and a brand new perspective on the beautiful life I have for you. A new chapter of life is coming that will cause unprecedented favor and love that you have so needed. So watch, it comes soon, and receive. The time to rejoice has come!

3/9/20

Hearing this sound, and releasing the word that has come forth. The breath of God has exhaled and caused a disturbance in the atmosphere. The place where the enemy has struck a mighty blow of fear will all of a sudden be concentrated, and filled with confidence, safety, peace and comfort to those that seek the protection and guidance of the one who holds the stars in His hands. No weapon formed against you will prosper! You are in a good season, nothing will change that!

3/11/20

There are spiritual puzzle pieces being placed in position right now. Stay clear-minded, focused, and rely on God. Do everything that is required of you in this season. You are being positioned for promotion and special opportunities. There is more favor upon you and around you than you can actually see. Trust God, everything is about to come to fruition and reveal the new thing of God in your life.

3/14/20

I prophesy over you now, that a double portion of grace, peace, and favor will be released in epic proportions over you and your family. In the midst of the storm that is presently testing your faith, close the door to fear, worry, and anxiety, and the peace that surpasses all understanding will give you everything you need. Your faith and the glory that comes off of you will be exactly what the unbeliever needs! Faith, power, and love! Now go and be that light! They are waiting for you!

3/19/20— In D.C.

Is there not an importance on the things that I say are true and just? You have been given signs and words. Many say that chaos will continue and perilous times will remain. For this is not so! For in its time, those times will come, but not yet! There are many things that must come to pass before these scenarios come and remain. This President has, and will continue to move forward and address everything and anything that comes on his watch. For he is needed. For in the likes of Joseph, when he ruled over Egypt as a source of hope and trust, this too is happening now in this nation. He will be a Joseph in a dark time, and he will bring comfort and support, and he will listen to My leading.

Pharaoh put complete trust in Joseph simply because he knew that the God of Joseph was higher than any name, more powerful than the forces of Egypt. He made a decree for the people to go to this man and find help that they needed. In that time, famine was no match to the power, love, and grace of the King of kings. You will see in the days ahead, what was not expected will arrive and reveal the glory of My power. Watch, for many will see this man called Trump make a sound, and a sound again! For He is praying, for he is listening. For I am listening, and I am moving! April comes and goes, but wait for it, it comes, it reveals, it declares. Watch the skies, feel the winds, watch the birds of the air! For rejoicing comes in the air first, then to the people. Pray, declare, rise up and believe! I Am with you.

3/21/20

The churches will open up once again! They will come back at the correct time, the pivotal moment. This time, with a power and demonstration of glory not seen for many seasons that have gone by. For this was not to be looked down upon, for I have seen and heard everything that was before anything was revealed. Who has the last say? Who holds the future in His hands? You must not fill yourself with fear any longer.

I Am your source, I Am your strength! As was spoken once before, look to the skies, for they give the signs that something is happening. Look to April, for it is a very critical month for this nation. Many will watch, many will seek! Keep your eyes on the ones that sing above, for they hold mysteries, for they hold answers. As the olive branch was brought back in a day of trouble, it revealed a sign that all was not lost, and hope abounds! So watch, our friends have begun singing their new song. They have been directed by Me to guide. Pay close attention.

3/28/20

You must keep your eye on the day called 30. March comes and it goes, but it does not end without signs that give clues to glory. Then comes the month called April. What takes place has been required to move swiftly.

Many things are stirring in the atmosphere and the spirit realm. The signs will be from the ones who sing gently and bring a new song. Be sensitive and stay focused on the leading of the Spirit. For a battle takes place, for a war shall be won.

4/3/20— In D.C.

The sounds by day, the sounds at night! For there is a song being sung by the ones who hold clues. For this is no strange thing, for it has been happening for generations and generations. One must come to understand the mysteries that hang in the balance, and the ones that have been revealed. Many watch, they wait, and they do not discern the times. Many speak foolish things, and they mislead the many, but in its time, the nations will come to understand that what is about to be revealed, shall be sovereign.

It can only be sovereign, and sovereign it shall be! Keep praying for your President, for he is weary. Many are speaking behind closed doors about defeat. They plan secretly, watching, preparing, sheep in wolves clothing. They do not have eyes to see, or ears to hear. Their hearts are cold, they wander as if in a wasteland looking to devour anything that is good. What they seek, they shall not find, and what they desire, shall not come to pass. I have sent reinforcements of angelic beings to guard the spirit realm and protect the natural realm. For this man that is called Trump, he shall be heard most powerfully before your month called April is complete.

He is ridiculed, discredited again, but he is listening to the still, small voice, and that is what keeps him going. In a time that is most critical for the healing of nations, and a very important nation called the United States, one must come to accept that it is a time where all must focus on life presently, the common good of mankind. What I Am about to do will do just that. This President was allowed to be placed in office by Me and only Me, simply because he would humble himself and allow Me to move on the people. Being used to bring reality of life and the value of existence. A comfort that no man can give, only the help that I can bring. Being positioned so My glory can be revealed in a greater way! Many are crying out to Me from all over the world. I have heard their cries. It is not I that has brought this hardship to the nations, but it will be My power that removes it. Signs given, songs sung. Keep your hearts pure, your minds clear. For in the suddenly of time, I shall exhale and the air shall be pure once again!

4/10/20

What can be seen? What will be heard? I want you to keep watch and be aware of your surroundings. Many have spoken about this month called April. Many have shared their thoughts, their theories, and their concerns. Will they put their trust in Me? Some do, some don't, but that doesn't change anything. There is a stream flowing that brings life to all that it touches. The water, the wind, the skies, and the birds above have already been spoken to by My voice, and they have been prepared to show all that is necessary in this month.

Everything that has been declared regarding generations past are significant and true, but that was for a time long ago. What was done then carried no grace, but I Am the Author of grace. What comes in this month shows an initiative for all people to understand and partake of My grace. Is this month significant? Is it a part of a plan that reveals the greater glory? Yes! It surely does! But most importantly, what I Am doing is not just healing a land, but opening up the eyes of the ones that call me Lord. For there is too much doubt, uncertainty, and the inability to truly hear My voice. I have given grace and mercy, and now the time has come to open up your eyes and ears truly to Me, and that comes by humbling yourself.

You must stop trying to figure this all out. This you cannot, nor will I allow it. My thoughts are not yours, My plans are very different than yours. What is the same, is the desire and the passion for all to understand the mystery of love, and the price I paid was severe. Take this time to share that love from a healed heart. Let them be jealous for that very thing, and in its time, you will see a great awakening unfold before your very eyes.

4/17/20

Set your sights on the water's edge. Remember the time when you looked out upon the waters and watched the sun begin to set. For in its time, the season will come, the sun shall be high above, and the heat of summer will give you much comfort. Now listen to these words, for the heat shall surely come, more than expected. It will be your sign that I Am purifying the atmosphere and setting the stage for greater glory during the fall season.

4/20/20

In the light of day, a source of hope, strength, and peace comes to fill you with the comfort that is needed. Many have responded well to the current situation at hand. You have overcome, remained diligent, and considered the cost of isolation. It has brought you to a new level of understanding, compassion, and thankfulness. In the new season ahead, which is sooner than you know, you will find even a greater peace. Collect your jars, for the windows of Heaven shall open, and oil shall come and bring overflow to what was once considered empty.

4/24/20— America

The tactics of fear will not interfere with the plans that are in place for this nation called America. Do not be moved by words that promote chaos, doubt, and worry. I have the last say, and nothing can change that. Where there was mercy, now there will be judgement. I will once again uncover and reveal hidden agendas and expose darkness. The glory of the Lord will not be hindered. Keep your eyes on the northeast, for I am watching closely. For what is hidden shall be visible, and what is spoken shall be heard. Sudden changes come, for they surely shall come. For a new sound is coming to this region, it shall replace an old sound. Look to the north, for it comes in the months ahead. It shall challenge, and it shall prevail. It shall cause a stirring and bring a fresh wind of comfort to the masses. Keep watch, listen closely, the day comes quickly, and a new era begins.

4/26/20— America

Are you ready for a landslide of epic proportions? Going against a sound that brought down the walls of Jericho is not in your best interest. What was dishonored, was not just about a man, but about I Am. The proud will be ashamed, the arrogant will be humbled, and the glory of the Lord will remain. Those that rose up against what I have positioned in place will not be a voice of influence as they once were. For a great, great change is coming to this nation. Healing, deliverance, and an increased realm of freedom will be present. For many are crying out for justice, and justice they shall see.

5/4/20— In D.C. & S. Korea

The land that's called South Korea! Not many look to her as a source of strength. Not many consider her a power that can defend herself. But this is not so! For there is scheming on the borders of North Korea and South Korea. For one who planned has delegated authority to another to plan secretly, under the radar, but I say it is foolishness in My sight. For I Am watching every move. I will expose every deceptive, deceiving plan against what My plans are for the next several years. Keep your eyes on the summer months. For a very strong defense shall come and cause a counter to an injustice.

Where one considered, and another prepared, two shall rise up and act quickly and expose wickedness. For in the summer months, a great freedom shall come to the nation of the South. Now watch, for in the days ahead, a stronger relationship forms with South Korea and the President that is called Trump. There is communication that fills the atmosphere with the sounds of righteousness and justice. There will be no harm, there will be no hardship.

Another level of alignment is forming, and what is formed between the two, cannot, and will not be broken. This special land that has been given great grace to overcome, shall be a mighty voice of reason. She will be honored and given a double portion of justice. In her delight, she will be rewarded, and in the depths of passion of the people, she will govern wisely. Never to be mocked, ridiculed, or dishonored any longer. For her time is now. The leaders of the two nations called United States and South Korea shall lock arms. In this you can trust, and in this, there will be great comfort.

5/5/20

What is hanging in the balance shall be released suddenly. Prepare for a harvest of opportunity and outpouring! Where there was silence, there will be a new sound. Where there was a calm, there shall be a mighty river of overflow. May is your month of significance. It shall go down as one to remember! Watch closely, the sound has been ordered to be heard.

5/9/20

Who has the last say? Who controls the wind, the stars, and the skies? There are many that try to use their power to control and manipulate, but this will not accomplish the agendas that they seek. Watch, for in the summer, the voices shall be heard no longer. Stay strong, keep watch, for I am observing everything, and in its time. Freedom will come when I say it's to come.

John Natale

5/15/20

As the winds swirl, and the sun gives off its heat, pay close attention to what is revealed in the skies. For again, as with so many times before, My sovereignty will once again show who is in control of the atmosphere. Plans and hidden agendas will not be allowed to come to fruition. If only they would concede to the very fact that the prophets have spoken the truth. For the truth will set you free. Watch, for the sound comes forth and sheds much light to questions that need to be answered, and surely will be answered.

5/22/20— In America

There is no change with the birds of the air, no hindrance to their being. Things are moving, hearts are groaning, sounds can be heard. I'm watching everything, listening to all things. What is happening in this nation is not destruction, for this was desired from many. Hoping that people would give up hope, give up passion. But this is not so! For what comes forth from the people is hunger in its highest form. For what they seek, they shall find! For what they pursue, they will establish.

You seek a sign, a sign shall be given. It will confirm what has been spoken already. That I Am, and in this, you can trust. But you must watch closely. For as the health of the atmosphere strengthens, leaders of this great nation that did not trust in Me, their power will weaken suddenly. For they have already chosen their path, and their path was not My will. Pray, stay sensitive to Me and all will be well.

5/24/20— In D.C.

There's a Judas in Washington, in the land called D.C. He will be exposed soon enough. For I will expose him, and his laughter will be turned to sorrow. You cannot hide from the spiritual authority that is present. For the mysteries are spoken to the prophets. For they have been granted favor, knowledge, and insight.

5/29/20

Get ready for another level of breakthrough this weekend. What was closed, shall open, and what opens, brings much joy to your situation. It was all about timing. As with seedtime and harvest, what you have sacrificed and poured out is now coming back to you in overflow measures.

6/5/20— In D.C.

Keep your eyes open and your ears attentive to the sound that appears in the sky! For the atmosphere is rumbling and the exposure comes soon, and the storm follows. For there is a great war going on presently in the spirit realm. For the ramifications of wickedness shall not be tolerated. Righteousness shall overcome darkness and in this you can trust. Grace shall be given to those who seek Me. You will be given a sign, and another sign shall follow these revealings of darkness. For the enemy has been given authority simply because a door is open. This door will shut soon enough and a surge of peace shall come, but not until divine order is restored.

6/10/20— In America

Wickedness comes and seeks to devour and destroy, but what it does not accomplish is a very simple absolute. I Am that I Am! All around you is pain, anger, and uncertainty. But watch, as the Summer continues, something not expected will come forth and a calm will come to land called the United States. A restoration of hearts, friendships, and family. A new beginning, a new chapter, a new day. I can bring good from what evil tried to destroy. I can change all things, and I shall do this because love is the greatest tool that is used to heal a heart.

All around, eyes will open, ears will open to the sound of a voice that brings comfort and hope. They will say it will take years to restore what was damaged, but I say, this will not be so! For something has already started. Many will have dreams in the night, and many will have visions by day. They will come to understand the mystery of love and grace. They will choose life, and they will choose Me. So as you pray for this nation, for the people of this land, pray with an expectant heart and watch what unfolds. What comes suddenly is filled with a sovereign presence of My very being.

6/13/20— In America

This I say to you, as with the Prophet Elijah. He was brought to a cave to understand a mystery. There was much trouble in the land, a great spirit of Jezebel was operating to remove truth and fill the atmosphere with wickedness and delusion. For it shall not be so! For there shall be a sign in the air and on the ground, just like Elijah experienced on the mountaintop. My power and presence revealed My authority. Now listen, now watch, for as a Prophet was instructed to anoint three new individuals to carry on the mandate of the Kingdom, so it will be so in the land called the United States.

There was grace for those who would not succumb to wickedness, but where there is wickedness, these new voices will be used to remove the influence of disunity in this land. For My will is faith, hope, and love, and it will be carried out. In the days ahead, watch, for strong decisions will be made that will suddenly appear and change everything. Silence will come and peace will replace anger. This spirit of Jezebel has had much influence in this nation to control, manipulate, and dishonor true authority. It brings a strong deceptive spirit that misleads, misguides, and causes eyes and ears to be blind.

Now, just as Elijah heard the sound, this nation will hear a sound again, but it will be nothing that has been heard before. It has no history, and nothing familiar to mankind. It is a new sound. For it comes from My hands, My voice. So the time has come, as with Elijah, he was directed to return to a land and start the process of justice. I say now, the process has started, and the placement of these new voices shall come.

6/19/20— In America

The plans of the enemy to divide and destroy this nation shall not, and will not come to pass. The hearts of men and women alike are crying out for justice. Justice they shall see. As everything is watched by Me, many ask, "When is help coming? Why is there so much suffering?" Many hearts in significant places of authority have become cold and calloused. They rule like a pharaoh, not pursuing the camaraderie of all people. They seek their own agendas with plans that are hidden behind closed doors.

But this shall not come to pass, for I have chosen one particular voice that shall be a voice of reason. She will activate hidden mysteries that will displace the unrighteousness and expose the wicked ones. A platform has been given, and many will try to discredit and dishonor her voice, but this will not come to pass. For her sound comes from My heart, and nothing can stop this authority. Keep your eyes clear, your ears attentive to the sound that comes forth. For in the Summer months, great progress will be made and what was lost, shall be restored.

6/25/20— In America

The woman raised up as an Esther will have a sudden meeting with the President. Together, they will strategize and plan. Keep watch, for her platform grows each day. Many are threatened by her, and they plan and speak against her, but this only makes her stronger. Her voice is like thunder and her eyes like lightning. For she has been anointed for such a time as this.

John Natale

7/1/20— July 2020

As you look back at the status of the year called 2020, you see all types of scenarios that include laughter, tears, pain and frustration. An atmosphere filled with uncertainty, so it seems to the ones who see with natural eyes. But the question is, what do you see? Are you confident in Me? Does the drama that is presently active in this nation concern you? I have some good news for you! July, July! You have come!

From the distance, from the stars, from the palm of My hand. A mystery to be revealed. It will be one that is remembered for time and time again. For you shall see My glory revealed, and this will establish a great opportunity to present itself to you and your family. Some have felt that their heart has been ripped out from inside, but this is not so. For the enemy is working constantly to convince you that you have lost precious time, precious moments, but this is not truth. Time has come and gone, and seasons have changed, but you have not!

My plan is going according to My will, and in this, you can trust. What comes in this month, brings joy, unspeakable joy to you and to your situation. Change that you seek, shall come. Shifting that you desire, shall take place. The opportunity that has been prepared for you in advance, shall come forth! Watch, for the waiting will end, and the comfort and advancement shall suddenly be activated.

7/7/2020— For California

Your voice has been heard, your songs sung in the night, but you have distanced yourself from Me. You walk a path that does not bring Me joy. Where is your heart, California? Where has it gone? Many cry for justice, many cry for help, but their voice goes unheard. The desperate ones seeking peace, seeking unity in the way only I can bring. I tell you this, even the rocks cry out for My presence to fill the land. There will be a calm, there will be a great reformation as one steps in and sits in the highest seat of authority. For this will not happen until the ground rumbles and shows its signs.

For I am watching, preparing, and positioning the land called California to be awakened to true freedom. It shall be of historic proportions. So let it be so! For one man shall take a stand and be a voice preparing the way for another. For he is well-versed, well-spoken, and even respected by both sides. For he shall rise up and release a sound that shall grab the attention of the faces that rule and reign in Hollywood. For he is already positioned to do such a thing, and when he comes forth, watch, for a new found freedom comes to life and seasons of wickedness come to an end.

7/9/20

In the midst of darkness, light still prevails. In the midst of a storm, a calm always comes. Prepare yourself as the peace that surpasses all understanding surrounds you in this very significant month. For voices are coming forth to challenge wickedness. What you have been seeing and watching, this will all of a sudden change. Light shall come in the Summer, it shall surely come! There is a holy anger rising up, for the people are being dishonored, devalued, and in this deception, I shall have the last say. For they cry inwardly and outwardly for help, and help shall come and shape this nation once again! In this, you can trust!

7/15/20— In America

The great spirit of deception and delusion that is causing a significant disturbance in this nation shall be dealt with in the coming days. The people shall see a quick justice come forth and I shall silence the voices of those that came to divide and bring disunity. For they still believe that their agendas shall come to pass, but they have not been given authority to accomplish this. For in its time, they shall govern, but not in this season, or a season ahead. For My plans that are in place now, continue, until I say they are complete.

7/24/20

There are at times, negative circumstances, that seem like they can be endless and wearisome, can all of a sudden change and produce positive results. Even in the midst of great turbulence, things are happening behind the scenes that will bear fruit that remains. Present scenarios in this Nation, with the Government, and most of all, with your life, are all subject to change, if you believe! I Am working out mighty things that will bring restoration, hope, justice, and peace.

What transpires before Summer's end, is not to be taken lightly. For it shall be good, and all shall see just how significant it is when you pray, you seek, and you put a demand on Me! Just like the woman pressed through the crowd to get to Me. She never gave up, she never lost hope. What she did find was healing, grace and peace for her circumstance. That too, is available right now, for every heart that is in need of My touch. So reach out your hand and take mine. It's here right now!

7/26/20

Overcoming adversity does not have to be difficult or strenuous. With My grace that is sufficient for you, all things are achievable, if you believe, and you contend for your breakthrough. Your month called July soon comes to an end, but will not finish until the plans that are in place according to My will come to fruition. Stay strong and stay alert! I Am with you!

7/31/20— In D.C.

In a vision, I saw a wave, much greater than ever seen. Turbulent, powerful and mighty. Yet it had a gentleness to it that was accompanied by peace. I could see it coming, and with

EACH MOMENT THAT PASSED, IT GAINED STRENGTH FROM THE PRAYERS OF MANY PEOPLE THAT HAVE CRIED OUT FOR JUSTICE, AND THOSE THAT HAVE SACRIFICED EVERYTHING FOR THE SAKE OF THE CALL FOR FREEDOM.

To those that have no eyes to see, or ears to hear, the wave comes unexpectedly, and it brings significant ramifications to the injustice that has been brought to the people, to the land called United States. For in the months ahead, it gains more strength, until the day when it crashes and changes everything. There will be freedom, there will be the exposure of wickedness that hides, but cannot hide much longer. You see, water is used to clean that which is unclean. It also is used to reveal what is hidden. It represents Holy Spirit. What is now about to happen in the months ahead, will be of enormous proportions. Keep your eyes fixed on the month called November, as the water crashes, so does the plans of the enemy to divide a Nation. For this will not be so! A victory shall be so significant, so extreme, and so monumental, it will shake the arrogant ones, the hypocrites, the liars, and the deceivers to the core. They shall be put to shame, and their plans to conquer shall be disrupted and dismantled. For My plans to establish My glory shall come in like a flood, and the fruit shall remain, until I say it is complete.

8/11/20

I'm putting everything in place for you now. This is good news! The significance of this, so you can have a peaceful and prosperous August and September. These months will shape and form the fulfillment of many wonderful things that take place in the season called Autumn. Watch and see the glory that comes and brings the establishment of joyful new beginnings!

8/16/20— Trump the Trumpet

Years have come and gone, and life does not stop, nor does it change its course. It continues, it perseveres, it fights for what is right, it overcomes what seems impossible, and it continues to move forward. Some years ago, a certain man named Donald Trump made a choice to take a stand for justice, for restoration. He made that choice, and in that choice, it positioned him to take on an assignment far greater than those around him believed could be achieved.

With much adversity and resistance, he has overcome the plans to divide, to remove. Many do not understand the mystery, that this man is being used for the common good of all people. His capacity, his diligence, is not generated by natural strength, but by spiritual authority. He is in place for many reasons. Some have come to fruition, and many will come in the days ahead. This Nation called the United States, has overcome many adversities, many trials. It is watched by many, and in the days ahead, a new chapter shall be revealed. One that changes everything. For he has been prepared from a time long ago, before the foundations of mankind. To be a voice that shapes the future. Upon this foundation, I have placed My word, My plans for this country, and in this, natural means cannot remove what has been placed by Me. These words have been spoken for many years, that this is the time of a new beginning. It will shape the Nation, the economy, and most of all, the hearts of mankind.

It will position, prepare, and bring a global awakening of truth. You see, the truth always sets you free! The mysteries have been revealed by many individuals that have been instructed to speak this truth. As you prepare for the months ahead, you must understand that a plan that is in place, shall not and will not be shaken. For what is necessary to take place over the next several years shall come to pass, simply because what is in place now is a vessel that will accommodate this plan.

For righteousness and justice shall come in like a flood, and those that dishonored this Nation with their false, deceptive schemes shall be brought to justice. They misled, misguided, and did not seek unity, but only division. For this is not the plan for this Nation. It will come back again, stronger than ever before, because their eyes will be opened, not by

man, but by Me. So listen for the sound, for it comes again, louder than ever! For in this you can trust, for in this, it shall be done.

8/17/20

IN A VOICE TONIGHT THAT SPOKE SO CLEAR, SO STRONG, YET SO GENTLE, I HEARD THESE WORDS; *"Anoint with oil every entry point into your home. Every doorway, even the entry point of the driveway or walk that leads to your front door. For I am preparing something that will bring significant glory over the land."*

8/30/20— In D.C.

So many voices, so many words. It can be heard across the land; it can be heard throughout the Nations. What comes of this? What shall be placed? For there is a time coming soon enough when a trumpet shall sound again. It shall be heard much louder than ever! It will in its next season, resonate with the sound of peace and prosperity. Not only in this Nation, but the Nations of the world. It will bring comfort, hope, and justice. It will finish its course; it will finish well.

So, what happens when the trumpet is put away and has completed its assignment? It shall come back and be placed in a very familiar hand to steward. This man is now prepared, this man is filled with integrity and honor. For he sits in the seat of second command of this Nation, the Nation called the United States. For what he has seen, for what he has heard, for what he has learned, will take him to a higher place of authority and govern the people with an honor and respect for the people! He loves his country, he loves justice. For he has prayed earnestly, diligently, and what he has heard, shall come to pass soon enough. So watch the days, the months, and the years that go by, with a peace that surpasses all understanding. For great days are ahead, and in this, you can trust.

9/9/20

As long as you stay close to Me, what exists presently in this Nation, shall not, and will not interfere with the plans that I have for you. It has been said, things will not change even after the curtain rises and displays a continued authority in the land. Promoted pain, hatred, and disunity have been working day and night, seeking who it can devour. That is their hope, that is their plan. That is what they want, but it is not what I want!

*Your year called 2020 was one that tested everyone, and exposed the true heart of mankind. There shall be a beautiful ending to this year! It shall never be forgotten, never looked at as if it was a failure. In fact, it made people cry out for more justice, righteousness, peace, and what is not spoken of, the word **UNITY**. Many people have tried to bring division in this Nation to last for generations, but I have intervened, and I moved on the hearts to hear My voice so they can turn from wickedness to righteousness.*

It is being established. It is being positioned. As the year draws to a close, pay close attention to the voices that speak venom, for their power is diminishing and their influence fading. For they shall be silenced, so the people can come back into freedom, peace, and joy. It shall be so. It shall not fail!

9/16/20

Today is a day to rejoice and be glad in it! Don't take a single second for granted. Life is so precious, there cannot be any waste. Many of you have been reflecting on your life, your past, your time. It seems that it has gone too fast, wishing you were back at pivotal moments. Like the time when your children were young, or when you walked down the aisle to be married. Things have come, and they have gone, but that does not mean that great things are not present, or yet to come to pass.

You can't go back, but you certainly can go forward. This special word for you today, is here to remind you wholeheartedly, that there are many people around you that need you, rely on you, and love you more than you know! Take heart, there is so much that is coming your way, so much joy and comfort. Your heart will be satisfied, and your soul will be at peace. Simply because greater love is coming for you! It will pour over you like oil, and penetrate all of the hardened places. A new season comes, it presents itself with arms opened wide, and a laughter that can, and will be heard throughout time!

9/17/20— Prophetic Presidential Word

The President who is called Trump has been placed in an office by the highest authority in the land; the spiritual authority that manifests in the natural. It has been spoken into existence before time began. These words are of significance in this hour. Listen closely! For in the likes of Joseph, and who he was called to be, many tried to stop the fruition of things to come, but I would not allow it.

I gave Joseph the strength and the tenacity to keep fighting, keep believing, and keep moving forward. This is what takes place every day with this man. His strength, his resilience, his perseverance gets stronger and stronger simply because I Am the one who gives him what he needs. Today is a reminder, that this man called Trump, is just like Joseph, nothing will stop the destiny of his life, and what he was created to do for this Nation, and the nations of the world.

9/21/20

Do not accept defeat in this hour! The enemy is a liar! Stay strong, speak life to your situation, and expect My strong hand to intervene on your behalf. Peace shall come and displace the whirlwind.

9/29/20

Significant progress and steps have been made by you! You thought things weren't going to change, and then, all of a sudden, breakthrough comes! But this is just the beginning. Watch what unfolds before November ends! For you have entered into a season of greatness! Remember that woman who was called great? She doubted, struggled, and was hopeless. Then, suddenly, faith came, and changed everything! This is where you're at! This is where you begin! You are loved more than you can possibly imagine! Never forget that! Now keep moving, there's much to obtain, much to learn!

9/30/20— In D.C. Trump | Biden

For his head was down when truth was spoken! That was your sign of submission! He cannot handle the truth; he cannot handle the pressure. For he will cave in, he will become undone. For the unrighteousness and wickedness that came forth from his decisions, and the lies that he speaks forth, all come to the surface. I revealed to this Nation called the United States, who the lion is, and everyone heard that roar. This President called Trump is not afraid, he is fearless. He has been given authority, tenacity, and a power to rule and reign. As with David, no giant can stand in his way! His voice of truth and justice carried a sound that was heard for generations, and in the days ahead, that come quickly, that same sound continues and continues. Watch, for the instigator of disgrace shall be silenced and his influence completely dismantled. For this man that comes to take away the seat of a President has not been given authority, nor shall he ever have influence again.

10/1/20— Press Secretary

Her name is Kayleigh McEnany! She is a daughter that has been given favor to defeat the forces of evil. In these next few weeks, watch how she handles the darkness, and with her sensitivity to My voice, she not only will cause the media to dismantle, but those that sit in high levels of authority. One that is the Speaker of the House. Keep watch, for her authority increases, and her voice silences the sound of disunity and hidden agendas.

10/2/20— President Trump | The Turning

I will use this present situation that is currently affecting the whole Nation in a way that is not expected. I will strengthen the President even more, and the hearts of the people that were against him, will now honor him. This is about compassion now! When hearts turn and mindsets shift. You must trust in Me. It's not a time of concern for the ones who see and hear, but a time of concern for those that are against My plans.

Watch, for in the days ahead, many will come forth and turn towards righteousness, unity, and peace. For this Man called President Donald J. Trump, and this Woman called Melania Trump are protected. They are cared for. What comes of this is more than the darkness can handle. For both increase in authority and support. They shall move quickly.

10/7/20— In D.C.

Deception and delusion is hard at work to deceive the American people. Stay focused, listen to My voice, and the truth will set you free. A great exposure is about to take place with those that manipulate to achieve their own agendas. I will not allow darkness to prevail. For the glory of the Lord is about to be demonstrated in significant ways, and the eyes of the people opened.

John Natale

10/14/20— In D.C. "Influential Esthers"

I am using several very influential women in government to expose significant darkness, deception, and delusion. Watch, for in the next several days, all attention comes to those that have planned, schemed, and hid behind closed doors. A very interesting piece of information comes forth and finalizes what has already been established. The manipulators, the deceivers, the liars, they are scrambling, shaking, and imploding. For their time is coming to a close. Many that had positions of authority will no longer be a voice, and their history forgotten. For they chose a wrong path.

They were offered grace, but their blind eyes could not be opened. They choose wickedness instead of righteousness. So the dust is shaken, and the path now has been cleared. The sun arises in the morning, and it brings light to the direction of the one who travels. Watch, again I say watch, for she is being elevated, and her voice comes forth like a double-edged sword. She has begun a new assignment that is needed at this time. They are afraid of her. They will turn their attention to her, but she is prepared, she is positioned, and she will conquer.

10/19/20— In D.C. "Benghazi Justice"

There is a coming justice that centers around Benghazi. For many are trying to keep it hidden, but in the next several weeks, an unexpected individual pays a visit and provides a very interesting piece of information that has been silenced long enough. Justice comes, it surely comes!

10/21/20— SCOTUS

Amy Coney Barrett has been given a platform. She is confusing the enemy and bringing widespread panic among those that seek to divide and destroy. Not only will she be one of the greatest judges ever placed in power, but her influence and example will cause the hearts and minds of

274

many to reevaluate their position on many current scenarios in America. Keep watch, for one particular individual tries to stop the confirmation, but arrogance turns to humility very quickly.

10/22/20— In D.C. | Exposure & Favor

For October shows many signs, those that will change everything. It has been said, that there is protection for those that believe their power and influence cannot be dismissed. Oh, but there is something coming that will shake everything, and everything will be shaken. Eyes are on November, but the time now is focused on October! For again, I say that this month, this pivotal, and critical month, will not end without great exposure that produces revelation and understanding to a mystery. A sudden shift of favor comes to the one who sits on the highest seat of authority in the land called the United States.

11/2/20— Trump 2020

The angels rejoice! The atmosphere shifts! For the time has come, it has surely come, when you will see a powerful move of My spirit in the hearts of men and women alike. For the hearts have turned towards righteousness. Perspective has changed! Revelation has been given! The people have heard the sound, they have heard the truth! Many have turned, recognized true freedom! They have made a decision that will cause a great stirring in the land! For this man called President Donald J. Trump continues his journey to complete his destiny.

He has been given a double portion of favor, and in these next four years, all the dishonor that was spoken, will be replaced with a cup that runneth over. Unity will come back to a nation that was divided by those that did not have a heart for people, but for their own agendas and passion for power. But I have dismantled their hidden plans once again. So rejoice! As with Israel, the cry has been heard, and I have answered.

11/5/20— Election 2020

Stay alert, focused, and sensitive to Holy Spirit. Many things are about to be uncovered, and in this process, the enemy will be releasing a spirit of fear among the people. He is aware that he has lost, and exposed again, but he will not stop without a strong attempt to keep deception and delusion present. Keep your eyes on Me! You will see victory, and you will hear the sound of freedom being sung that will shake the atmosphere!

11/5/20— Trump | False Prophets

As with the false prophets that challenged the voice that carried truth, you will see a glory that will destroy the darkness, and humble the arrogant. An altar has been built before the people to see the greater glory. It has been waiting for the kairos moment of time to reveal a mystery. There was one that was sent to an altar to put to test, the true God! That day, the darkness, the deception, and the lies that came forth to make a mockery of the credibility and value of the Lord God came to a sudden end. It was a step of faith to take a stand for righteousness. You have seen this now manifest in the present. The battle has begun, the display of authority will come when it is time, and the destruction and removal of wickedness will follow. Keep your eyes on the progress, for clues are given, and faith, confidence, and power is poured into the one who has said, "I will go!"

11/13/20— For America

What you are presently seeing is the beginning of a great reversal in the spirit, it will change everything. A battle raging on, a fight for the heart of men and women alike. To discourage, to suppress, and to ultimately rob you of your joy, but this will not end in the way that many think! There is a glory coming! A greater glory! A shifting, a great turning! Who is on the

Throne? Who sees all? Who knows all? Faith has been tested, many have given up, given in, but there are those that have given all! They have stood firmly on the soil, and they have come with an expectant heart attitude, a strength, and a faith that can move mountains! They have cried out, and they have been heard. Today, rejoice, for I tell you to rejoice! For I Am in control, and all things submit to My voice! Be still, and know that I Am God!

11/15/20

I am bringing a spirit of confusion on the camp of the betrayer. There will be a turning, one against the other. Their sleep shall be hindered, their peace, removed. Watch, for one comes out and speaks words of remorse.

11/17/20— In America

Who makes the crooked places straight? Who holds all things? Take all focus off the natural, and hold tightly to the spiritual things that truly give peace and comfort. The enemy is trying desperately to take control of the mind and establish fear and hopelessness. Do not give in to this plan. For My strength is sufficient for you. I Am speaking, just listen closely. I'm not a respecter of persons. Everyone in this hour should be hearing My voice clearly. Be sensitive to My Holy Spirit, I Am with you.

11/19/20— Election 2020

Keep your eyes and ears attentive to November 22-28. It's a Thanksgiving week that brings a whirlwind of revelation, and Elijah calls down the Fire!

11/29/20— Prophetic Update | Election 2020 BREAKING: Prophetic Dream

On Friday evening, November 27th, I had a very significant dream. I was standing inside a building in Washington, D.C. where the portraits of past

Presidents are on display. It was then that I came upon the portrait of President Trump. As I was looking at the picture, I heard the Holy Spirit speak these words.

> *"This President has been placed in this hall prematurely by the mindsets of men and women alike that have chosen to give up fighting for righteousness and justice. This battle is not natural, but spiritual. It is I that chooses when this fight is over, and it is I that decides the outcome. For he has not finished his course yet, and in its time, he will be remembered for what he stood for, and what he accomplished. For many are praying, and I have heard that prayer."*

Then suddenly, the picture started to take form, and the President came forth out of the picture and looked at me. You could see the determination in his eyes, and the diligence to overcome. He carried a demeanor of confidence, and an attribute of humility to show honor, integrity, and passion for the mandate he has been given to steward.

11/30/20— Election 2020

The fraud will not just reveal the facts, but expose the "Untouchables"!For they have been watched by the one who sees all things! Their hidden plans uncovered, and their wickedness revealed! Watch, for days come, and panic sets in!

12/1/20

The month of December brings revelation and understanding regarding the exposure of the "Untouchables". For there is one who will get a knock on the door soon enough! For he thinks he is untouchable! And I, the Lord, will deal with him, as he seeks to be hidden.

12/2/20— United States

In the midst of all the tension, concerns, and doubts, I Am a God that hears the cries, and sees the tears. It is a difficult time for many, but yet, an exciting time for others. It's not hard to hear My voice, or sense My presence. It's time to disconnect from the sources that only bring confusion, doubt, and worry. For My grace is sufficient for you, and My voice a perfect source of comfort. I Am speaking loud and clear to this nation! Many have chosen to listen, many have not, but this day, I encourage you to be sensitive to Holy Spirit, and what you need, you shall have.

12/6/20— President Trump | Hanukkah

As the celebration of life comes forth on the day called the 25th of December, the days leading up to that are recognized as "THE DAYS OF MIRACLES". What many expected to happen in the natural did not take place, simply because God's grace and His supernatural power intervened to show how spiritual authority outweighed natural circumstances. Watch, for in the days ahead, there will be a consistent surge of God's glory keeping the oil from running out. These will be signs that will be a source of hope and inspiration to a nation that has been crying out for justice.

12/8/20— Trump | Biden | Netanyahu

Your President is praying! He is seeking Me, pursuing Me! The signs will be given in the skies, and the earth will speak as well. When spiritual eyes are not open, many react in the natural, and in most cases, prematurely. This is so with a man that I watch closely. His name is Benjamin Netanyahu. For he is questioning everything without speaking. But he will speak soon enough! He has responded out of pressure, but he will soon see the light, and he will revisit an old friend! For this you can trust! So now I tell you this!

This one called Biden, his heart is calloused, and he is troubled. For panic is upon them, and they are fully aware that their time is coming to a close. They will try to distract, and engage again with intimidation, but I have sent Angels all around this nation, and around your President called Trump. For a war is raging in the spirit realm, but understand this, the enemy is losing ground everyday! I am allowing the battle to continue for more reasons than you can comprehend. You must understand the mystery that I see far ahead, and what I Am allowing is uncovering a significant, deep realm of darkness that has been hidden for many seasons. For it is I, My power, My voice, that has uncovered the darkness that many thought was not possible to reveal. The hidden agendas, plans, and decisions that are schemed each day, are coming to an end.

In the days ahead, as righteousness sweeps through a nation, many leaders will address the facts, and admit the wrongs. Some will be given grace, some will be given mercy, but there will be those that pay a price for wickedness. Keep your eye fixed to the December month, for it shall never be forgotten.

12/13/20— United States

The enemy is exposing the very ones he is using in this hour against justice and freedom. Watch, for in the next few days, much is revealed to the nation, and truth keeps marching on!

12/17/20— Prepare for Glory

The enemy has mocked, ridiculed, and slandered the one placed in an office to serve the people. But he is powerless in his attempt to remove what I have positioned. For he has been chosen, not to rule over them, but to help a nation understand freedom, passion, and the pursuit for justice! The enemy has strengthened the attack on the body of Christ, some have fallen prey to the tactics, the intimidation, the doubts, the fears, but I have released a strong wave of glory that will penetrate the darkness and crush it before the eyes of men and women alike! Even the younger ones will see My glory in this nation! It will cause such a stirring, a shaking! Do not relent, keep your passion strong! Keep fighting, praying, believing! A nation is crying out! Do you not believe that I hear that cry? And that I have not acted already in the spirit? For I have, and the manifestation comes quickly!

12/24/20

Mr. President, wisdom is coming to knock on your door. The strategy will be released. Stay focused, stay sensitive, respond to the voice that speaks within. You will be given the sign. You shall respond at the kairos moment of time. You shall move forward.

Part Nine
Prophetic Words — 2021

1/2/21— President Trump

For I have put a hedge of protection around President Trump. Nothing shall hinder his tenure or his destiny. Woe to those that speak negative words and make their threats, for they are dealing with a spiritual authority that is beyond their understanding, and an army that is innumerable in size. Watch very closely, as he is given peace, grace, and confidence in the days ahead. For a nation is praying, and I Am responding. There are trying days ahead, but rejoice, for I overcome the world. For great days are coming that will be seen around the world, and the praying church will be on display for people to see, that faith is the substance of things hoped for, the evidence of things unseen.

1/12/21

As the January month continues, watch how unexpected favor and grace pays a visit to your family. Increase which has not been seen, and not forecasted has been released in its perfect time, to set the stage for a perfect season!

1/16/21— President Trump

For My eyes are on him, he is in the cleft of the rock. For his heart has been tenderized. He is waiting, watching, but he is okay! He is trusting, praying, and yielding to My will. For it is I that has the last say! Do not look at your times, your dates, your mindset, for I am fully aware what is transpiring, what is happening. Now I tell you this simple truth, have faith, and believe in Me!

I see what's ahead, what is in the future! You are in a time now that you must pause and listen. Do not be pulled to the left or to the right, keep your eyes fixed on Me and watch the glory unfold. I Am good, and in Me, you can put all trust.

1/23/21— America The Beautiful

Your eyes shall be opened! Your ears attentive to a sound that comes shortly! There is no weeping in My house, no pain, no suffering! Why do you allow the enemy to convince you otherwise? Have I not already spoken? Have I given up on the plans for this nation? Certainly not! Then why have you? Does not My word say in the last days, they shall call evil, good, and good, evil? This nation has entered into a time of great deception. This was released many times by the voices that release the mysteries of Heaven. You must listen attentively to Holy Spirit, and stay strong! Many things are working for the good for this nation, and will be revealed shortly.

As with Moses, he directed the people to stay still, stay calm, that word is Selah! You have been positioned now to watch, and wait. The enemy has been positioned as well! Pharaoh postured himself in a place of un-authorization, and made a choice not to follow the word of the Lord. What he saw that day was a full release of supernatural glory that was not expected, simply because he thought he was greater than My word! His plans became nothing, his authority deauthorized! That day he learned differently. That very special day, My people waited, and watched, and saw the manifestation of what was deemed impossible, become the possible!

1/31/21— The Land Of The Free

Just when you think it's over, a suddenly comes into existence and changes everything! There's a lot of movement in the spirit realm, things we cannot see, but will be revealed in its time! The Winter is in its full capacity now, but underneath the ground, things are happening, moving, preparing. Signs will be given in this season to prepare what's coming in the Spring! The next season will shock many, encourage some, discourage others! But it will come, and it will complete a plan that was orchestrated before time. Do not be concerned about what is seen, but be faithful in what is unseen!

2/4/21

I'm watching, guiding, and preparing! There are those that have fled as Elijah did when Jezebel raised her voice. Even when a significant victory came forth and silenced the false prophets of Baal. You must understand how this spirit operates, and how it manifests. For it is strong in this nation now! It has been spoken of many times in the past, and warnings have been given. It will intimidate, threaten, and will do anything to silence the voice of truth! But there is a day coming, and coming, there shall be a day! For one shall rise up and not be hindered. For he shall be heard, even when the many try to silence his voice. As with Elijah, he was anointed with power, ability, perseverance, and boldness, and when the kairos moment of time came, another one was placed into position to complete a task of justice and righteousness! For one is waiting, but two shall be used to restore what was stolen! Like that same day, long ago, a great and mighty spirit was reigning in the atmosphere to bring fear and control, but I have positioned My voices once again, and My angels, and justice is coming in the days ahead! In this, you can trust!

2/11/21

There's still plenty of time to accomplish the things that I have planned for your life! Do not fall for that trap that speaks in your ear, that time is critical. Don't look back, but look forward, and allow Me to show you the very significant days ahead. The enemy is a liar! What was spoken, was true! What will be revealed, is awesome! Keep going, keep believing! It's close!

2/17/21— United We Stand

A bit of disturbance with your peace has caused some frustrations and weariness, but I have come at this moment to replace the struggle with refreshing waters! An attack on your joy is actually targeting progress and destiny. In this hour, the enemy is concerned that breakthrough is close, so there is an assault on your mindset. Know that I am here to deflect and break the stronghold that is present. Victory is now, and a restoration shall be complete. There is a great warfare taking place in the spiritual realm centered around the freedom and justice of the land called the United States. Great battles against what is good, what is pure, are raging on and causing significant disturbances in the atmosphere. Stand in faith, posture in hope, for I am aware of all things, and I have each day aligned perfectly to what will transpire for the revealing of what is My plan, My purpose! What they say doesn't matter, only what I say is truth! My truth sets people free, My truth sets a nation free! And who the Son sets free, is free indeed!

2/17/21— United States

America shall not be divided in any way, shape or form! Divine interruption shall suddenly come and erase the plans that have been hidden behind closed doors. Keep watch, for China is planning and scheming, but this will not come to pass. For there is one who is watching everything, and another who keeps watch on a wall that is not in public view.

2/20/21— Mystery Of The 13

Keep your eye on the states of Pennsylvania and Georgia. For there is a mystery that will present itself soon enough. The original 13 colonies are coming back into play, and will be a topic of conversation as events come into existence that represent liberty and freedom!

2/28/21— Sound The Trumpet

The shaking has started and the trumpet has made its sound, loud and clear! Now watch, for one becomes agitated, and another defensive, but what is coming forth is a wave that cannot be stopped. For a season has begun that brings even a greater exposure! An alliance becomes stronger, and a relationship strengthened, as leaders from around the world embrace a voice that speaks truth, and carries an authority that is honored around the nations!

3/4/21

Your hour is coming that will bring much comfort and peace. I need you to understand that I Am with you, around you, and within you! There is no need to panic, no need to worry, nor is there any reason to be confused by what you see. Am I not in control? Am I not moving at all times? You must settle within yourself, your mindset, and your heart, that I have heard the prayers of the people. I have not walked away, I have not stopped listening. For in its season, things come to pass, but not the hour in which you see, for there is no clock on My wall, and there is no concern or worry that I carry.

You must ask yourself a simple question, do you believe in My word? Are you moved by natural things or natural words that come from deaf ears? Allow My peace to give you rest, and watch the transpiring. Do not give up or give in to the tricks of the enemy, for plans are in place, and plans will be carried out when eyes and ears are not expecting anything to manifest. For great things take place suddenly! Remember, as was spoken before, keep your eyes on the Eastern Shore, there are surprises coming forth that are hidden in My hands.

3/8/21

Any ground that the enemy was able to obtain over this past weekend shall be returned. Your joy, your peace, and your progress shall be blessed with a double portion from the hands of the Father!

3/9/21— Land Of The Free

The enemy is silencing many voices in this hour! Remember the days of Elijah, when My power and My presence manifested in ways that overwhelmed the enemy? Then all of a sudden, the enemy strategically chose a different path and achieved a short-lived victory. That was until I intervened and brought havoc on the hour of darkness again! You must have faith, persevere, and stay focused. For I Am speaking, positioning, and preparing for some certain surprises that will not be revealed until specific people are positioned in specific places that carry spiritual and natural authority. Have I not told you to keep your eyes on the Eastern Shore? Winter comes, and winter goes, then comes life and mysteries that have remained hidden until I release them to make their appearances.

3/10/21

Keep your eyes on the Eastern Shore of the United States. There are hidden mysteries that will be revealed shortly. What is hidden, is revealed. What is revealed, brings revelation.

3/11/21

The "Untouchables" hide in secret places believing that they will never be revealed. But there is a day coming, in which Holy Spirit will uncover significant voices that hide behind brick walls. As each day continues, more and more is being exposed. Darkness is not capable of holding its ground, so as time goes by, I Am exposing one by one, and the wickedness that accompanies darkness.

3/15/21— Time To Speak

Do not allow the enemy to silence your voice. Holy Spirit is making a way in this season for authentic voices to come forward and release the sound of the Lord. The enemy is perplexed by what's taking place in the atmosphere, and there is opportunity to take back ground that he has stolen. It's a critical hour that will bring much truth, much revelation. Take your place, posture correctly. A great victory is about to come forth.

3/19/21— United States

Transition is coming! It is expected, but does not carry favor. As darkness surrounds the atmosphere, stay calm, stay alert, watch Holy Spirit dissect the structure and reveal the source.

3/25/21— United We Stand

Spring has come, and with no surprise, the gentle winds accompany the sounds of songs being sung in the trees. But wait, a mystery that has been hidden in its shortened season shall come to pass. For a new sound shall come forth, and bring life to a disrupted atmosphere! For there is much to be thankful for, even when natural circumstances don't reveal the beauty of victory. The time is coming, when the winds show their face, and the sound that comes from it, speaks to a nation!

Behold, I have not forgotten you, for I have weighed all things in the balance. A time is coming when specific things will be addressed by My authority. Stay clear minded, strong, and filled with faith! Don't let these things steal your joy! Release the frustrations to Me, and let Me deal with the wickedness. As was spoken before, the enemy and his plans are folding and coming undone. One by one, clues are given to the inevitable revealing of darkness. Now rise up! The enemy wants you silent, stagnant, and motionless. There is fear coming from his camp, they are aware that exposure is eminent! Let the sound of My voice come forth from your heart! Rise up I say, and show the enemy the very nature of who lives within you!

3/31/21

There's a healing that is about to take place in the area of your heart that has been wounded by abandonment. What was ripped apart and stolen will be restored seven times! April is a significant month of restoration. For your journey suddenly becomes lighter.

3/31/21

They are afraid, for much concern has entered their minds! For what they think is controlled, is only getting stronger. They are trying to keep the Lion silenced, but the Pride has surrounded the Lion with wisdom. What they thought was a memory, shall become a reality once again! Do not forget who is in control, and who holds all things together! The writing has already been written on the wall.

4/6/21

I'm exposing darkness day by day in each state that will reveal the true identity of those that seek power, and not freedom. Those that are tearing down the foundations of peace and unity. Keep watch, for the stage is being set, the curtain rises, and one is brought forth to tear the veil. The season of colors will not end without the full display of its worth, and then, the land will be prepared to receive its reward.

4/13/21

Nothing was done in vain! There is an ending to a story that is not expected. There are victories, there is also defeat. Where there is defeat, there is revelation. Where there is revelation, there is strategy. Where there is strategy, there is victory!

4/20/21

We continue to stay strong, and fight for justice! We were not called to be silent. We are called to be light in a dark place! Righteousness will prevail over darkness! It's not time for that season to come! The deceiver shall be exposed and the truth shall come forth! The hour of breakthrough is showing its face in the distance. We rise, we speak, we prevail! God wins!

4/21/21— Justice is Coming

The veil of deception that has deceived a nation is about to be exposed! The hour is coming that will shake everything. Warring angels have been released in this season to overwhelm that which has been compromised. Watch, for what is fighting in the spirit shall manifest in the natural with sudden victories. Stay sensitive, alert to the months ahead. For sudden focus shall be placed on a very specific person.

5/8/21

The enemy is trying to steal the joy that Jesus has restored in you. There has been a great shift in your life, both physically and spiritually. This caused a new assignment to be implemented against you, but Holy Spirit has given you the strength, the tenacity, and the revelation to overcome! A flood of peace, laughter, and vision shall suddenly rise up and bring you to another level of grace.

5/11/21— Israel's Victory

You dare come against what is protected and positioned in the palm of My hand? You have no understanding of what is happening in the spirit realm! For a man who his leading a nation, he shall make a decision, it shall come quickly, and it shall make a sound that resonates throughout the Middle

East! They will say, "They are not movable, they have a God that protects them." As it was in the beginning, it shall be on display again! Your natural weapons have no power over My authority, and in the days ahead, you will understand that My authority rules and reigns over wickedness! Now listen, there is one who sits in power, who has more influence than they think! They believe he is powerless, but I recognize his heart, his prayers, his revelation of Israel. And for this, grace is offered, but grace will run out in its season. When this takes place, eyes will be placed on your own land. In this, you will see justice that comes in like a flood. For the enemy has postured itself thinking that victory is at hand, but I have already given victory to the land called Israel.

5/15/21— America Restored

The enemy has been allowed to posture in a place of power, but will soon fall to the voice of truth! As with Goliath, he stood on a hill, mocking, dishonoring, and disgracing that which was righteous. Until one day, when everything changed! That day is coming! That day will be remembered for generations! That day cannot be stopped.

5/15/21— Goliath Silenced

Goliath taunted and challenged the people every day with arrogance, dishonor, and discredit. He was allowed to position himself in a posture of strength, just like the voice that speaks to a nation presently. Then truth came suddenly, when it wasn't expected, and spoke to the voice of delusion and deception, to remind him that divine intervention was coming, and when it comes, Truth wins!

5/17/21

A quick, sudden shift of grace and favor shall supernaturally be released and handed to you. In the moment of despair and hopelessness, the timing is once again perfect for you and your family. For what I see is far different from what you see. All things are subject to change even when your thoughts say different. So rejoice, for the release comes like wind, and will not go without giving a blanket of peace that comforts your weary heart.

5/25/21

Great peace being released right now. God's favor is upon you! Strength, joy, and rest shall accompany you. You have overcome an intense season, and you have overcome adversity. Prepare for the door to open that has been prophesied over you. All things are aligned and prepared to be given unto you.

5/27/21

Justice will start from the top, but there's even one that is higher, and he will be dealt with as well. They think power is invincible, but they do not understand the mystery of true authority.

6/4/21

The prophets shall begin a new work in this new season. They will speak the truth, and they will cause a great stirring! Like John, they will be a voice crying out in the wilderness. They will prepare the way! Their calling is not glamorous, nor is it popular. There is a separating taking place now, that which will reveal truly those that have been called for this time. For more will come against than those that are for. Great words shall come forth that will expose the wickedness of men, and reveal what is coming in the months ahead. Many eyes will be opened, and great revelation shall accompany those that have eyes to see!

6/7/21

So many people, they come and they go. Struggling, worrying and living as if there is no hope in sight. You were not created just to exist, you were created to thrive. Today, I remind you that if you believe and do not doubt, you will see great days and you will see great victories. Just believe! John 5:1-15.

6/8/21

I Am with you always. I have no beginning, nor do I have an end. I Am always and forever. Your spirit shall be revived and you shall seek Me in a greater way that will open up new and exciting realms of glory. Understanding and wisdom shall be your friend, and you shall see much breakthrough in the days ahead. You are in a new season of maturity and discernment. I have given you what you need and I have restored much in your life. You shall see the manifestation of great things take place as you move forward, My Child.

6/10/21

Significant breakthrough in the realm of peace is about to address your situation. It shall suddenly come forth and calm the lingering storm. As this chapter comes to an end, a new season comes forth that will move quickly, and bring much fruit to the table.

6/12/21

And the prophets shall congregate on the National Mall, and they will prophesy, and they will speak to the darkness. For in their voices, mysteries will come, and it will penetrate the atmosphere, and bring hope and justice to a nation. The sound will be heard throughout a nation, and it shall bring great revelation to those that have eyes to see!

6/14/21

Every situation that the enemy has used against you in the last several days will be turned around for your good, and opportunity and breakthrough will arise from the ashes. The beauty and fragrance of God shall overwhelm all discouragement and despair.

6/29/21— Capitol Secrets

A great turn of events unfold as exposure takes place in the north! They will say, "How did they know? How did they find out? It has been hidden for 12 years!" *But I have spoiled the plans once again! In the short days ahead, two shall come forth and become one voice, and what was hidden to bring down one, shall be exposed to bring justice to another and another!*

7/2/21

There's quite a bit of movement in the atmosphere right now! A battle is about to be won in the spirit realm. July is a month called **Victory**. Celebrate this day, as the sun is lowered, and the sky is darkened. Signs will follow, eyes shall be opened!

7/8/21— Awakening in D.C.

A very strong release of the presence of Jesus shall come shortly and interrupt the agenda of one very specific individual in Washington D.C. A reconciliation will take place with the Messiah. Watch closely, for in the Capitol District of the United States, a hardened heart becomes soft and calls out to the One who sets the captives free. The effect will shake many, and the waters will be stirred up. But what comes from it, shall have long lasting effects on perspective and direction that facilitates justice. So watch, for he is angry, he is out to dismantle honor, but in the days ahead, his own heart shall be restored and healed.

7/10/21

Keep your eyes on Washington, D.C. For the month of July is very significant to a very special person who speaks against what is true! For his heart is being softened, and My voice shall be heard!

7/16/21— The Season of Salt

As was spoken earlier, these mysteries shall not be avoided, but understood! My people are struggling, but in a short time, they shall see My wonder! They have lost the sense of time, the ability to discern the time. I tell you these things, that there is nothing lost, nothing broken that cannot be fixed. For your eyes shall be fixed to one place soon, and in that day, it will be even harder to comprehend if you watch with natural eyes. You must see in the spirit, allow Holy Spirit to reveal to you what's coming. Justice is coming! A great change! A change for all! Set your sights on the land called Israel, for signs will be given, and a sudden disturbance in leadership becomes present. For an exposure will be revealed that will have ramifications on United States soil. For I am uncovering all wickedness, and as the Summer months continue, justice suddenly comes, as one very significant voice has a change of heart, and speaks from the heart of Truth!

7/17/21— The Lion's Roar

Do you not think that I see everything that is plotted, planned and schemed? For all will be dealt with! Each and every one that has his hand in the pot of destruction! They all shall be accountable for wickedness! For in the spirit realm, there is a measure that is established to bring accountability to those who do not pursue righteousness. For the season has come, where angels have been released to surround the gates! The

297

sound of a Lion shall be heard! It shall give fair warning to those to repent and speak truth! Now watch! For in the days to come, the waters will be stirred, and the clouds moved, and this will be your sign that the Lion has positioned itself to bring forth the sound!

7/25/21— The New Assignment

A season of steps that are taken give insight to the new assignment that is required. Don't question what seems small at first, but rejoice, for it becomes increasingly significant soon enough. What you are about to enter into is more than you can imagine! Stay focused, and don't allow the enemy to steal your joy. For the manifestation of the supernatural realm is revealed shortly.

7/29/21— Season of Change

Stay strong in a time of consequences! Challenges come, but will be conquered and defeated if you keep your eyes on Me! The enemy is trying once again to intimidate with tactics of false power, and control, but Holy Spirit is awakening the hearts and minds of many! The plan is to place fear in the people and cause their mindsets to give in to the spirit of delusion and deception. By wearing you down, they can set the hook of control in your mindset, but what they don't understand nor see, is the mystery of faith and trust. There is One that is greater than this false power, and there is One that is higher than their natural thinking! If you trust Me in this hour, and stay sensitive to Holy Spirit, you will overcome the storm in the Summer and Autumn months. The key to breakthrough is Me! Stay close to Me, stay sensitive to Me, and this too shall pass. For Summer ends, and Autumn comes, but does not close nor begin without divine intervention!

8/1/21— Prophetic Visitation | The Declaration

In a sudden encounter I had with Holy Spirit on Friday night, I saw a very large crowd in Washington, D.C. There was a sea of people cheering and excited about the current state of affairs in the United States. Hope was returned, and peace was in the air. Then all of a sudden, there was a person speaking at a podium, declaring that justice was present, and the future was filled with hope and peace. As I looked further and deeper into the vision, I could see that the man facing the crowd was Donald J. Trump. He had a different sound coming forth from his lungs. It was polished, sharpened, and confident. What was being released, was not capable of being stopped by man. The crowd too big for anyone to hold back. The sound echoed across the land. There was a protection around him far greater than the protection offered by man, in fact, what was protecting him, was angels encircling 360 degrees. His voice could not be stopped, and what was spoken, was needed for such a time as this. The land shook, the mountains vibrated, and the winds blew responding to the declaration that was given and released into the atmosphere. So in this time, rejoice, for sudden changes come, and mysteries revealed, to the eyes of the seers!

8/9/21

Have you ever felt like Nathaniel under the fig tree? Good news is coming! The sudden encounter with Holy Spirit when you least expect it shall take you by surprise! I declare and speak over you that your pain and struggle is about end, and your breakthrough comes forth! Do not give up!

8/13/21

Things are happening all around you! You must have eyes to see in this season. What you don't think you have, you have been given much. Get ready for a great disturbance in the atmosphere, as My presence manifests spiritually and naturally.

John Natale

8/16/21— Middle East Exposure

I Am allowing specific things to take place presently, in order for significant events to be revealed. As you watch closely to the scenarios of the Middle East, it will uncover hidden mysteries that will ultimately expose one of the "Untouchables". For My eyes are on him, and My stare shall penetrate his wickedness. They will see in the short time ahead, that the plans of the enemy, and what is taking place now, will soon backfire and reveal sources of wickedness. Light always overwhelms darkness!

8/19/21

Holy Spirit releasing peace and joy in great proportions right now! It will be like the oil that ran down Aaron's beard! Receive and be glad! It's right on time!

8/21/21— Prophetic Dream

Had a dream last night about the one holding the office of the President. I spoke with him regarding the present state of the nation and current events abroad. He seemed confident and calm. As the conversation continued, I could see the protection that was in the room start to get concerned. He was unusually clear with his voice and his reasoning, until he was questioned regarding integrity and honor. At that point, those in the room started walking back and forth, as if they had no understanding of what to do next. It seemed as if they all of a sudden understood the realm of honor! True honor, true integrity, and true character. He started speaking in words that did not make sense, as if all clarity left, and his ability to reason ceased. I had compassion for him, knowing that God was working on his heart, but the fight that was taking place internally, was taking a toll on his self worth. As he continued to speak, he placed his sunglasses on so his eyes could not be seen by me, as he did not want to look eye to eye. What was hidden was brokenness, and the inability to allow the heart to be transparent. He then grabbed his belongings, and left the room with those around him.

8/23/21

Do not worry, for what you see is not permanent, but only temporary! As time continues, the unexpected shall be present, and what was considered lost, shall be recovered! America, your days of restoration are upon you! It has begun! They are panicking! They are lost! Their mindsets are confused, and confidence has been replaced with fear. For wave after wave, I Am using specific individuals to uncover all of the hidden plans and schemes. One by one, each and every one, will be exposed, and righteousness shall be present among the people. Do not be concerned or impatient, for I Am in control of all that is present, and I have not turned My face from the wickedness that was allowed to come in to this nation. The story does not end with what you see, it shall end, by what was said was impossible!

8/30/21

I know it's been hard, sometimes unbearable, but you will overcome these moments of despair. In the midst of all that's going on. There is a voice inside of you that reminds you, this too shall pass. I'm giving you what you need now in the moment. You shall be given strength, grace and peace. Your eyes will be opened to My plans, and My victory that is scheduled to arrive shortly in your life, and your family. Now is a good time to rejoice, for angels are all around to lift their swords high and give a victory shout! The enemy has lost another battle again!

9/2/21

The spiritual atmosphere has been cleared out. Expect breakthrough today as certain scenarios that have been heavy, all of a sudden become very light.

9/3/21

The season is over and the enemy has lost yet again. The battle was Mine all along, you just didn't believe it at times, but that is okay. I knew you would have your doubts. In My grace, there is understanding and unconditional love. All I wanted you to do was to keep looking at Me, and you have done just that. Now it's time to reap what you have sown. Your tears have been collected, it's time to water the ground and watch the beauty come forth. Well done, Child, you were never going to be defeated anyhow, simply because I would not allow it.

9/4/21

Sensitivity is being released so hidden mysteries can be revealed. Pay close attention to the inner voice. It speaks loud and clear, and these next few days are critical to significant breakthrough.

9/6/21— The Broken Administration

Soon there will be more exposure to the administration that operates in deception and delusion. Their hearts will grow in fear as Holy Spirit reveals more hidden secrets. The weight of conviction will suddenly appear on one that is struggling already. For she will give in, and reveal what she already knows.

9/7/21

Here is what He is saying right now! "COME TO ME, ALL YOU WHO LABOR AND ARE HEAVY LADEN, AND I WILL GIVE YOU REST." Matthew 11:28

9/7/21— Turmoil in D.C.

They thought they silenced a nation in November, and all they did was awaken the people. A sound that is unstoppable, unchanging, and continually growing. The depth of deception and lies have come to the surface, and they know now, one by one, they will be exposed, and the one who watches all, will have His way! For the people are shouting for justice, and justice they are seeing! Autumn! Your season is here! Show your colors, for you are preparing to bring clarity and vibrance to the nation. Then, as Winter draws near, "Untouchables" come forth, and their authority suddenly ceases.

9/10/21-The Pharaoh's Heart

Many times Moses went to Pharaoh to make a bold statement. "LET MY PEOPLE GO!" He would not listen, and he mocked the words of wisdom. As the struggle continued, the heart of Pharaoh grew colder and colder. For he was fighting against a mandate that came from I Am! As with this man that abuses his authority, and also has become a Pharaoh, he will also have a heart that grows cold, and then one day, he will have no choice but to give in, simply because the power of God was too much for natural authority to resist. He will see that the cries of the righteous have been heard, and he will see the power of God enabled right before his eyes, and freedom come to those that put their trust in Me!

9/16/21

Jesus wanted me to remind you that He has not forgotten about your situation. Some very interesting scenarios are about to take place, and cause you to soar like an Eagle. The mandate on your life has just been increased! Things will no longer be as they were!

9/17/21

One door closes, two are opened! Favor, increase, and honor shall knock on your door momentarily!

9/17/21

Holy Spirit wants to bring revelation and understanding to your current situation. What seems disheartening and frustrating shall suddenly take a joyful turn and place you right where you need to be in this next season. Honor shall be restored, and increase shall be given back sevenfold from what the locusts devoured in your last season. Rejoice, for you are now about to soar like an eagle, and the wind shall carry you farther than what you expected.

9/20/21— Mysteries Revealed

In the natural, it looks like the enemy won a battle in your life, and defeat came knocking on your door. But what actually happened was that Holy Spirit allowed specific circumstances to come forth and set the stage for a very serious exposure to take place. What came against you shall be dealt with, and what comes to bless you shall bring significant opportunity. Rejoice, for the season has changed for you, and you shall be glad in it!

9/22/21— His Presence in D.C.

A sudden surge of signs and wonders are about to influence a nation! Prepare yourself, for very specific individuals are about to make a big impact at the National Mall of the District called D.C. It will shake some, stir much, and heal many!

10/7/21— Season of Change

I know it has been tough over the past few weeks, but My grace is sufficient for you! With everything that is going on, and everything that is out of your control, it seems overwhelming. Yes, maybe more than seems, but I promise you, there is a breakthrough coming to you, one that you cannot see now, but is active and alive! It awaits My voice to be released, and as you ponder and question specific things that have shifted unexpectedly, a sudden wind shall come and My presence shall change everything. You have been given strength to keep going, to keep moving forward, even when you feel as if nothing is happening. But things are!

I will restore joy, peace, and confidence to you in this season. What you thought was separation was actually a beautiful plan in place to bring preparation for restoration. You will see over the next few weeks what Holy Spirit has been doing in the spirit realm. Wonderful, very special revelations and scenarios shall unfold to bring your heart back to a place of comfort.

10/18/21

There is a shift that has taken place in the spirit realm. Watch, as some very interesting events take place in the nation shortly. The "Untouchables" carry a spirit of fear now, for they know that a significant revealing is imminent!

10/21/21

Get ready for the supernatural to be natural! Sudden opportunities will come that reveal the heart of people and how they seek truth! For divine appointments will be present all weekend long, and show the glory of

God! They are coming simply because you have been faithful with your pursuit of truth, and your capacity to show love.

11/5/21— New Jersey

Holy Spirit is exposing wickedness and unrighteousness in the state of New Jersey. It's been hidden and under the radar, until the day came that changed everything. Over the next several days, you will understand the mysteries of how things are revealed. Pay attention to the "Untouchables", for they never thought these things would take place.

11/5/21

What took place in New Jersey will reveal what is hidden. Do not lose hope in righteousness and justice, for in the days ahead, mysteries are revealed that focuses on, not one, but two!

11/6/21

The "Untouchables" are doing everything they can do before the last quarter of 2021 is over. What you have just seen is desperate measures in desperate times! They know that a very serious change is coming to America because the people have awakened! Watch closely! They are fearful, and they know that their agendas have all been exposed. This is why they are furious, trying to accomplish many things that are not in the best interest of the people. For in the next several weeks, very interesting changes occur suddenly that brings hope, and signs will be given regarding the 1st quarter of 2022. I say again, You must stay strong, and believe! January, February, March! The Season of Honor!

11/14/21

His eyes are upon you! Looking directly into your heart! Penetrating the very depths of your soul! Prepare for a sudden surprise visit from the One who holds all things in the palm of His hands. For He is positioning you for something very unique in this season. Your alignment, and the position you hold is critical in this hour. Your sensitivity to His presence shall increase dramatically over the next few days. For He is about to show you how much you are needed, your value, and the impact you are actually making. For increase comes in the measure of your calling. For new doors open, and you will walk in them, and operate in a capacity that was never dreamed of! For your time of deeper realms of glory are now upon you!

11/17/21

The enemy is trying diligently to come against your integrity and value. Stay strong, hold your ground, and keep your eyes fixed on *I AM*. Your breakthrough is about to come forth! Suddenly, when you least expect it!

11/23/21

Many people will not meet your expectations, and fall short of the task at hand. There are also many people that will be used to help you in this new season coming! Certain doors will be open, and some to close. Don't be discouraged by what doesn't come to pass, for there is far greater a door coming that will open up many mysteries about your future! Find your peace in Him, He is your refuge, and your strength in time of need!

11/25/21

As the Sun rises, the Sun sets! Seasons come, and they go! Now, as you have entered into a day of thanksgiving, the mysteries of Heaven are now upon you. The Son is truly rising in a unique way, regarding circumstances and scenarios that need closure, and to some, to reopen. Be watchful. Pay

John Natale

close attention to the sudden events that come forth in your life! For many wonderful things are in place now, to help facilitate new beginnings and restoration that is needed for the year ahead! For I have very special plans for you! Many plans that you had no idea were coming!

11/27/21— Max Is Back

Keep your eyes on the one who stirred the waters seasons ago! For he is planning, preparing for yet another significant shift! 2022 is a time where his voice again shall cause quite a bit of turbulence! They have tried to silence him with intimidation, but what he is about to bring to the table will change everything! For even when he was young in his career, he was called "Max". He brought justice, and had no idea that his destiny would involve revealing truth! Watch, for he has been granted a double portion to carry out the plans that have been set before him!

12/3/21

Signs and wonders occur in the month called December, and spread throughout the United States. It will transition into the 1st Quarter of 2022. Pay close attention to the land called "The District of Columbia" For strange events take place, and unexpected shifts are revealed! Rejoicing shall be heard in the streets, along with the cries of many! Tears will fall from the eyes of those that persevered and remained strong in a turbulent time. And to some called the "Intercessors," for you shall be glad! For your contention did not go unheard, it watered the earth and helped facilitate the breakthrough that has come!

12/15/21

For those that are broken, discouraged and doubting. I Am here! As with Thomas, I will suddenly appear and bring great comfort and the

308

reestablishment of hope. Fear not, your tears have reached my hands, and joy shall replace sorrow! It's time to shake the dust off of your feet and move forward once again!

12/19/21

Restrictions, requirements, and expectations are standards among conditional love. These are the many things that we place on ourselves, and at times, on others. Jesus loves with an unconditional love! Allow Him to penetrate your very being. We have now entered into a time where He is causing us to be vulnerable. This is critical as we enter into a brand new year! The place where revelation comes, and advancement follows! He loves you today! Just as you are! Allow Him to take you in His arms, sit on His lap, and hear His heart beat! There's nothing better!

12/23/21

Prepare for a sudden shift of positioning and the increase in the storehouse. December does not end without you finishing well. The unexpected turn of events that you thought could not happen, will not only arrive, but will stay positioned for several seasons!

12/27/21

Now prepare, watch, and stay sensitive to My voice. For the time has come when the hourglass shows the sand it holds, and reveals its finished journey. The things positioned for you and your family are prepared to be released. You did not grow weary in well doing, and your faithfulness has been rewarded! It's your time to reap a harvest!

Part Ten
Prophetic Words — 2022

1/1/2022— The Year Of Revelation And Restoration

Revelation and Restoration is coming in ways not dreamed of! A time where the hearts and minds of people come to an understanding and see significant shifts take place in their lives, their communities, and their nation! Watch closely, for as the year continues, major developments take place, and unexpected changes occur! The people shall be the voice heard loud and clear! Their cries shall be heard around the globe!

They will soon position themselves in such a posture of authority, that it will cause a frantic stirring to the ones who release oppression, delusion, and deception. The media and other voices shall no longer have their effect to oppress and hinder, simply because the presence of *I Am* shall rule in the hearts of the people! There will be a sovereign reign of glory in this new year, and restore what was stolen in 2021.

The sound of trumpets shall be heard again, and in this victory shout, there shall be a movement of people that move forward and cross many lines of victories! For many new faces shall come forth to facilitate freedom, and one familiar face shall be the focus of liberty! As with those that were on the boat that day, and saw *I AM* on the beach, their eyes were opened up to a great victory and celebration! This is your word for this time! A great celebration comes, when great revelation is revealed!

1/7/22— Season Of Instructions

For those that are feeling displaced and unvalued, this doesn't change the plans I have for you! Yes, you have felt like an elephant is sitting on your chest, and oppression is at an all time high. But what is about to take place in your life will change everything! The very things that are going on in your heart and mind are about to take on a radical shift towards Me! As this breakthrough comes forth, the manifestation of these things will be so much greater, and far more impacting than what you have experienced in the past!

The enemy has been trying everything to win a battle in your life, but I haven given you grace to get through the storm. The target was your self-worth, value, and fear of the future. The year called 2022 has not been what you were expecting. What manifested was minimized vision, and the loss of expectancy that you carried for such a time as this. I know it's been hard, but you are still on course for what I have destined for this time! You shall have your strength renewed, your confidence restored, and your joy revived! This shall come upon you suddenly, and even now to some, as My words are received! Don't be alarmed when I ask you to stay awake with Me during the 4th watch! For you have also entered into a season of instructions. Stay sensitive to Holy Spirit, for there is much to say in this hour!

1/8/22

This man called Denzel shall be used greatly in the year called 2022. He carries no fear, and will be a column of faith for others to gain encouragement from. Watch, for his platform increases, and his voice shall penetrate the darkness. For I am going to use the entertainment industry to preach a message of truth! And truth he shall bring!

1/22/22

Keep your eyes open, and your ears attentive to the voice that comes from the land called Washington, D.C. For there is one who resembles a Jason Bourne! He is seeking truth! For He shall find his way, cause quite the stirring, and reveal much!

1/30/22— Resist & Receive

The enemy is trying to crush you, and at the moment, it feels like he is winning. But a sudden wind is about to come in, so powerful and so beautiful, that the glory that it carries shall change everything, and restore what was stolen!

John Natale

1/31/22— The Great Shift

Many things come forth, and many things finish their course in the year called 2022. Watch, for the mandates shall lose their strength, and suddenly disappear into the wind. Voices of authority shall be replaced with voices of reason that strengthen, and uphold honor. Not only will the land called the United States be repositioned and restored, but keep your eyes on Canada, Australia, and the land called Israel. For a breakthrough comes to the Holy Land. Eyes open to truth, fear replaced with faith! For the people are speaking, acting, rising up in ways never thought possible! As was spoken before, the nations, one at a time, are being awakened by My voice, My authority. They thought they had power, control, but they never considered the power and presence of the I AM!

They believed I AM not aware, not interested, but they are ignorant, and they do not know Truth, the one who is Truth! For the tears, the cries, and prayers of the many have been heard, and I have prepared much for such a time as this, to act and to move puzzle pieces into new positions. For they shall say "What has happened, didn't we have a plan that would win?" They did have a plan, but My authority crushes plans that are not My plans! So in this time, when you have been weary, and you have questioned everything, including Me, I will restore your faith, and restore your expectation, for in this time, you are needed.

For many will look to you and seek your peace, the peace that only I can establish. Many are rising up! Many new leaders shall have a platform and be My voice! The season is nearly upon you, prepare and shake the dust off of your feet. There is work to be done, things to come back into place, and hearts to beat again. America, great days are upon you! As Israel prayed for deliverance in the land of bondage and was heard, deliverance is coming! You are about to take a great step forward to promise!

2/2/22

Have you ever thought of why John was at the feet of Jesus while He was on the cross? What was needed that day would change his world forever! As he looked into the eyes of Jesus, never leaving His gaze for a moment, all things became new! He was meant to be there, meant to understand the depths of love! Do you think he saw the future? What he would have to do for the One he loved so very much?

Put yourself in that place right now, and look into those piercing eyes that laid everything down for you. Allow the love that flowed that day to penetrate your heart! John's perspective and destiny all came into existence that day, simply because he opened every area of his life to the One who gave all His life for you and me! Sometimes, we get stuck, and fall back because of the troubles of life, but we can always turn to the eyes of love for hope and direction!

He is good! And His love never fails! So many of you will have that experience in the days ahead! Whether it's a vision or dream, prepare for that encounter. It's needed for the days we have entered into.

2/10/22

Keep your eyes and ears on Nancy! For the voice comes forth that reveals clues to the year called 2022. Mysteries being revealed that was not expected! Holy Spirit is causing truth to be on display in many unusual ways in this season.

2/18/22

Holy Spirit just said *"Help is on the Way!"* Angels surrounding you, lifting up your arms that are heavy. The broken pieces shall be fixed, and the peace that was stolen, returned sevenfold! It comes Suddenly!

John Natale

2/22/22— United States

Don't be concerned about the smoke screen that is present with current scenarios in the nation. Many new strategies are being used to deflect the exposures that shall take place, and with very specific people. The spiritual battle is much greater now, and is manifesting in ways that is trying to take focus off other critical issues. The coming year called 2022, is already marked for significant breakthrough, it shall not pass without great defeats *and* great victories. Pay close attention to one who speaks in riddles, and the one who speaks with no clarity, for a clue is given unexpectedly, and will reveal answers to very important questions at hand! Isaiah 22:22.

3/2/22— Mystery

What answers are you looking for? What questions do you have? Some will say, "Say it isn't so!" Many have had their minds brought into a level of anger, some confused, but in its time, the answers shall be given! They look to Russia, seeking answers to actions, but in fact, the answers will be redirected to questions. Questions that will be asked to others that have answers. Answers that many did not expect would come forth so quickly. And quickly they shall come, and reveal such truth. For it is truth that sets all things in motion! For it is the work of Holy Spirit in this hour preparing, shifting, and realigning what is needed in a critical season. For Holy Spirit has all authority, all access! My word reveals, restores, and revives that which is needed in its time! The time has come now, for the season has come, and the season bears much fruit!

3/8/22— The Hand & Root

You can choose to accept defeat or choose to rejoice. The words have been spoken already regarding the great deception that has plagued the nation. In its time, all truth comes to pass. You must remember, I Am, who I Am, is fully aware of what has, and what will take place. People are awakening throughout the world about the plans, and the events that changed everything. But, one must not shrink back, nor settle for what is upon you!

For you see, a great and mighty wind comes, it shall clear the air, remove the smoke! Remember the smoke? It was spoken of not too long ago! And the one who is going to speak, he is not accepted, nor is he considered to be one that reasons wisely. There is a great movement of angelic activity that resides over the land, the land that is the focus of the nations! Choose wisely regarding what is My attention! It seems to many that emptiness, and barrenness is all around! Many have questioned those that have spoken against the darkness, and have placed their feet firmly into the soil! For their words will not come back void! For they chose wisely, sensitive to My voice, and stood firm!

Now, stay sensitive to My voice, and My leading! What seems impossible, is possible, if you believe! Put the pieces to the puzzle in place, and understand the mystery! Things are allowed to take place simply because man has free will, and in these choices, many things come forth to reveal other things, things that are not visible. So the questions come and they go! You ask,

"Why didn't *I AM* stop it? Why didn't *I AM* fix it? Does *I AM* fix what is broken? Just to be repaired? or shall the King of Glory pull the root out from the ground?"

Oh it shall be so! Some roots have been exposed, and many see what's under the soil. But there is a stronger root, and he has been growing for many seasons! My hand is about to penetrate the soil, and pull up the root from the base. For it has grown into many branches, branches that seek to gain in strength, but it has grown to its capacity! It has no more room, and no more guidance from the base! For it feels the strength of the hand of God all around it. It holds things in place until the appointed time to lift and reveal. For that time is coming! For the season draws close! Watch and listen! For as the ground speaks, it reveals the season of uprooting!

3/20/22— The United States

Sudden events take place, as the season draws to close. What has been hidden will unexpectedly make a sound that reveals what has been hiding behind closed doors. The enemy is using fear tactics to keep the light from engaging, But I have positioned two very different individuals that will be used to engage the source! Prepare for the season to end, and another to begin. There is one who is about to get considerably frustrated and weary, for he is losing his strength. For one weakens, and another strengthens, and in its time, one comes forth, and exposes the weak one. And his words shall be used to reveal the cracks in the foundation!

You were looking for answers to come forth from certain soil, but in fact, simple truths come forth from soil that was not expected. So don't be alarmed about what you see, and what you hear. For in its time, the dust settles, and the skies clear. Voices will be heard sharply, faces will be seen clearly, and they shall not be received. For their words will fall on deaf ears; their sound insignificant, and incapable of penetrating the mindsets of mankind. Your season is coming upon you, it has been spoken of before, now it manifests in unique ways!

3/24/22

Do not be intimidated by the sound or the presence of the enemy. He is fully aware of your strength in this season. The enemy will use the tactics of affecting others around you to get to your faith. Stay focused, and stay strong, your season shall not be disrupted in anyway.

3/25/22

Keep your eyes on Florida, and Governor Ron DeSantis! For authority increases, expands, and the platform strengthens. For in the days ahead, an announcement is released, but the roots in the ground shall remain. For the enemy is desiring that the tree be uprooted and planted, but destiny has already been chosen. His authority is protected, and his wisdom grows each day. In the weeks ahead, one will try to undo with words of condemnation against what has been established, and what shall be accomplished. For this will not prevail!

For he has been positioned strategically for such a time as this. To be a watchman on the wall, to be a voice of hope, to be a voice that comes against the darkness. For he knows his place, and he knows his assignment, and in this he has been given great insight. For he has been given keys to unlock the mysteries of deception and delusion that have ruled and reigned in the season of despair. So pay close attention to his words, for he shall prophesy, and give a sudden word that stirs the water, and then a surge of freedom shall be ignited!

3/28/22— The Untouchables

Who are they? What are they? What secrets do they have? When are they revealed? As time has gone by, and voices come and go, blueprints have been shown through the lives of many, the hidden clues to the ones called the "Untouchables". For they have postured in power, shown their strength, and raised their voices. But as seasons come and go, the spirit realm also changes its season. For the time has come now, as Holy Spirit is moving in many unusual ways, ways to bring sudden changes that were not considered possible.

Voices that were thought to be powerless are coming to facilitate a knocking on the door. One by one, each one will be revealed, and one by one, they will turn on each other. Holy Spirit is causing their alliance to become weakened at the root. And in the days ahead, the root, that which

was hidden for several years, speaks and reveals truth to what many have
been seeking.

4/1/22

A sudden shift that changes everything! Weariness is gone, and joy has
come! April is a month of restoration, restored hope, and revived hearts!
The floodgates of Heaven are open!

4/11/22— Authority in Florida

The assignment for Ron DeSantis is Florida! If he chooses to abandon his
post, his authority shall cease. He has been given a very significant
mandate in this season, and the season ahead. His post carries great
authority that is used significantly to be a lighthouse for the nation. You
must pray and intercede for this man. Discernment and wisdom is critical
in this hour. He already knows what to do, but manipulation and ungodly
wisdom wants to change that!

But *I Am* will not allow destiny to be disrupted! His heart has been molded
to reflect the heart of God towards the common good of mankind. Prayer
and intercession is key to his tenure. Keep watch for him, for he makes an
announcement soon, and his posture reveals his intentions. For they are
afraid of him, because he carries the boldness that David did! He will
confront a giant, and in that day, he shall see a great victory!

4/14/22

During the months of April, May, and June, Holy Spirit will cause many
things to take place in the spirit realm that will manifest in the natural
realm. These months ahead will bring forth divine connections,
opportunities, and appointments. They are critical in your life, and will be

used to set up the next seven seasons of Jubilee. Prepare your hearts, and take every thought captive that comes to distract and discourage. For you will see My goodness, and My love bring forth such overwhelming, extravagant peace, joy, and abundance in your life.

4/16/22— The Floridian Anchor

The Prophetic Posture of Governor Ron DeSantis is a much needed critical anchor in the sand. In its time, the anchor will be released, the sails shall catch the wind, and the vessel shall be pointed to a new course of direction. In this time, the posture is positioned as a column of strength and support for one who has not finished his journey. You will see as time goes by how they are used for each other. An increase in camaraderie, trust, and strategy shall be evident in the days ahead that lead to great victories.

4/18/22— He Is Near

When you feel alone, I Am there! When you can't hear My voice, I Am still speaking! When you can't see any hope for your situation, I Am preparing you for a great breakthrough! When all seems lost, there is always a way that I Am found! What you felt was missing, depleted, and exhausted, shall suddenly take on new life! Yes, you have gone through quite a season, one you thought had no end in sight. But all things become new! All things can change at any moment! And that time is now! All it takes is just one touch, one word, one sudden breath from the winds of change! Holy Spirit is doing that right now! So receive that now! Hearts healed, bones healed! Lives made whole, and the unexpected healing that was not expected! Sudden opportunity and breakthrough that comes in a way that is a mystery to you! For what you thought was not possible was walking right alongside of you the whole time!

John Natale

4/21/22

There's such a sweet peace today! Expect breakthrough to come as the hours pass! Specific things that you've been waiting for have been directed to manifest and come to fruition.

4/21/22— The United States

There is great movement in the spirit realm, as angels have been released to stand guard in strategic locations across the land. For there is one who expects a victory to be imminent, but the plans have already been witnessed by My gaze. They are powerless, and have no authority. It has already been spoken, that these things shall not continue. For light overcomes darkness, and the darkness cannot comprehend it! You have seen many things take place that changed everything, but that didn't change My plans for this nation.

In everything, there is a time, a season, and in this, it can be a mystery that is not always understood. What is important is that you stay strong, stay alert, and see things with spiritual eyes. Many have settled, let go because of weariness, but I will revive their faith! This nation will return to a place of honor once again! The things that took place were allowed to come to fruition for many reasons. It revealed many things, many hearts that became cold, lifeless, and divided. But what was once good, shall be again! So prepare your jars, just as the prophet spoke to the woman who thought the end was near!

Fresh oil is coming, and more than you can imagine! So rejoice, for what was taken shall be retuned! So as the enemy comes to steal, kill, and destroy, I Am here to give life, and give it abundantly! The season is nearly at hand, the time draws near, and many know that change is coming. It is one that cannot be stopped nor hindered. There is one who knows what he is called to do. For he has been active, strategic, and sharper than in the previous season. So keep your attention on him, for he will make a very profound declaration! For he is not weary, he has

322

been given a double portion of grace, peace, and confidence. For he knows the outcome already, and knows that in its time, the curtain rises once again.

5/1/22— United States

Watch in the coming days, for Holy Spirit will reveal a very interesting piece of the puzzle. Then the wind shall blow, and clear the air to see what is hidden.

5/9/22

Keep your eyes on the one called Trump! For his hand is on a chess piece, and he is about to make a move that is not expected. It will confuse some, but to others who know the game, the strategy is epic!

5/11/22

Many of you keep looking back to regain what seems lost, but I Am here to tell you that greater days are ahead. You have not lost anything! You actually have gained much! Many additions shall come forth in this month called May, and you will see and experience an unplanned opportunity filled with a double portion of grace.

5/15/22

It's going to be a glorious Sunday! What you didn't expect shall come to fruition, and what was expected shall manifest in a greater measure. Stay faithful! He is there to supply all your needs! Listen closely to Holy Spirit, Over the next few days, specific directives take place. Doors open, doors close, and the answer to what you have been seeking shall be heard very clearly. Peace then fills your heart, and your path shall be not disturbed any longer. The next steps shall be joy, laughter, and a double portion of grace.

5/19/22— Sudden Changes

Do not be discouraged or troubled when sudden changes are placed upon you. For all things are in My hands, and I Am guiding your steps. For these days ahead are ordered by Me, and they will be fruitful and bountiful. Trust me and know, that all is well. Don't look back, but look ahead! The future is now!

5/21/22

The angel of the Lord wrestled with Jacob at the Jabbok River to get rid of fear that was influencing his life. Don't allow the enemy to lie to you about your future. Your present circumstances are not what your future has in store. What's coming is more than you expected, and the door is wide open to walk through! Get ready! **It's Go time!**

5/28/22

We are called to do exploits in His name! It doesn't matter who you are, how old or young you are, Just Go! Do it! The enemy is trembling! The path is clear! GO!

5/31/22

Though there has been much adversity, there is advancement and victory! You have struck the giant! There are many cheering for you, and believing with you. The enemy cannot understand why you are still fighting, and in this, the present attacks and tribulations are coming to an end. Rejoice, for you have overcome once again!

6/4/22

Holy Spirit is about to do something very significant in the last stages of the second quarter! The spirit of delusion is being allowed to operate a little longer, then it comes crashing down! The enemy has nothing left to give, his plans have been compromised, eradicated, and dissolved. What you see is the final performance of what has been watched, and bridled for many seasons. Take notice of sudden pockets of My glory, as it manifests in specific parts of the nation and reveals angelic activity. Keep your eyes fixed on Florida, California, and Nebraska! They have been prepared to reveal supernatural activity.

6/8/22

God will not be mocked! A strong shaking is coming! It comes like a thief in the night, and it comes to overwhelm the darkness. Grace has been given, grace has been lifted.

6/15/22— Armor Up!

Keep careful that you are not being used by others so they can elevate their ministries. Your calling and gifting must be guarded at all times! There are many out there that haven't paid the price, but use the history of others to get an all-expense paid trip to the big show! Discernment is critical in this hour, and the separation of impure motives is presently in process.

6/17/22

Brand new strategical assignments are now in the works! Prepare your mindsets, and stay alert! For a door opens suddenly that will take you into territory that was not ever thought of, a promotion in the spirit realm that parallels your natural duties. This will be one heck of a journey! The breathtaking, awesome ride is about to begin! Hang on! It's about to get real!

6/17/22

Holy Spirit is about to reveal secret codes that uncover secret lives!

6/29/22— United States

Keep watch! For one is planning far more than what is being revealed. She has a hidden agenda behind the scenes, that which is operating to dismantle truth. You must pay attention to the words, the language, the movements. For there are clues, and there are puzzle pieces that reveal who the focus is on. It will reveal who is the concern, who they fear, who causes them to tremble! Light overcomes darkness, and the darkness cannot comprehend it. In the months ahead, you will see such a turnaround that shakes the nation! It moves in the spirit, then manifests in the natural.

For they are afraid of what is coming! The first of many dominoes has already fallen! Now get ready, for two more shall fall, and that will be your sign that prepares for the greatest victory in the land called the United States. Restoration shall come, alliances that were made with other nations shall cease, and a strength shall be restored with a double portion. As this unfolds, the nation called Israel shall speak loud and clear once again, and a camaraderie shall become present once again.

7/7/22

There is a door before you that is open! Don't be afraid to walk in it, and don't talk yourself out of it. It might not seem like what everyone was expecting for you, but this is not about them! This about you, and your destiny! Take each step wisely, don't overanalyze, don't think so hard! What is critical is simple. Keep your ears attentive to the voice that speaks truth! His name is above all names! His name is Jesus! If that offends someone, so be it! This is your time now!

You have waited, you have been faithful! You have heard from Holy Spirit, and you have responded correctly! It will be a very joyful and fruitful journey! What you see now is just the beginning of very significant days ahead! Remember the name Joseph! He had a dream! He carried an expectancy! He carried destiny on his shoulders and never gave up! What came to pass was more than he could have ever imagined! You have entered into the significant season! It's your season! Rejoice! It was planned for such a time as this Now GO!

7/18/22

Sickness and disease are not attributes of the Kingdom of Heaven. Do not accept them, do not tolerate them. The enemy has deceived many people in believing that this is part of life, but it is not the plan that I put in place. When you get a true revelation of the authority you carry, and the understanding that the enemy has no authority to take life, the door closes to the entrance point in which the adversary has entered into so many lives. Get that revelation today and close the door! it's not acceptable. You must remember, you are in this world, but not of it. The rules never changed!

7/27/22

The enemy is working hard to convince you that you're off the path. Stop questioning your faith! Resist him, and he will flee! You are right where you are suppose to be in this season! Keep moving, keep pressing in, and stay sensitive to My leading! Breakthrough is here, and sudden manifestations of My love and joy for you are about to knock on your door!

John Natale

7/30/22

The blessing is about to pour out in ways you never thought or imagined! Get ready for a very interesting, and refreshing correspondence! Sudden surprises and breakthrough shall overwhelm you in the hours and days ahead! Your faith was stronger than you thought, and your ability to overcome all things has always been present! Stay in a mindset of peace and joy! I Am right by your side!

7/31/22

Don't let the enemy steal your confidence! The decision you made has great blessing ahead! Holy Spirit already gave you the victory! You won, and the enemy lost badly!

8/7/22

Expect the door that is presently open for you to release significant favor and opportunity! The door that seems to be not fully open is about to swing wide! Walk in it and watch what unfolds! A double portion blessing is on a collision course in your life!

8/8/22— Benghazi Justice

Holy Spirit reminded me this morning that this subject is far from over! There is a sudden source that comes out and exposes secrets that were hidden from open ears! Keep your eyes attentive to the ones who saw it all! For they are being prepared to speak again! For they shall inherit the peace that has been stolen from them!

8/18/22

Let's stand together in faith and say

"Yes God! You will fill my day with peace, joy, and breakthrough."

For those of you that need supernatural grace today, it's time to press through, press in, and pull on the hem of the garment like the woman with the issue of blood did. She was given grace and strength to change her mindset, to make a choice, to never give up! Today is that day! Let's go!

8/21/22

If you need a breakthrough, it's time for the manifestation of blessing to come forth! No more doubt, no more fear, no more worry! Something has broken in the spirit realm that has caused hindrance and delay! The windows of Heaven are about to open! Get your empty jars! The oil is going to overflow!

8/22/22

Oh how the change has come! Many are experiencing it now, and many will see the curtain rise over the next few days ahead. This month called August will show you how things must be in alignment. The big things, the little things, they are all important to Me! So you have just a fragment of days left in this month, and some believe that it will end the same way it started, but this is not so! What comes at the end is the very thing that was not expected. For a great celebration shall be heard from the voices of many! It will not end with disappointment, but in jubilee and victory!

8/28/22

I have postured you to be a voice that speaks truth! Do not change the way I have made you for anyone! It doesn't matter what anyone says or thinks! The only thing that matters is what I have called you to be! The only thing that matters is ME!

8/29/22

There has been negative words from the accuser that have been in the atmosphere, and have been manifesting naturally. These are now ceasing and coming to an end! There is freedom now that will overtake you, bring advancement, and overwhelming blessing.

9/3/22

Pharaoh eventually caved in and realized he could not defeat the power of I Am! Do you see the similarities present? Watch closely! For the people shall be set free, and a very great victory is coming in the weeks ahead! Not only is freedom sounding in the heavens, but the sound of the shofar has been released to prepare the way! Angels are coming in epic proportions, and a justice revealed that was established long before the scenarios were even present! For I know all things, and I dictate all things according My plans and purposes!

9/5/22— Sovereign Healing

Generational demonic forces that have been hidden and causing much destruction in your life have been exposed and dealt with! Angels of war have dealt with them swiftly! They were lingering for years, strengthened by wounds of rejection. They had access because of the authority that was given to them, based on the wound of the heart. But that is over now! I have given you the victory, and the enemy has lost a battle he was never going to win! The generational curse is broken, and the sovereign healing has come! The season of color is upon you!

September is a month that you will see great restoration! In your life, and in those that are close to you! Times of refreshing are now in the winds that have been ordered to blow upon you! You will feel a great calm to a storm that seemed would never end! You will shake the dust off of your feet, rise up, and walk with a peace that surpasses all understanding! You will have a joy that is overwhelming! You will have a confidence in Me that was missing! You will be the head, and not the tail! You will be blessed going in, and blessed going out! In this new you, your perspective will change! Your mindset will change! How you see yourself will change! All because of a foundational spiritual darkness that was crushed by My voice! Rejoice! For the winds of change have come!

9/15/22

When you least expect it, breakthrough comes in ways not imagined, in levels not even considered, and in measures not dreamed of! For in the moments ahead, a very significant shift comes and changes everything! You have been faithful, even when you thought you gave up! You have been strong, when you thought you were weak! You were courageous, when you thought you caved into fear! Rejoice! For the days of reconciliation have come!

9/18/22

VISION AND DIRECTION IS BEING MADE CLEAR FOR YOU NOW! GET READY FOR A NEW ASSIGNMENT THAT BRINGS IN A GREAT HARVEST! UNUSUAL OCCURRENCES AND OPPORTUNITIES THAT YOU HAVE NO HISTORY WITH!

In a vision, I was shown two barn owls. One was looking directly at me, and the other to the right. They represent vision and direction. Also, I was shown a garage door that I needed to get to. Once inside, the door closed quickly. This is a representation of a door closing very quickly. This new season is coming with such speed, and all the details will be released soon enough! Do not be concerned about the door closing, for it is needed now! For what is coming! Wow! That is what is glorious! For that is beyond your comprehension! It is an outpouring of a double portion of the floodgates of Heaven! The road ahead is so clear, so full of abundance! NEVER FORGET THIS SEASON! IT SHAPES THE NEXT TEN YEARS OF YOUR LIFE!

9/26/22

The spirit of religion is very cunning! Pay close attention to scenarios over the next few days that reveal false motives. Your sensitivity and activation is critical to defeating the adversary. I will give you discernment and revelation to understand how to address the issues at hand. The key to victory is simple. **You need Me more than you need anything!**

9/28/22

Get ready for a great October thru December! The word for these months comes from **John 2:1-10**.

The choicest of wines are about to be revealed to the body of Christ. Those that have endured, persevered, and not given up, a great season is upon you! On a national level, watch what takes place! For there is one who many have considered defeated, but a strategy has been given that only comes from the place called "Mystery." For he is prepared to make a move on the chess board!

The season is now upon you, the one spoken about! It's time to shake the dust off of your feet and prepare for a supernatural victory! The wind changes its course, and the voices shall change from one sound to another! One particular voice shall be heard loud and clear in the next three months! It shall be much louder than before, and it shall clear the path that has been disrupted!

10/7/22

A surge of opportunity, advancement, and breakthrough is present! Watch for the sudden manifestation of glory that comes and overtakes you and your family! Faith is being rewarded! The enemy tried to bring a defeat to your posture of grace, but what was revealed was diligence, determination, and dedication! You have overcome, and the enemy has been pushed back! Take full advantage of the time! The windows of Heaven are fully open!

10/13/22

Stay diligent in your pursuit of what you know is an assignment from Holy Spirit. The enemy is working overtime to convince you to give up, but strength, confidence, and an unexpected breakthrough comes suddenly! Get ready!

10/16/22

Your codependency with man will suffocate you with religion, but your reliance on Holy Spirit will disperse you into revelation!

10/16/22

There are times that you feel as if you are just not good enough, or do not measure up. That is a lie from the pit! Today is a reminder that you have been created perfectly, with an amazing destiny ahead! There is nothing that can change that! The enemy diligently tries to bring self-condemnation to your self worth, but My presence brings all things together, and gives you beautiful peace. So right now, for those of you that have been struggling with who you are, there is an in-filling of strength, comfort, and confidence that will change how you see yourself, and ultimately how you see Me! Now get ready, for significant breakthroughs shall take place over the next few days!

John Natale

10/24/22

Over the next few weeks, a separation of the sheep and the goats shall take place! It will bring great concern to some, but for others, confirmation of what they had heard in the spirit. Hidden agendas, false motives, and impure desires shall come to the surface, and reveal unrighteousness in the camp! Holy Spirit is preparing the church for a great victory, and a sudden surge of glory! This will come, but it will not be completed without some house cleaning taking place!

Then the new season shall arise! One that was said was not going to happen, but is was already planned by the speaking of My voice! Destined, orchestrated by an authority that is above all authority! You must not fear any longer, you must stay sensitive to the voice that speaks within! For it speaks truth, and this truth that has been questioned shall come forth with such a victory, such a glory, that man will not be able to take ownership of! The year closes, yes it does, like all seasons do. But this year that you call 2022 doesn't end, it only begins the process of restoration of what was stolen!

11/15/22

We are in a Numbers 21:4-9 Season! Something very unusual is about to happen! What was not expected shall be a source of hope and restoration!

11/18/22

We have now entered into the season of great Truth and Justice! Get rid of all the doubt, discouragement, and murmuring, and prepare your hearts for events not seen before! This will take time, but grace, courage, and boldness has been given to some that will cause the atmosphere to become quite erratic. Do not be concerned for this, and its responses. In the spirit realm, a great battle is taking place, but the end is very close. Watch closely who is being used, one addresses a nation, and the other addresses unrighteousness. But both achieve a great victory!

11/23/22

Doors that you thought were closed, have never shut! It was the enemy's plan all along to convince you otherwise. I have given you diligence to keep moving forward. In this, you have kept the faith, even though you saw nothing manifest. A knowledge and understanding was inside of you that could not be silenced.

From this, a suddenly door has opened for some, and will open for others in the moments ahead! Don't try to reason with the door that is upon you! It will look as if it is more than you can handle, but this is from Me, and it has been granted, simply because you have been faithful with what you have been given. And now it's time to pour out the overflow! Get ready, for it is so much more than your mindset tried to figure out!

11/27/22

Your ability to succeed is determined by your diligence to overcome. Stay focused, keep pushing, and win this battle! It's your time!

11/30/22

When the journey is over, you will stand before Christ looking back on how you lived, loved, and labored. It's that simple! It's that easy! Choose wisely while you walk the road called Destiny!

John Natale

12/2/22

The door that you are about to travel through is open! It might not be visible now, but it comes suddenly, without any hint of when. I'm causing you to trust Me! Don't let discouragement steal your momentum! Very specific details are needed to be put into place, and adjustments made before you start a new season of special assignments.

12/8/22

Looking back at everything you have endured, gone through, overcame, and conquered; is what you are going through right now going to break you? Of course not! Your greatest challenge has set you up for the greatest victory in your journey! You were never alone, even though the walls seemed like they were caving in. The foundation has always been strong! The season is coming to an end, and in the end you will finish above and beyond your own expectations! There are quite a bit of surprises coming your way! Some that you thought were long gone, and beyond reach.

Now as the day closes, and the night reaches its full, remember these words;

> BLESSED ARE YOU WHEN PEOPLE INSULT YOU, PERSECUTE YOU AND FALSELY SAY ALL KINDS OF EVIL AGAINST YOU BECAUSE OF ME. REJOICE AND BE GLAD, BECAUSE GREAT IS YOUR REWARD IN HEAVEN, FOR IN THE SAME WAY THEY PERSECUTED THE PROPHETS WHO WERE BEFORE YOU.

Take these words now, and allow them to penetrate your heart! I have calmed the storm!

12/10/22

There is time coming very soon that the Prophets will engage and implement 1 Kings 18:17-18. This will bring quite a stirring among the Pharisees, and reveal where the heart is truly grafted in!

12/14/22

Keep pursuing, and walking towards the door that is presently open! It might not seem much is happening, but what is happening behind the scenes is amazing! This is your trust moment! You have done what you needed to do so far! Now let Me handle the rest! The correspondence that you are seeking and hoping for is coming sooner than you think! When this happens, let My presence, and my guidance dictate every word that comes forth from your mouth! This will allow the opportunity to come to fruition, and start a new assignment.

12/22/22

Do not be afraid! For I am with you wherever you go! Very unusual scenarios come your way, and unexpected supernatural manifestations take place as you step out into faith! I Am bringing many people to you! Do not be afraid to share what you hear inside your heart! For what is about to happen changes everything, changes you!

12/27/22

A sudden supernatural release of favor is coming to change your course of direction and provide in epic ways. You have been faithful with little, now you shall be given much. But where much is given, much is required. Doors shall open wide for you suddenly, and the doors already open, shall be adjusted to accommodate what is already active. Have faith, and believe! Nothing shall be removed, only added. Your season of increase has arrived!

Part Eleven
Prophetic Words — 2023

John Natale

1/1/23– 2023 The Year Of Opportunity And Promotion

You are going to see significant breakthrough, restoration, promotion, advancement, and cancellation of debt. It shall be an epic year that is the polar opposite of 2022. Where there was decrease, there shall be increase! Where there was disappointment, there shall be excitement! Where there was rejection, there shall be an open door that will confirm a that was given years ago. In the days ahead, it is critical to be sensitive and trust My guidance and course of direction. You will have correspondence with not one, but several people, that will present opportunities to new and exciting assignments. Favor shall be flowing like oil in this new season!

You have been faithful with everything that has been required of you! Now much is given, and much is required. The door of opportunity that is coming has those that are presenting it fascinated and mesmerized by what you carry! Laughter shall echo throughout the house, as what was not expected shall pour out on epic levels, and overwhelm the heart! The storehouse shall be filled again! The support shall be more than imagined! The light that you carry shall burn brighter, and carry very significant influence in areas and regions that were once closed and dormant!

The full restoration comes to the family! Prodigals return! Marriages healed! Unity restored to the foundation that was broken by disappointments! The full measure of what was prayed for, hoped for, shall all come to pass!

1/17/23

Watch and see how the bread and fish multiplies! There are times that I will cause the storehouse to empty, so it can be filled with sudden resources that were not on your mindset! This is your time of faith! Remember that I Am your Source! You have seen it before many times, today is no different! Your faith shall be a visual component of hope for others! Take this time now and rise up with confidence, I saw you in your despair, just like I saw Nathaniel. He was brought to a new level of revelation and understanding, just like you are about to experience! Peace I give, Peace covers you!

1/19/23

For those that have lost their ability to walk, Holy Spirit is healing your legs right now!

1/20/23

The trumpet cannot be silenced, because the musician has been instructed to keep playing! There are new sounds about to be heard. With these new notes released, they shall be a sweet melody to some, and to others, an irritable shriek of defeat. So prepare your hearts, be attentive with your ears, for the sound that goes forth into the atmosphere shall be loud, clear, and graced with authority.

1/22/23

I know you're tired, but Holy Spirit is giving you strength to overcome your adversity. Your wineskin shall be changed, and new wine added to give you everything that is required of you in this season. When you least expect it, the floodgates of Heaven shall open up and overwhelm you!

1/24/23

What is coming into existence is merely a smokescreen of what's to come. Do not be surprised when certain individuals are placed into power to continue the present pattern. Now pay close attention! Holy Spirit has revealed all things, spoken all things, and nothing shall change the course of direction that shall come and bring back integrity and honor to a nation that was founded on the principles of righteousness.

John Natale

1/28/23

I Am the God of second chances! Never forget that! What seems impossible, is completely possible to Me! So in these precious days ahead, prepare for the unbelievable to come forth!

For I Am! For I Am good!

1/28/23

People are trying to influence you in directives that are not My will. What I Am looking for is a generation that will put their trust in Holy Spirit, not be co-dependent on the ways of man! You have come to a time in your walk where you will see many false things come to the surface and reveal where the heart truly is.

Discernment is being sharpened significantly to allow you to make adjustments on your path. Don't be concerned about sudden shifts in your connections, for they are needed in this season. You shall move forward now with greater intensity, and sudden bursts of favor that bring clear paths!

2/5/23

Keep your eyes on the one called Trump. For he has a hand of cards that will take everyone by surprise! Do not be concerned about the distractions that are presently active regarding his forward progress. The enemy is trying to take focus off of him, and place it on someone that has not been called into the season of seasons. He will strengthen considerably in the weeks ahead, and cause quite the disturbance to those that are seeking to keep the current system active.

2/9/23

The enemy is on assignment to bring turmoil, anger, and bitterness to present scenarios that has you troubled. But there is a great peace and victory coming in the moments ahead! A sudden surge of breakthrough shall cause an overwhelming defeat to the adversary. The winds shall cease, and the storm shall pass!

2/23/23— United States

There's quite a disruption taking place in the spirit realm! The fight is extremely intense! What is happening presently, and in the days ahead will reveal a spirit of confusion, and ultimately, a clear sight of restoration and justice! The enemy has actually begun to implode on his own plans! What was designed to take down righteousness has changed its course, and now is in full manifestation mode of accelerating the target on wickedness.

As was spoken in the days gone by, one is weakening, and the other is strengthening! You will see one gather people together, encourage, help, and strengthen the hope of lives across the nation! The other will seek the counsel of the one who has been hidden, but visible to some. He will seek advisement on decisions that are ahead, but this will not change the outcome of what Holy Spirit has aligned to come forth. So watch, and listen closely, for there is one who resides off the land, he plans, he watches, and he prepares!

For he has a word, an informative word that some do not want to hear. But it will be released, and when it is heard, a clue shall be given to understand what is coming! This puzzle piece will be used significantly to realign the wheel that is needed to spin with balance!

3/3/23

A season of support and direction is upon you! What is needed, and what is available now, shall take care of you and your family for many months ahead! It's the direction that is critical! You will have new opportunities to grow, but you will have past connections to learn from! As was spoken about in the prior season, this is polar opposite of what you were experiencing. What you didn't realize about the season past was simple! You were not doing anything wrong, you were just being molded and prepared for the outpouring of blessing! Just because significant favor wasn't evident physically, doesn't mean that spiritual favor wasn't present! It was! And now the preparation is over, and the floodgates are open!

3/5/23

The enemy tried to corrupt the day with a blindside attack, but Holy Spirit disrupted those plans and de-escalated the situation! Now onto the next assignment! A week of significant breakthrough!

3/13/23

Supernatural grace, peace, and favor shall flow like oil that ran down Aaron's beard! Get ready for some very interesting turn of events that facilitate the outpouring you have been expecting!

3/24/23

The enemy is trying to bring you back to your past, and ultimately cause you to cave in. The struggle has been quite intense, with feelings of hopelessness, but Holy Spirit has something very special in store that changes everything! What took place years ago has seemed as if it has kept lingering, and wouldn't go away, but today is a new day! A new beginning! It's time to close that chapter and move forward!

I'm removing grave clothes that stayed longer than it should, and placing on you now a new coat that reveals strength, peace, and joy! It's the joy that will mark you now! It's the laughter that will identify you now! This all comes from My heart for you! My plans for you! So lift up your head, and look up, the Son shines brightly! You are a Child of God!

4/2/23

The Joseph Moment is now present! Prepare for a sudden opportunity that will facilitate a very significant assignment! As Pharaoh was used to enable the destiny and calling of Joseph, you too are about to see how your gift will make room for you! April is a very critical month that reveals the opportunity and promotion that was spoken of earlier!

4/18/23

It doesn't matter how well you speak behind a pulpit! What does matter is if you are releasing what Holy Spirit is saying! It must reflect the character and attributes of Jesus. Anything else is natural, lifeless words!

4/23/23

The dam is breaking and the water is about to overwhelm you! What was held back is no longer delayed! The outpouring of favor is now available for you and your family! Watch, for in the present day, and the days ahead, the opportunities come and the doors swing wide open!

4/29/23

You might not have seen the great breakthrough you were expecting, but what you didn't know was that your diligence and perseverance shall be rewarded in a way that was not expected! Get ready for a very significant week ahead! The door is open, and a peace that surpasses all understanding shall overwhelm you in these days ahead! The road is clear now, and the path is wide open! You overcame the obstacles and pain of the past, and now as the maturity in your life is evident, the timing has become present!

It's your time now! I have watched you, guided you, and helped you! Now I am blessing you! But in this new opportunity, share your testimony, share your heart! For there will be many that I will bring to you, for you to support, and help in their season of struggle. But as the time, and support continues, they too will experience the open door as well. So stay sensitive, stay tender, and never take your eyes off of Me! I'm watching you! I'm with you! Always!

5/3/23

I heard the Holy Spirit say *"The month of May shall be called **AMAZING**."*

You will be overwhelmed by My goodness and the amount of blessing that overtakes you! When the circumstances around you cause you to feel that there is no hope....I Am there! When there is silence and you hear nothing....I Am there! When discouragement tries to consume you....I Am there to give you peace! Watch as I unlock the hidden treasures that you have been waiting patiently for. I Am directing you in a promise land that is more than you can imagine! Do not be afraid, and do not worry any longer! You have won, My Child! Your faith has made the way for you, and has caused Me to reveal great glory for you! It has been fashioned for you before time began.

5/7/23

Stay focused and determined! Your character and attitude at times are being judged because of the passion you carry! Don't relent, and do not stop being who you are! You must continue to rely on Holy Spirit. Many take that place, and interfere with your life! They pull you to them, instead of pushing you toward Me!

Don't be surprised in this season, as you are directed to step away from specific individuals. For there is a pruning once again in the garden! This will cause a bit of disturbance and concern, but peace shall flow like a river over the scenario. Your life is directed by Me! Your destiny given by Me! Never forget that! So now, in its present time, there are significant matters at hand, things that you have faithfully, with diligence, kept believing for!

The enemy has tried as well with diligence to delay and stop this assignment and blessing, but the battle has been won, and as the dust settles, the breakthrough comes! So prepare for great movement and acceleration! For what has been waiting, has come!

5/16/23

The enemy is trying to sabotage your authority by using complaints and harassment, but I have overwhelmed his attack with truth and justice! A door will open for you that has such significant favor and blessing! This door carries great authority, and will be used for your breakthrough and promotion!

5/21/23

You might of thought you were finished, but one of the greatest milestones in your life is about to make a grand appearance!

6/3/23— United States

Stay sensitive, and focused to the Holy Spirit during the season that's upon you, and the season ahead! For it is a very critical time in this nation! It's not time for the anchor to be removed from the sand! There's still a ship that needs to finish its course! Once that ship has reached its destination, it will be decommissioned. Once these events are completed, the ship that is waiting in the sand and feels the strength of the sun shall be released to set a new course.

6/6/23

The enemy is shaking and trembling because you have stayed diligent, remained focused, and kept the faith! Even though you have at times, questioned the validity of the sovereign word spoken over you, sudden strength and revelation kept you aligned properly to continue the direction you are headed in. For the new significant assignment that's about to be revealed has great authority and power that will be demonstrated while you carry out this assignment. So speak life, speak words of thankfulness, and rejoice! For this new work in your life has, and will be monumental in its fruition!

6/12/23

Every hindrance that the enemy has used to come against relationships in your family is broken now! The sacrifices you have made to help bring unity to your family has not gone unnoticed! What seems a bit chaotic now shall suddenly change, and a full restoration shall come to fruition! Holy Spirit is doing a work behind the scenes that involves watering the seeds that you have planted.

Even though there is some significant frustration and weariness that has settled in, you will see the manifestation of healthy, joyful, and harmonious relationships in the moments ahead! It is My plan to have everyone in one accord, and carry a healthy heart and spirit as you enter into the next several seasons. You will learn to draw from each other, strengthen each other, and most importantly, encourage one another! Transparency shall flow like a river, and many hearts shall be made whole during this time of regeneration!

6/14/23

We are in the time of times that reveal the wheat and the tares, the sheep and the goats! You must pay close attention to what the enemy is trying to accomplish, and the true objective to his plan! Many will give into deception and delusion!

Stay very sensitive to the voice of Holy Spirit, and you will see through revelation and understanding what is happening in the nation presently. The realm of intercession is critical, and the pursuit of righteousness and justice through the spirit is made available through the strength of I Am!

6/19/23

Your life matters, your purpose is significant, and your testimony precious to many! There has been so much that has come against you to stop your faith, but your heart, and the light inside of you has pierced the darkness, and given hope to many! Now prepare yourself for a very significant, sudden breakthrough that takes you to the next level of your calling and destiny!

6/25/23

There is an unusual, not expected movement in the atmosphere today! Holy Spirit is causing things to shift in your favor! Movement for you has begun in a significant way! New things, new assignments, new faces! Get ready, HE has heard your cry, and the door is fully open!

6/28/23

The Lord has made the way for you to experience a dramatic breakthrough in your finances! A sudden burst of breakthrough comes and the windows of Heaven opened! You stayed faithful, diligent in hope, and persevered when strength seemed lost.

Now it's your time to see the "More than Enough"overwhelm you!

6/30/23

So the fireworks come, and they go! But what is coming in the days ahead, brings more than just a show! Keep close attention to the one who speaks and brings his own fireworks! He is positioned now, and after some very interesting accusations he has been released to share what he has been holding back! The sound of independence, the sound of freedom is upon you! But this does not end just yet!

For the likes of a Nebuchadnezzar has intensified the fire, and his spiritual eyes shall not open to see the fourth man in the fire! Then the word of the Lord came suddenly, and spoke these words!

> THEY SHALL DRIVE YOU FROM MEN, YOUR DWELLING SHALL BE WITH THE BEASTS OF THE FIELD, AND THEY SHALL MAKE YOU EAT GRASS LIKE OXEN. THEY SHALL WET YOU WITH THE DEW OF HEAVEN, AND SEVEN TIMES SHALL PASS OVER YOU, TILL YOU KNOW THAT THE MOST HIGH RULES IN THE KINGDOM OF MEN, AND GIVES IT TO WHOMEVER HE CHOOSES. Daniel 4:25

7/6/23

The movie, *Sound of Freedom,* will be used by Holy Spirit to convict, reveal, and bring to justice the many that believed they were the elite

350

called, "The Untouchables". For over the Summer months, several shall be brought to justice! This will be your sign that the I Am has not forgotten nor turned His face from this nation! What was once lost, shall be found!

7/15/23

Continue to pursue the passion and calling that has been placed inside of you! Just because it hasn't manifested in the natural just yet doesn't mean the door is closed! The enemy has used many people to try and convince you otherwise, but I have made the way to bring this all to fruition! The reason you have not given up is because the plan that is in place for you, and the diligence to carry on is centered around a very critical assignment!

For I have strengthened you! You will see this door open suddenly, and when it opens, you must be very sensitive, and in tune with Holy Spirit. For you will be used in ways never dreamed of, nor imagined! It is much bigger, and the impact far greater! In the next few days ahead, correspondence shall come suddenly, and give direction to the steps needed to be taken!

7/20/23

It's time to take that step of faith! I know you are concerned about how it will all come to pass, but what you don't know is this! I have a plan and purpose for this assignment! Something that you haven't been able to see, simply because you have been watching with natural eyes!

Now it's time to turn on the spiritual eyes that you have always had from the beginning! It's time to see this very significant purpose and blessing come to fruition! YOU MUST REMEMBER, IT WAS SPOKEN OVER YOU MANY YEARS AGO!

Now it's time!

Final Words

9/18/23 - Prophetic Dream | Trump

HOLY SPIRIT ALLOWED ME TO SEE IN THIS DREAM SOME VERY interesting scenarios. First, I was walking in a field, kind of like a farm, or an Autumn Festival. It was early evening, dusk. The field was very large, there was a platform in the distance used for a speaker. I noticed that the atmosphere was peaceful, as if a great calm came after a storm.

There were no people in attendance, but I could sense a large presence of Holy Spirit and Angelic activity. Then I noticed several rows of steel folding chairs. As I gazed at the chairs, I could see Donald Trump sitting in the back row. There were members of his staff sitting with him, as well as security. I then saw myself sitting directly in front of him. I wasn't sure if he had spoken already, or he was getting ready to speak, but I do know it was not the year 2023 or 2024! It was in the future! There was an incredible peace all around! I knew that things had changed, and he was now in an office of authority.

I was then informed that the symbolism of my position in front of him meant a few things; Spiritual guidance, spiritual protection, the Lord going

353

ahead of him, not behind him, and the prophetic word of the Lord manifesting naturally, but operating spiritually! Holy Spirit showed me that he was humbled and in the place or posture of trust. He was putting his trust in God, not man! I also saw his suit that he was wearing, blue, and his face, the countenance on his face, serious, with determination in his eyes! He was sharpened, sensitive to Holy Spirit, but still determined, and diligent as are his everyday attributes.

All of them suddenly stood up, and I found myself standing up as well. We were finished there, now needing to go back to business as usual. Everyone including myself walked back to the vehicles that were present. I was then shown that my purpose in the dream was to reveal the heart, the mindset, and what is needed in the days ahead. A prophetic picture of destiny, fearlessness, the Spirit of Elijah! That Holy Spirit was always in control, and had great plans!

The Future! The Breakthrough! The New Thing of God!

As with the dream I had about him in 2015, asking him very specific questions about his future, and getting a glimpse of what's to come, this dream took me to the future, to see what had already taken place!

10/8/2023 - Prophetic Word | Israel

Benjamin Netanyahu! He has been chosen! Many do not believe this! Many have made their words resonate in the atmosphere of their displeasure! But he is chosen! He has been chosen because of this very scenario! He is not intimidated by the wickedness that is all around the land called Israel! He will make a statement, he will act, and he will see a swift victory that restores the land of Israel! You must pay close attention to him, and why this has come in this Season! Israel shall be restored! All fear that has been imparted into the people from the past administration shall be restored 100-fold! Not only will the land be restored, but a great sign shall come in the months ahead! This sign shall give you a very interesting clue to what is coming in 2024! The relationship continues! The bond of friendship continues! Strength, favor, victory! Israel will also be a sign to the United States! A sudden shift of significant breakthrough!

Thank You!

I want to thank each and every one of you that uses this tool for your own journey! Everyone has the ability to be used by God to change the world! To be a light in a dark place! Speak life, declare freedom, and be used to open the eyes of the blind!

"Light penetrates the darkness, and the darkness does not comprehend it." John 1:5

Let your light shine!

Never give up on yourself!

God is good!

About the Author

John Natale is the Founder and President of John Natale Ministries, Inc. and United States Law Enforcement organization. John travels for Ministry and Law Enforcement assignments.

With inspiration, encouragement, and the prophetic word of Holy Spirit, he believes the mandate he has been given helps with revelation and understanding, and facilitates destiny!

He has written two books: *Journey of Destiny* and a Prophetic Manual called *Listen:Learn:Obey.*

John and his wife Nancy are blessed with six wonderful Children, CJ, Ryan, Chase, Noah, Luke, and Jacob.